Early Childhood Bilingual Education

A Hispanic Perspective

W9-DGS-428

Bilingual Education Series

GARY D. KELLER, *Editor*

GUADALUPE VALDÉS, ANTHONY G. LOZANO, and RODOLFO GARCÍA-MOYA, editors, *Teaching Spanish to the Hispanic Bilingual: Issues, Aims, and Methods*

JOSHUA A. FISHMAN and GARY D. KELLER, editors, *Bilingual Education for Hispanic Students in the United States*

FLORENCE BARKIN, ELIZABETH A. BRANDT, and JACOB ORNSTEIN-GALICIA, editors, *Bilingualism and Language Contact: Spanish, English, and Native American Languages*

√ GARY D. KELLER, *Leo y Entiendo,* a bilingual reading program for kindergarten through grade 3

MAE CHU-CHANG, editor, *Asian- and Pacific-American Perspectives in Bilingual Education: Comparative Research*

THERESA HERRERA ESCOBEDO, editor, *Early Childhood Bilingual Education: A Hispanic Perspective*

Early Childhood Bilingual Education

A Hispanic Perspective

Edited by
THERESA HERRERA ESCOBEDO
The University of Texas at Austin

Teachers College, Columbia University
New York and London   1983

Published by Teachers College Press, 1234 Amsterdam Avenue, New
York, N.Y. 10027

Library of Congress Cataloging in Publication Data

Main entry under title:

Early childhood bilingual education.

   (Bilingual education series)
   Bibliography: p.
   Includes index.
   1. Education, Bilingual—United States—Addresses,
essays, lectures. 2. Education, Primary—United States
—Addresses, essays, lectures. I. Escobedo, Theresa
Herrera. II. Series: Bilingual education series
(Columbia University. Teachers College)
LC3731.E27 1983   371.97'00973   82-25624

ISBN 0-8077-2721-0 (pbk.)

Manufactured in the United States of America
88 87 86 85 84 83   1 2 3 4 5 6

Dedication

To my family, Nati, Toni and Gloria,
my mother Beatrice Herrera
and in loving memory of my father,
Antonio Gloria Herrera.

Contents

Acknowledgments

An edited volume requires the cooperation of many individuals—individuals who may or may not be dedicated to similar goals and theoretical orientations. The volume editor's job is to incorporate the works of these diverse contributors into a comprehensive unit. The task is made immensely easier when the individuals are willing to collaborate and make the seemingly endless revisions that ultimately become the united whole. Therefore, my first debt of gratitude is to the contributors whose works appear herein and also to those whose equally valuable contributions were not incorporated in the interest of the overall cohesiveness of the volume. I am grateful to the authors for their willingness to write the papers and suffer through the various reviews and revisions, and especially grateful to Jim Patterson for his patience in typing and retyping the manuscript.

I am especially indebted to Gary Keller, editor of Teachers College Press's Bilingual Education Series, for his support of the initial manuscript and his guidance in the review and final selection of the papers. This debt of gratitude extends to Teachers College Press for its support of bilingual education and willingness to develop and disseminate materials in this comparatively new field: to Carol Napier and Louise Craft, who made communications with the press a pleasure, and to Jane Barry and Kerry Kern, who both made valuable suggestions during the technical editing phase.

I also wish to acknowledge the contributions made to the development of this work by the Mexican Studies Center at the University of Texas at Austin and the Experimental Program for Opportunities in Advanced Study and Research in Education, a Grant Program Emphasizing Increased Participation of Minorities and Women in Research on Problems of Education, funded by the National Institute of Education (NIE). The aid given by NIE to researchers in the Project for Minorities and Women in Research (PMWR) at the University of Texas at Austin proved instrumental in the conceptualization of this volume. Equally important was the support provided by the University of Texas PMWR fellows through their friendship, intellectual contributions, and active participation at training sessions, national conferences, and informal discussions. I am indeed fortunate to have had the opportunity through the NIE grants program to develop a supporting network of friends not only at the local level but also at the national level with other NIE project directors and participants; in particular I acknowledge Dr. Gwendolyn Baker at the City University of New York, Dr. Silas Abrego at the University of Southern California, and Dr. Frank Alejandro, NIE Project Director.

This publication was supported in part by a grant from the NIE, Grant No. G78-0227.

Finally, I am grateful to my family for their support of my work and tolerance of my neglect of them: my mother, Beatrice Herrera; my two daughters, Toni and Gloria; and my husband, Nati, who all make living worthwhile.

Introduction

Early childhood education in the United States had its formal beginnings in a bilingual setting. In 1854 Margaretha Schurz established the first U.S. kindergarten, in which she implemented procedures and materials developed by Friedrich Froebel and used the German language for instruction. A bilingual approach was later utilized by the German-English academies of the 1860s and 1870s. The emphasis of these early endeavors, however, and that of Maria Montessori later, was not so much on language as on methods and materials.

Outside of the United States, interest in early childhood bilingualism existed much earlier, as indicated by European documents on bilingual schooling that go back at least three centuries. The interest continued with various periods of intensified activity. Concern for international understanding after World War II focused new attention on bilingualism. Conferences held in European countries discussed problems of bilingualism, the relationship of bilingualism to school and society, and the use of a foreign language as a medium of instruction.

In the United States several years after the post-World War II period, the Bilingual Education Act of 1968 and the revised version of 1974 brought official recognition and federal support to bilingual education. Interested educators have since been involved with the same concerns encountered by individuals of earlier eras. The three facets of bilingual education—language, culture, and instructional practices—are still of major importance; questions and reservations related to them are expressed by supporters and critics alike. The initial urgency of meeting the needs of bilingual children and developing functional programs for that purpose took precedence over investigations into appropriate procedures. Thus, after a decade of efforts and progress in program implementation, research in bilingual education is still very much a fertile field.

A large amount of the research presently being conducted has not been incorporated into the existing literature on bilingualism. A good deal of what is available is in the area of language. However, much is still not known about the dual-language acquisition process and the development of language in early childhood-bilingual classrooms. In addition, researchers have only recently begun to investigate the influence of culture on young children's learning and the effects of instructional strategies in bilingual classrooms.

The present volume brings together the work of various authors who address vital questions in the areas of language, culture, and instructional strategies as related to Hispanic children. The chapters, all original, were specifically written for this volume and are based on research findings, scholarly investigation of the existing literature, and the authors' knowledge of young children. The defining theme, bilingual education for the Hispanic child, establishes the framework for the volume and integrates the various papers, which are organized into three major sections on language, culture, and instructional strategies. The major goal of this effort is to provide information on current research and practices that will aid researchers, practitioners, and aspiring students in their efforts to enhance the education of Hispanic children.

LANGUAGE

The area of language acquisition and development has perhaps raised more questions for bilingual educators than any other. What language influences need to be considered in developing instruction that allows children to learn a second language while presenting new content and concepts? What unique features are there about learning two languages simultaneously? The first section of this collected work addresses these questions. It includes papers that explore approaches to language instruction and specific aspects of language acquisition and use.

Chapter one focuses on language instruction, while the next three address bilingual acquisition and language usage. Garcia's contribution examines the available literature regarding the nature of bilingualism in early childhood and describes a study related to both bilingual acquisition and instruction. Ana Huerta-Macías presents a qualitative, longitudinal study of a child acquiring two languages in a setting where both languages were alternated indiscriminately; the focus is on the effect of a linguistic environment without separation of codes on a child's speech. Sara Hudelson explores the use of videotaping as an observation tool for the assessment of language and presents a descriptive study of the code-switching behavior of the children who were videotaped in a natural setting. Amodeo and Cárdenas report findings regarding the private and social speech production of preschoolers during a series of increasingly difficult tasks in a sample that included monolingual and bilingual students of Hispanic, Asian, and Anglo ethnicity.

CULTURE

The sociocultural setting is of great importance, and nowhere is this more evident than in bilingual education. The impact of culture on learning has long been of interest to educators. What cultural variables can determine children's behavior in educational settings and how can these be incorporated into bilingual classrooms?

The papers in this section address these issues. The first two report findings of field research and the next two literary research. Jackson and Espino use an ethnographic approach to examine the life histories of ten third-grade Mexican American children and explore the relationship between such cultural variables as child-rearing practices, interaction styles, and schools to the constructs of field dependence and field independence. The paper focuses on each child's experiences in home, school, and community. Frank Gonzales reports findings of a study implemented to determine what cultural elements of two varying degrees were evident in bilingual classrooms. Gloria Contreras reviews common biases associated with multicultural education programs and suggests alternative structures with special consideration for young children. Escobedo and Huggans review cognitive learning style and subsequent intrinsic cultural variables associated with a specific style and with Mexican American children. The focus is on the theoretical developments of field dependence and independence and research findings as these support or reject the theory related to Mexican Americans.

CLASSROOM STRATEGIES

The instructional process that occurs in bilingual classrooms has been of grave concern to educators since the implementation of bilingual programs. This has been particularly important for individuals involved in the education of children in the early years. Children at this stage of development require special instructional strategies that take into account their need for concreteness and active interaction with the environment; they gain information through touching, tasting, feeling, smelling, and hearing. The integration of classroom practices that provide the needed sensory interactive experiences with the more formal structure for academic instruction is critical to children's future learning achievement. The implementation of these practices in bilingual classrooms is even more vital for Hispanic children, who have had in the past a high dropout rate and a history of underachievement.

The papers in the third section of this volume focus on classroom practices during the early childhood period; most are data-based, while others have a theoretical and experiential framework. Alberta Castaneda establishes a rationale for developmentally appropriate instruction for young children and, drawing on her knowledge of children as well as her background in the writing of kindergarten mathematics materials, elaborates strategies for enhancing premathematical concepts and premathematical language. Gilbert Cuevas also focuses on the importance of language for the development of mathematical concepts and reports a study that examined the acquisition of concepts of numbers and numeration by a sample of first- and and second-grade Hispanic students. His paper also examines the study's implications for teaching strategies.

The next four papers address the area of early reading and reading instruction for Hispanic children in bilingual classrooms. Rosalinda Barrera presents a critical analysis of current reading pedagogy in Spanish-English bilingual programs. The focus is on several prevailing notions in bilingual classrooms, which are examined closely as to their value to children's reading-language learning. Aurelia de Silva summarizes current research on the process of learning to read Spanish as it relates to Spanish-speaking Mexican American children and reports a study involving Spanish reading miscues. Olivia Saracho and Arlinda Eaton both explore learning style and aspects of reading. Saracho reports a study of the relationship of Mexican American children's perception of reading and their cognitive style that utilized an open interview to obtain measures of perception and to map cognitive style. Eaton presents findings of a study that explored the relationship of oral reading miscues to the cognitive style dimension of field dependence and independence.

This edited volume represents the most current, original work of researchers whose major interest is early childhood and/or bilingual education; many are nationally recognized for their contributions to these areas and related disciplines. Most of the chapters present research findings; some make a unique contribution by exploring current state-of-the-art practices or theoretical topics. Information is presented that would be of interest to individuals in such areas as foreign-language education, child language acquisition, teacher training, and multicultural education.

It is anticipated that in a growing field such as early childhood-bilingual education there will be an ever-increasing number of scholarly contributions that will need to be periodically collected, organized, and made available. Other volumes focusing on a wide range of topics, including those addressed in this volume, and perhaps expanded to include other language groups, could provide valuable resources for practitioners and researchers. It is hoped that the information presented in this volume will serve to shed some new knowledge on concerns related to the education of young Hispanic children in bilingual classrooms.

—T.H.E.

I | Language

1 | Bilingual Acquisition and Bilingual Instruction

EUGENE E. GARCIA
Arizona State University

Language acquisition is one of the most impressive aspects of child development. It seems remarkable that drastic changes in linguistic competence can be clearly identified within the first few years of life (Menyuk, 1971). Although the exact variables influencing this development are still not evident, research in this field has been voluminous and theoretically varied (deVilliers and deVilliers, 1978; Lenneberg and Lenneberg, 1975). The main focus of this research has been single language acquisition (Brown, 1973), although more recent research has employed cross-linguistic analysis with children who are learning different languages (Bowerman, 1975; Braine, 1976). Compared to these bodies of literature, very little systematic research is available regarding children who are acquiring two or more languages, simultaneously, during the early part of their lives. The following is an attempt to review research in bilingual acquisition, with a specific attention to some of my own work, and then to relate the empirical findings to the area of bilingual instruction.

For clarity, early childhood bilingualism will be defined within the boundaries of the following conditions.

1. *Linguistic character:* Children are able to comprehend and/or produce some aspects of each language beyond the ability to discriminate that either one language or another is being spoken. This condition allows many degrees of linguistic competence within the boundaries of bilingualism, including that of a child who has memorized one or more lexical utterances in a second language.
2. *Social character:* Children are exposed "naturally" to the two languages as they are used in social interaction during early childhood. This condition requires a substantive bilingual environment in the child's first three to five years of life. In most cases this exposure occurs within the nuclear or extended family, but this need not be the case; visitors and extended visits to foreign countries are examples of alternative models and environments.

3

3. *Psychological/developmental character:* Simultaneous development must be apparent in both languages. (This is contrasted with the case in which a native speaker of one language begins a course of second-language acquisition.) This bilingual development occurs concurrently with cognitive/conceptual changes regarding the perception and processing of linguistic information.

These conditions define the population of interest here. It is clear from this definition that an attempt is made to consider children's linguistic abilities in conjunction with their social environment during this psychologically important segment of their lives.

Several theoretical formulations are presently available to account for the process of bilingual acquisition. McLaughlin (1978) best accounted for the incongruencies in these formulations, by admitting the unavailability of empirical information on second-language acquisition. All have been generated through extensions of previous work with children acquiring their native language and with adults acquiring a second language. Only recently have major research efforts focused on children between the ages of two and five who are acquiring a second language. Therefore, it is not possible at present to provide a single, unclouded view of this important developmental phenomenon. Instead, various views, each worthy of consideration, emerge. The following discussion is an attempt to bring these views into focus and critically assess their value.

STUDIES OF BILINGUAL ACQUISITION

It is clear that children learn more than one linguistic communicative form in many societies throughout the world. Sorenson (1967) describes the acquisition of three or four languages by young children in the Northwest Amazon region of South America. Although the Tukano tribal language serves as the *lingua franca,* there continue to exist some twenty-five clearly distinguishable linguistic groups in this Brazilian-Colombian border area. In the United States Skrabanek (1970) reports a hundred years of acquisition and support of both English and Spanish language systems among young preschool children in the Southwest, with no indication that this phenomenon will be disrupted. Although not apparent from a cursory examination of linguistic literature, research with bilinguals is not a recent subarea of linguistic or psychological inquiry. Ronjat (1913) reports the development of French and German in his own son. He found little deleterious effect from this bilingual development, attributing the positive outcome to the separation of the languages; in this case one parent consistently spoke French and the other German. Pavlovitch (1920) reports the development of French and Serbian in his son under similar circumstances. The languages reportedly developed simultaneously with minimal confusion. Geissler (1938) reports, anecdotally, that as a teacher of foreign languages he observed young children acquiring up to four languages simultaneously without difficulty. It is only Smith (1935), in a study of missionary families who spoke English and Chinese, who reports difficulty during simultaneous acquisition. This difficulty was most apparent in the language-mixing character of the children's speech.

One of the first systematic investigations of bilingual acquisition in young children was reported by Leopold (1939, 1949a, 1949b). This author set out to study the simultaneous acquisition of English and German in his own daughter. These initial descriptive reports indicated that as the subject was exposed to both languages during infancy, she seemed to weld them into one system during initial language production periods; early language forms, for instance, were characterized by free mixing. Language production during later periods seemed to indicate that the use of English and German grammatical forms was developing independently.

More recent studies have systematically addressed several issues relevant to bilingual acquisition. Carrow (1971, 1972) restricted her study to the receptive domain of young bilingual Mexican American children in the Southwest. Children (aged 3 years 10 months to 6 years 9 months) from bilingual Spanish-English home environments were given the Auditory Test for Language Comprehension. This test consists of a series of pictures representing referential categories that can be signaled by words, morphological constructions, grammatical categories, and syntactical structures, including verbs, adjectives, adverbs, nouns, pronouns, morphological endings, prepositions, and interrogatives in both languages. A comparison of English and Spanish comprehension on this task (Carrow, 1971) revealed: (1) children were very heterogeneous— some scored better in one language than another, others were equal in both; (2) a greater proportion of children scored higher on English measures, even though Spanish was not used as a medium of instruction for children who were in educational programs.

In a cross-sectional comparison of English-only and bilingual (Spanish-English) children (aged 3 years 10 months to 6 years 9 months), Carrow (1972) reports a positive developmental trend for both Spanish and English in bilingual children. Bilingual children aged 3 years 10 months to 5 years 9 months tended to score lower than monolingual children on English measures, but in the final age comparison group (to 6 years 9 months), bilinguals and monolinguals did not differ significantly on these same English measures. These combined results seem to indicate that at the receptive level, Spanish-English bilingual children were: (1) progressing (increasing their competence) in both Spanish and English; (2) heterogeneous as a group, but tending to favor one language (predominantly English) over the other; and (3) lagging behind monolingual children in their acquisition of English, but eventually catching up. Although this research was limited and its specific conclusion cannot be readily generalized to other populations of bilingual children, it does offer some empirical information relevant to the study of early childhood bilingual development.

With respect to expressive development, Padilla and Liebman (1975) report a longitudinal analysis of Spanish-English acquisition in two three-year-old bilingual children. These researchers followed the model of Brown (1973) in recording children's linguistic interactions over a five-month period. By an analysis of several dependent linguistic variables (phonological, grammatical, syntactic, and semantic characteristics) over this period, they observed gains in both languages, although several English forms were in evidence while similar Spanish forms were not. They also report the differentiation of linguistic systems at phonological, lexical, and syntactic levels. They conclude that "the appropriate use of both languages even in mixed utterances was evident, that is, correct word order was preserved. For example, there were no occurrences of 'raining esta' or 'es a baby.' There was also absence of the redundance of unnecessary words which might tend to confuse meaning" (p. 51).

Garcia (1983) reports development data related to the acquisition of Spanish and English by Spanish-English bilingual preschoolers (three- to four-year-olds) and the acquisition of English by a group of matched English-only speakers. The result of that study can be summarized as follows: (1) acquisition of both Spanish and English was evidenced based on the quantity and quality of obtained morphological and syntactic instances of language productions; and (2) there was no quantitative or qualitative difference in English language productions between the bilinguals and the English-only controls.

Huerta (1977) has provided a report of a longitudinal analysis for a bilingual (Spanish-English) two-year-old child. She reports a similar pattern of continuous Spanish-English development, although identifiable stages appeared in which one language forged ahead of the other. Moreover, she reports the significant occurrence of mixed-language utterances, which made use of both Spanish and English morphology. In all such cases these mixed utterances were well formed and communicative. Garcia, Maez, and Gonzalez (1982), in a national study of bilingual children four, five, and six years of age, found regional differences in the relative occurrences of switched language utterances. Spanish-English children from Texas, Arizona, Colorado, and New Mexico showed a higher (15–20 percent) incidence of language switched utterances than children from California, Illinois, New York, and Florida, especially at the prekindergarten level. These findings suggest that some children may very well develop an "interlanguage," in addition acquiring two independent language systems later on.

The above developmental findings can be capsulized succinctly, but not without acknowledging their tentative nature:

1. Children can and do acquire more than one language during early childhood.
2. The acquisition of two languages need not hamper the acquisition of either language.
3. The acquisition of two languages can be parallel but need not be. That is, one language may lag behind, surge ahead, or develop simultaneously with the other language.
4. The acquisition of two languages may result in an "interlanguage" incorporating structural aspects of both languages, or languages may develop separately, with mixed forms a rarity.

A careful review of the third and fourth conclusions indicates that contradictions concerning the empirical reports are the rule rather than the exception. If one disregards the possible procedural incongruities that may account for such contradictions (and at present this is not a recommended strategy), what conclusions are actually possible? The specific discrepancies in the data on parallel versus nonparallel development and separate versus interlanguage development may well have their origin in the different bilingual milieus occupied by individuals or groups of children during early childhood. The task of empirical researchers is therefore to isolate the social variables that individually or in combination, directly or indirectly, influence bilingual acquisition.

A CROSS-SECTIONAL EVALUATION OF SPANISH-ENGLISH ACQUISITION

Subject and Procedures

I wish to describe in some detail a recent study related to both bilingual acquisition and instruction. The study worked with productive language data gathered in a national Spanish-English test standardization effort conducted by the Educational Testing Service. This agency was funded by the Department of Health, Education and Welfare to develop and standardize a series of easily administered tests to measure several cognitive and linguistic attributes in Spanish-English bilingual children throughout the United States (CIRCO, 1980). The standardization involved close to six thousand children of Hispanic descent (Chicano, Puerto Rican, and Cuban) between the ages of four and six years. The data of interest for this study were gathered through subtest 10C of the CIRCO. During this subtest, trained examiners interacted informally and individually with children and recorded all the children's utterances verbatim. The present study attempted to provide an analysis of speech recorded during these interactions for a selected number of children from sites located throughout the United States. In doing so, it provides one of the first detailed analyses of Spanish and English in different age groups and the different Spanish-English bilingual groups of the United States, Chicanos, Puerto Ricans, and Cubans.

All children who took either the Spanish or the English version of subtest 10C were initially successful in completing a Spanish-English receptive pretest of mild difficulty. Therefore, each was considered minimally bilingual. Additionally, all children were reported by parents as members of a home environment in which both Spanish and English were spoken. Subtest 10C of the CIRCO battery obtained a measure of "spontaneous speech" by having examiners engage each child tested in an informal conversation concerning a picture of a neighborhood setting (for the Spanish test) or a classroom one (for the English test). Subject transcripts from six regions were used: West (California), Southwest (Colorado, New Mexico, and Arizona), Texas, Midwest (Illinois), East (New York and New Jersey), and South (Florida). For each region subjects were randomly selected from preschoolers (from Headstart programs), kindergarteners, and first graders who had taken the test, with the following constraints: (1) twenty subjects who had taken the English test and twenty subjects who had taken the Spanish test were chosen; (2) half of the subjects selected resided in urban settings (areas with a population-by-acre ratio of 1,000 to 1 or higher), and half in rural settings (areas with a population-by-acre ratio of 50 to 1 or lower). For the Midwest and the East, no rural subjects were included in the testing. Thus, 600 subject transcripts were included in the study (see table 1 for the number and geographical distribution of subjects).

Of primary interest in this study was the analysis of Mean Length of Utterance (MLU). This measure has been proposed as a standard for the assessment of language development in children (Brown, 1973). It has as an index the number of morphemes per utterance, utterance being a unit of speech demarcated prosodically and by pauses. MLU was calculated for English and Spanish language samples (see table 2). One major problem with using this measure to compare Spanish and English is the difference in morpheme structure and the inequality in the availability of morphemes between the languages. For instance, the utterance "la muchacha" would receive a score of 4 using the adopted morpheme guide: the article "la" receives 1 point, the noun "muchacha" 1 point and 2 points for sex and number agreement. The equivalent English utterance, "the girl," would receive only a score of 2. Because of these inequalities, it is not permissible to compare Spanish and English MLU directly.

As previously indicated, it was the intent of this study to provide some exploratory comparison of Spanish and English measures of bilingual Spanish/English children at certain grade levels. Moreover, the study attempted to accomplish the above by gathering language productions from different regions

Table 1: Summary of Subjects: Prekindergarten, Kindergarten, and First Grade

REGION	TESTED IN SPANISH						TESTED IN ENGLISH						Σ
	Urban			Rural			Urban			Rural			
	P	K	F	P	K	F	P	K	F	P	K	F	
West (California)	10	10	10	10	10	10	10	10	10	10	10	10	120
Southwest (Arizona, Colorado, New Mexico)	10	10	10	10	10	10	10	10	10	10	10	10	120
Texas	10	10	10	10	10	10	10	10	10	10	10	10	120
Midwest (Chicago)	10	10	10				10	10	10				60
East (New York, New Jersey)	10	10	10				10	10	10				60
South (Florida)	10	10	10	10	10	10	10	10	10	10	10	10	120
Total	60	60	60	40	40	40	60	60	60	40	40	40	600

Table 2:   Rules for Calculating Mean Length of Utterance
(After Brown, 1973)

1. Start with the first utterance.

2. Only fully transcribed utterances are used; none with blanks. Portions of utterances, entered in parentheses to indicate doubtful transcription, are used.

3. Include all exact repetitions (mark with a plus sign in records). Stuttering is marked as a repeated effort at a single word; count the word once in the most complete form produced. In the few cases where a word is repeated for emphasis or the like ("no, no, no"), count each occurrence.

4. Do not count such fillers as "mm," "eh," or "oh," but do count "no," "yeah" ("sí," "oye," "ese"), and "hi" ("hola").

5 All compound words (two or more free morphemes), proper names, and ritualized reduplications count as single words: for example, "birthday," "racketyboom," "choo-choo," "quack-quack," "night-night," "pocketbook," "seesaw," "rompecabezas" (puzzle), "sacapuntas" (pencil sharpener), "cumpleaños" (birthday), "abrelatas" (can opener). There is no evidence that the constituent morphemes function as such for these children.

6. Count as one morpheme all irregular past forms of verbs: "got," "did," "went," "saw" ("hice," "fui," "puse"). There is no evidence that children relate these to present forms.

7. Count as one morpheme all diminutives ("doggie," "mommy," "perrito," "mamacita") because children do not seem to use diminutive suffixes productively; rather, they use diminutives as standard forms.

8. Count as separate morphemes all auxiliaries: "is," "have," "will," "can," "must," "would," "puede," "sabe," "podía," "pudo," "debía," "debería."
   The same rule applies to catenatives: "gonna," "wanna," "hafta." These are counted as single morphemes rather than as "going to" or "want to" because they seem to function that way for children. Count as separate morphemes all inflections: for example, English possessives (s), plural (s), third-person singular (s), regular past (d), and progressive (i), and Spanish plural (s, es) and progressive (iendo, ando).

9. In Spanish, count as separate morphemes all single articles ("el," "la," etc.), demonstrative pronouns ("esta," "este," etc.), and contractions ("del," "al"). These seem to be standard forms.

10. In Spanish, count as additional morphemes article-noun and pronoun-noun agreement for both number and gender ("el pato," "los patos": "el" is scored as two morphemes because it agrees in number and gender with "pato").

of the United States and from children within those regions, which were either classified as urban or rural areas. In doing so, the study represents one of the first attempts to document Spanish/English bilingualism in this country with regional and population considerations in mind. Moreover, it provides some initial (albeit tentative) comparisons of this linguistic nature between Spanish/ English ethnic groups (Chicanos, Puerto Ricans, and Cubans) in this country.

Results

At the most general levels, it seems appropriate to conclude that Spanish-English bilingualism is alive and well throughout the United States at all grade levels, and in all regions and environments studied. Mean scores for MLU were high enough to indicate that Spanish and English productions involved the use of complex morphological "rules." It is worthwhile to note that Spanish MLU scores were always higher than the English ones, although such differences are more likely to be attributable to morphological differences between the languages and MLU computational procedures rather than to higher proficiency in Spanish.

There is little evidence in the measures studied to indicate any strong regional or urban-rural differences, but a pattern was identifiable in grade-level comparisons. For English that pattern was one of progressively higher mean MLU scores from prekindergarten to kindergarten to first grade. For Spanish the pattern was distinctly different: the mean for MLU scores increased from prekindergarten to kindergarten and then dropped to below prekindergarten levels at first grade (see figures 1 and 2).

These different patterns might be related to issues of language acquisition and language loss. Carrow (1971, 1972) has reported on the increases in receptive ability for both Spanish and English correlated with increase in age in three- to six-year-old bilingual Chicano children in Texas. Padilla and Liebman (1975) have also reported the simultaneous development of Spanish and English. The present study further attests to the phenomenon of simultaneous acquisition. Prekindergarten children obtained relatively high MLU scores in both Spanish (10.0) and English (6.0). But the results also seem to suggest a decreased productive level in Spanish by first grade, indicating a "language gain" pattern for English and a "language loss" pattern for Spanish. This conclusion needs considerable tempering, since the decrease in MLU scores in Spanish-tested children was not dramatic; that is, the scores did not deteriorate drastically from high levels to low levels. But if the trend was to continue in the more advanced grades, this loss could seriously affect Spanish production.

It is not uncommon for bilingual adults to admit to some degree of language loss in Spanish, primarily attributed to the overbearing monolingual English

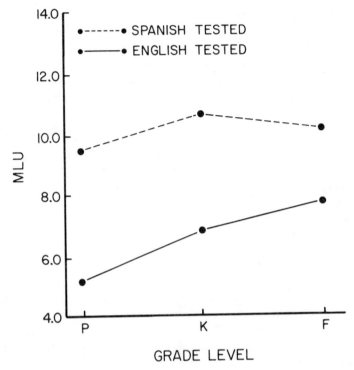

Figure 1: Mean MLU Scores for English- and Spanish-Tested Subjects by Grade Level: Prekindergarten, Kindergarten, and First Grade

curriculum. In fact, the drop in MLU in the present study is correlated with admission to the first-grade level, where the oral language experience of preschool and kindergarten is transformed to more formal written exercises.

Implications for Education

McLaughlin's review of research (1978) led him to conclude that many misconceptions about language and bilingual acquisition in early childhood are prevalent:

1. The child acquires a language more quickly and easily than an adult because the child is biologically programmed to acquire language, whereas the adult is not.
2. The younger the child, the more skilled he or she will be in acquiring the second language.

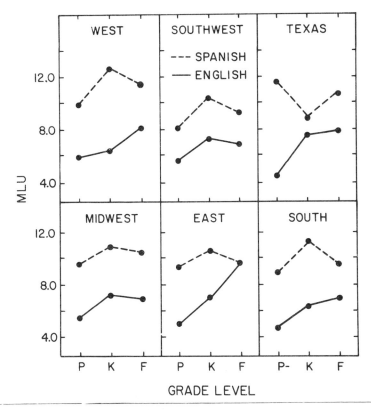

Figure 2: Mean MLU Scores for Spanish- and English-Tested Subjects for Each Region by Grade Level: Prekindergarten, Kindergarten, and First Grade

3. Second-language acquisition is a qualitatively different process from first-language acquisition.
4. Interference between first- and second-language instruction is an inevitable and ubiquitous part of second-language acquisition.
5. There is a single method of second-language instruction that is most effective with all children.
6. Bilingualism negatively (or positively) affects the child's educational attainment, emotional adjustment, and/or cognitive functioning. (McLaughlin, 1978, pp. 197–205)

In concluding that the above propositions are unproven, McLaughlin followed the strategy of any good scientist: Propositions extracted from empirical observation and experimentation are to be handled with extreme caution. It is possible that some or all of the above propositions are true, but to claim their truth at a time when empirical support is limited is clearly not in the best interest of future research and the applied technology of education.

With this in mind, it is possible to address some questions related to bilingual education in early childhood in terms of the available research. Three concerns are discussed:

1. Do bilingual education efforts in early childhood negatively affect linguistic and cognitive development?
2. Do bilingual education efforts in early childhood positively influence linguistic and cognitive development?
3. Should such efforts use immersion, transition/English as a Second Language (ESL), or transition/maintenance programs?

The research presented by Garcia (1983) regarding the first question reveals that exposure to two language systems and subsequent proficiency in these two languages do not retard linguistic development in either language. Children who were operating at complex levels in Spanish were not retarded in English as compared to matched monolingual English-speaking children. Important questions remain, however, about the relationship between the differences in the qualitative nature of the bilingual and monolingual experiences and linguistic and cognitive development, and the relationship of cognitive process variables to bilingual development.

The second question is somewhat the reverse of the first and focuses on the positive influence of bilingual education. Although there is no evidence that bilingual acquisition has a negative effect on general linguistic development, neither is there any evidence of advanced linguistic development for bilingual children when compared to matched monolingual children. Bilingual children do score significantly higher on several cognitive measures than matched monolingual peers (Cummins, 1979), especially on measures of ability to consider properties of the environment in a flexible manner. Critical questions remain, however. Are these advantages related to bilingualism itself or to other cultural variables associated with bilingualism? Are they related to proficiency levels of bilingualism? Are they limited to specific languages and specific cognitive tasks?

The type of program best for bilingual education is a matter of great concern to educators, researchers, and all individuals in the bilingual education field. There is very little evidence on which to base even the most cautious conclusion. Previous immersion efforts have been evaluated positively for elementary school children in French-English schools in Canada (Lambert and Tucker, 1972). A similar conclusion for Mexican American children in the United States in not warranted. Prior to the formal funding of bilingual education at the national level in 1968, the English-immersion program was the model for the education of language-minority children in U.S. public schools, and the program proved disastrous for those children.

Data from empirical research in bilingual and cognitive development shed some light on this question. Dulay and Burt (1972 and 1973), acknowledging the low incidence of second-language errors related to native-language structure, suggest that incidental teaching of a second language might prove most beneficial. That is, an immersion or transition effort that exposes the child to the second language seems the most effective strategy for second-language acquisition. Data presented by Garcia (1983) suggest that a formal maintenance instruction system that reinforces the native language produces parallel development in both languages. Cummins (1979) reviews several studies that indicate that cognitive flexibility is an attribute of only the proficient bilingual. Monolingual and unbalanced bilingual children scored significantly lower than proficient preschool bilinguals on Piagetian tests. Thus, transitional-maintenance efforts may both enhance the acquisition of new language structures and provide advantageous cognitive benefits. Sound evaluations of immersion, transition, and maintenance bilingual programs in early childhood are needed before we can reach any conclusions about the adequacy or relative effectiveness of these strategies.

Other curriculum questions remain. Should languages be temporally and contexually separated (e.g., teacher A speaks L_1, teacher B L_2; Monday and Friday L_1 is spoken, Tuesday and Thursday L_2)? Should content areas be repeated in both languages? What is the role of the transition approach as a curricular tool?

CONCLUSION

It remains difficult to apply findings concerning bilingual acquisition directly to bilingual education efforts in early childhood. More questions than answers have been generated by research, but such challenges will undoubtedly benefit all children who acquire the language(s) of their society. The variability of bilingual acquisition suggests the importance of social factors; that is, the specific character of bilingual acquisition for individuals or groups may have its origins in their various bilingual social milieus. This suggestion does not exclude the more traditional study of the acquisition of linguistic structures, but our research must be extended to include social and environmental variables if we are to gain specific knowledge of relevance to bilingual instruction. Thus, the study of bilingual acquisition will be more directly related to the needs of instructional personnel and the daily decisions they must make regarding bilingualism and education.

REFERENCES

Bowerman, M. Crosslinguistic similarities at two stages of syntactic development. In E. Lenneberg and E. Lenneberg (Eds.), *Foundations of language development.* London: UNESCO Press, 1975.

Braine, M. D. S. Children's first word combinations. *Monographs of the Society for Research in Child Development,* 1976.

Brown, R. A. *A first language: the early stages.* Cambridge, Mass.: Harvard University Press, 1973.

Carrow, E. Comprehension of English and Spanish by preschool Mexican-American children. *Modern Language Journal,* 1971, *55,* 299–306.

Carrow. E. Auditory comprehension of English by monolingual and bilingual preschool children. *Journal of Speech and Hearing Research,* 1972, *15,* 407–457.

CIRCO. Berkeley, Cal.: Educational Testing Service, 1980.

Cummins, J. Linguistic interdependence and the educational development of bilingual children. *Review of Educational Research,* 1979, *49,* 222–251.

deVilliers, J., and deVilliers, P. *Language acquisition.* Cambridge, Mass.: Harvard University Press, 1978.

Dulay, H. C., and Burt, M. K. Goofing: an indication of children's second language learning strategies. *Language Learning,* 1972, *22,* 235–252.

Dulay, H. C., and Burt, M. K. Should we teach children syntax. *Language Learning,* 1973, *23,* 245–258.

Garcia, E. *Early childhood bilingualism.* Albuquerque: University of New Mexico Press, 1983.

Garcia, E., Maez, L., and Gonzalez, G. Language switching in bilingual children: a national perspective. In E. Garcia and M. Vargas (Eds.), *The Mexican American child: language, cognitive and social development.* Tempe: Arizona State University Bilingual Education Center, 1982.

Geissler, H. *Zweisprachigkeit deutscher Kinder im Ausland.* Stuttgart: Kohlhammas, 1938.

Huerta, A. The development of codeswitching in a young bilingual. *Working Papers in Sociolinguistics,* no. 21, June 1977.

Lambert, W., and Tucker, G. *Bilingual education of children: the St. Lambert experiment.* Rowley, Mass.: Newbury House, 1972.

Lenneberg, E., and Lenneberg, E. (Eds.) *Foundations of language development,* vols. 1 and 2. London: UNESCO Press, 1975.

Leopold, W. F. *Speech Development of a bilingual child: a linguist's record,* vol. 1: *Vocabulary growth in the first two years.* Evanston, Ill.: Northwestern University Press, 1939.

Leopold, W. F. *Speech development of a bilingual child: a linguist's record,* vol. 2: *Sound learning in the first two years.* Evanston, Ill.: Northwestern University Press, 1949a.

Leopold, W. F. *Speech development of a bilingual child: a linguist's record,* vol. 3: *Grammars and general problems in the first two years.* Evanston, Ill.: Northwestern University Press, 1949b.

McLaughlin, B. *Second language learning in children.* Hillside, N.J.: Lawrence Erlbaum Associates, 1978.

Menyuk, P. *The acquisition and development of language.* Englewood Cliffs, N.J.: Prentice-Hall, Inc., 1971.

Padilla, A. M., and Liebman, E. Language acquisition in the bilingual child. *The Bilingual Review/La Revista Bilingue,* 1975, *2,* 34–55.

Pavlovitch, M. *Le language efantin: acquisition du serbe et du français par un enfant serbe.* Paris: Champion, 1920.

Ronjat, J. *Le developpement de langage observe chez un enfant bilingue.* Paris: Champion, 1913.

Skrabanek, R. L. Language maintenance among Mexican-Americans. *International Journal of Comparative Sociology,* 1970, *11,* 272–282.

Smith, M. D. A study of the speech of eight bilingual children of the same family. *Child Development,* 1935, *6,* 19–25.

Sorenson, A. P. Multilingualism in the Northwest Amazon. *American Anthropologist,* 1967, *69,* 678–684.

2 | Child Bilingualism: To Switch or Not to Switch?

ANA HUERTA-MACÍAS
The University of Texas

A relatively unexplored area in the field of bilingualism is the acquisition of bilingualism in children. Leopold's (1978) study of the acquisition of English and German by his daughter, Hildegard, remains a classic in this field. Longitudinal case studies of children who are in the process of acquiring two languages simultaneously are, however, very few. This literature, furthermore, has focused on cases where the one person–one language principle was in effect during the language-acquisition process. Leopold's study, for example, followed this principle in that he was the only person in the home to speak German to his daughter, while her mother most often spoke English to her. Ronjat (1978), who studied the acquisition of German and French by his son, Louie, also attributed much of the child's balanced development in both languages to the one language–one person principle. In Burling's (1978) study, it appears that the author was the only person who spoke Garo to the child; his mother used English with him. Imedadze (1967), who also observed the language development of her child, likewise noted that the people surrounding the subject invariably spoke one language or the other. Fantini (1974), who studied the acquisition of Spanish and English by his son, Mario, writes that Mario was strongly discouraged from mixing, or using both languages within a single utterance; his parents made a strong effort to separate the environments in which each language was used to the extent that Spanish was used at home within the family, while English was permitted outside the home with other speakers.

A few other contributions to the field of child bilingualism are particularly relevant to this paper in that they deal, to differing extents, with language alternations in children's speech. Swain and Wesche's (1975) study samples over a nine-month period the French and English speech of a three-year-old bilingual living in Canada. The languages here were also separated in the linguistic environment of the child, since the father addressed his son in French only, while

This study was partly supported by an NEH grant for a summer seminar on bilingualism.

the mother addressed him in English except when there were other French-speakers present. The parents conversed with each other in French, however, so that the child's linguistic milieu at 3 years 1 month was estimated by his mother to be 60 percent French. This study is significant in that the authors focus on the child's mixed-language utterances.

Two other studies that deal with the mixed-language speech of bilingual children are Bergman (1976) and Lindholm and Padilla (1978). The linguistic milieu of the child in Bergman's study is not clearly specified; nonetheless, one can infer that the two languages, Spanish and English, were separated according to the one language–one person principle from the author's statement (Bergman, 1976, p. 86) that it was her intention to raise her daughter, the subject of the study, so that her languages would develop independently of each other. Her daughter began to mix languages at certain periods of her language development, however, and observations are made on some of her mixed-language utterances as they occurred from about 1 year 2 months to 2 years 5 months.

Lindholm and Padilla's analysis of language alternations distinguishes among language mixing, language switching, and translation. The data in the report consist of speech samples of eighteen bilingual children between the ages of 2 years and 6 years 4 months. The linguistic environment of these children within the home is not specifically described, but it is stated that they were second-generation Mexican Americans and that ten of them had learned English and Spanish at home, so that there was presumably no rigorous separation of codes within the homes in these cases. Reference will be made to these studies where they are relevant to the observations reported on below.

Lacking in the literature are longitudinal studies of children raised in bilingual linguistic environments where no effort whatsoever has been made to separate the languages. This paper deals with such a case. Its purpose is to provide some insight into the bilingual acquisition process in a situation where a child is simultaneously acquiring two languages in a context where the one language–one person principle is not in effect, but where both languages are most often used indiscriminately by the adults around him. More specifically, I will focus on the effect of this environment on the sociolinguistic and linguistic patterns emerging in the child's speech. Does he differentiate sociolinguistically between the two codes? Is he able to separate them, and has he developed a model of when to use each of these languages? How do the two languages interact linguistically in his speech? Does he adhere to the grammar of either English or Spanish, particularly in his mixed-language utterances? In general, how is this child's linguistic environment reflected in his speech, and how has it influenced his language? This preliminary study, while touching on these questions, will also provide some insight and direction for future in-depth studies of children's bilingualism.

METHODS AND PROCEDURES

The study was a two-year longitudinal examination of one child, Christopher. Christopher, who at the start of the study was 3 years 3 months old, has been raised in a bilingual environment, where he has heard both Spanish and English from birth. All of Christopher's family is bilingual, including not only his parents, but maternal grandparents, uncles, and aunts as well; the latter are most often the child's caretakers when he is not with his parents and therefore are a major influence on his speech. Code switching[1] occurs extensively among Christopher's family members (see Huerta, 1978, for a descriptive analysis of the family's speech). Thus, Christopher has also been exposed to this style of speech from birth, and it is his developing bilingualism in this speech milieu that is the focus of this paper.

The procedure for this study consisted of recording Christopher in conversation with various members of his family. Accompanying notes were taken on the speech contexts during these recordings, with particular attention to the speakers or listeners present, the physical context, and the conversational situation. The recording sessions took place in Christopher's home or his maternal grandparents' home. All of the conversations involved either his parents or his maternal grandparents or both, the writer, and occasionally one of his uncles. There was no motive for inhibition on the subject's part, as he is very well acquainted with all these people, and so the dialogue recorded was natural and informal speech.

A verbatim transcription was made of all the recordings and then analyzed qualitatively; I felt that the qualitative approach would allow a descriptively rich and comprehensive interpretation of the data. The following report is based on an overview of the speech Christopher produced between the ages of 3 years 3 months and 5 years 3 months, when he had passed the two- and three-word stages and was producing longer strings of utterances. The analysis covers approximately nine hours of recorded speech in approximately twenty sessions, each about one month apart.

THE SOCIAL USE OF LANGUAGE

As I noted above, the speakers around Christopher can and often do use both Spanish and English when speaking to him. Some family members use one language with him more frequently than the other one—his grandparents, for

---

[1]The terms "code switching" and "language mixing" or "language alternation" will be treated as synonymous throughout this paper, since it is not intended to analyze the specific Spanish or English segments used in bilingual speech. Thus, recognition of the use of two languages in discourse is sufficient here, and a differential use of these terms is not necessary for my purposes.

example, use Spanish more often—but he is, nonetheless, very frequently spoken to in both languages by a single family member and within a single conversation. He is aware that these family members are bilingual, and he responds to them in both English and Spanish.

His speech at the ages being reported on here shows different language-use patterns from previous years (see Huerta, 1977, which reports on data gathered when Christopher was between two and three years old). He has begun to separate the languages to a greater extent; that is, he has begun to differentiate the use of Spanish and English according to the speaker addressed. This is most evident in the case of his grandparents, with whom he now uses Spanish most of the time. The child frequently switches from English to Spanish when he addresses either one of them in a conversation. Example (1) illustrates a switch to Spanish as Christopher turns from his mother to his grandfather. In (2) there is likewise a switch in the last utterance when the subject addresses his grandfather.[2] Note that there is also a switch in the first part of this dialogue, apparently triggered by language used by his aunt, the other conversational participant. The figures at right give Christopher's age at the time of the recording (in year and months).

(1) Ch: Mama, look how big it is![3]   (5:0)
         (twice, referring to a *piñata* and his mother's failure to pay
         attention to him)
         Grandpa, grandpa, mira que grandota están las orejas!
         (twice, addressing his grandfather)
(2) Ch: Nina Ana, wanna play blocks with me?[4]   (3:6)
      A: Ya me voy, Tipher.
     Ch: ¿'onde, huh, 'onde?
      A: Swimming.
     Ch: Well, play blocks with me.
         (turning to his grandfather)
         Grandpa, grandpa, quiere come and jugar blocks, grandpa, quiere
         jugar?

By this time Christopher has started to separate his codes along the lines of the one language–one person principle. This principle was never promoted by his family, nor was he ever told that he should not mix languages or that he should use a single language with certain speakers. This development in his speech patterns, then, came from his own growing sociolinguistic awareness of

---

[2]Although the last utterance contains English elements, what is of importance here is the child's effort to address his grandfather in Spanish. Similar examples will be discussed.

[3]"Ch" is used herein to refer to the subject's speech in dialogues. Other initials refer to the speech of the adult who is the other conversational participant.

[4]All instances of "me" in Christopher's speech represent the English, *not* the Spanish, pronoun.

who spoke what language most often. That is, Christopher's more frequent application of the one language–one person principle could have simply come from the fact that he often switched his language according to the language used in response to him, as illustrated in (2) above. He could, therefore, have started to use Spanish with his grandparents simply because they usually responded to him in that language.

It is also possible that Christopher began to associate the use of Spanish with his grandparents because he perceived them to be more fluent in that language. Data from Genishi (1976) lend support to this hypothesis; she found in her study of code switching among Mexican American children that these children often followed the rule of speaking the language that their interlocutor knew best. Likewise Fantini (1974) noted that Mario would switch to English if he perceived that the person addressed was not fluent in Spanish.

Another interesting development took place in Christopher's speech during the two-year period between the ages of 3 years 3 months and 5 years 3 months. He seems to have developed a linguistic awareness with regard to the use of his two languages. He was aware even in earlier stages of his language development that there were two "different ways" of saying the same thing, as illustrated by his comprehension of "orange" for "naranja" in the following example (from Huerta, 1977) of dialogue with his mother:

(3) M: ¿Ya almorzó?   (2:2)
     Ch: Ti. (sí)
     M: ¿Qué comió?
     Ch: 'Udo (menudo)
     M: ¿Menudo?
     Ch: Aha.
     M: ¿Y qué más?
     Ch: Naca. (naranja)
     M: Bacon?
     Ch: Naca. (louder)
     M: Coffee?
     Ch: ¡Naca! (yelling, frustrated at not being understood)
     M: Ooh, orange!
     Ch: Aha. (nodding)

However, he had never switched languages, given alternative forms upon request, or asked for translations, as he now does in (4), (5), and (6) below. Although there is no way of knowing whether he actually understood the concept of "language" in these examples, a type of linguistic awareness is nonetheless clearly shown in the interchanges. This is particularly true in (7), where the child actually refers to these two linguistic systems or "ways of saying things" by labeling them (although with the wrong label in this case) and where he moreover actually chooses to talk about different forms of expression, or language, on his own.

(4) A: Quiero que usted me hable en español. (3:5)
    Ch: OK. Casa, juguete, troca, carro.
    A: Pero platiqueme en español.
    Ch: I am! ¡Troca! You see?!

(5) A: ¿Y a dónde lo va a llevar su grandpa? (3:9)
    Ch: To the lake.
    A: ¿Cómo se dice eso?
    Ch: Patos.

(6) Ch: How do you call brown en español? (3:5)
      (looking at colors in a book)

(7) A: Look! Your grandpa bought tangerines. (4:6)
    Ch: (about thirty seconds later)
       They're naranjas, but in Spanish we call them tangerines.
    A: And what do you call peaches?
    Ch: Duraznos.
    A: In English or in Spanish?
    Ch: I don't know.
    A: In English?
    Ch: I don't know.
    A: In Spanish?
    Ch: I don't know!

From about the age of 4 years 6 months, then, he began to verbalize his linguistic awareness, even though at times, as in (7), he showed some confusion with regard to the Spanish-English classification of speech or simply refused to talk about different forms of expression. It appears that Christopher's linguistic environment did not preclude the acquisition of this "two codes" concept. Furthermore, he started to use these codes in a way not unlike that of children raised with the one language–one person principle: not only did he begin to associate the use of a language with certain speakers, but he was linguistically aware of the two codes in his speech and their differentiation. This is in agreement with Fantini (1974), who noted that his son first used the terms "español" and "inglés" at 3 years 6 months and 3 years 9 months, respectively, and used them correctly at 4 years 6 months. Fantini's child was asking for translations at 4 years 1 month, while Christopher was doing so at 3 years 5 months, as noted above. These data are also in accord with Swain and Wesche (1975), who noted spontaneous translations in Michael's speech at the stage from 3 years 5 months to 3 years 10 months. Thus, with regard to this aspect of language development, no differences were noted between Christopher and bilingual children reported on in previous studies.

Questions might now be raised about the subject's development in either language. It is not within the scope of this paper to compare his English or Spanish to that of monolingual children acquiring one of these languages or to that of children acquiring these two languages with the separation-of-codes principle in effect. (See Huerta, 1977, for a discussion of this topic.) Nonetheless, some general observations will be noted here with respect to the subject's development in Spanish and English.

Christopher's development seems to be uneven in that at certain periods of his life he has appeared to be more proficient in either English or Spanish. This observation has also been made, to varying degrees, of most children studied so far who are in the process of acquiring two languages simultaneously. Fantini (1974) noted that the development of English in his son was somewhat tardy in that he did not have much exposure to that language until he started attending preschool, at which time his English became more productive. The fluctuation in Christopher's development and use of either language is not unique to him and was a result of linguistic influences outside the home, rather than the lack of code separation at home. Like Fantini's son, he used and thereby developed his English much more than his Spanish during the periods when he was in a nursery school where only English was used. Later, when he did not attend nursery school but was taken care of during the day by his mother and other family members, his use of English declined. A turn to Spanish also occurred at the age of 3 years 11 months when he was taken on a two-week vacation to Mexico, where the family stayed with relatives, all of whom are monolingual Spanish-speakers. Not only did he use much more Spanish with his parents while he was there, but for awhile after the trip he used it much more at home, with his parents and others as well.

Therefore, the extent to which he used either language sometimes varied and the development of a language sometimes occurred in spurts. This variation is a result of short-term "immersions," or periods of intensive exposure to one or the other language outside the home. The alternate use of Spanish and English continued within the home, and Christopher generally followed this speech pattern there.

LINGUISTIC INTERACTION

Our focus now shifts to certain grammatical patterns in Christopher's speech. Christopher's tendency to separate his two languages according to the person addressed was discussed above along with other sociolinguistic aspects of his development. In the period beginning at 3 years 3 months and continuing through 5 years 3 months, he also began, to a greater degree than before, to separate the codes linguistically. That is, there was quantitatively less language alternation in his speech. Note (8) and (9), for example, where he produces all-English and all-Spanish speech, with the exception of the quotation in (9), which is retained in the language in which it was originally spoken and, of course, the proper noun.

(8) Ch: I'm going to go help you make the Christmas tree tomorrow and (4:1)
maybe I could go and then maybe my mommy could take me;
maybe I could wake up early and tomorrow I'm going to play and
today I'm playing and that's all. Wonder Woman is on right now.

(9) Ch: Ahh sí. Es que yo no estaba aquí y se fué mi mami a agarrarle (5:0)
unos pantalones y eran de Sesame Street y ella no se los quería
quitar y afuerzas con un ella, ella, ella, ella, le, le, le arrancó ese
pantalón con toi los calzones. Ella se estaba ahí y luego pasamos
enfrente de la gente y luego hizo un coraje y luego, y luego, y
luego la señora vino y le decía, "don't cry sweetie," y, y, y, y luego
ya paró.

There is also a qualitative difference in Christopher's mixed-language utterances in that these increasingly consist of English nouns or noun phrases inserted into otherwise Spanish (respectively) utterances, or vice versa, as in (10).

(10) A: ¿Y qué vió en el zoo? (4:5)
      Ch: Changos. I saw lions sleeping and I saw a big old elefante that was
trying to eat me with his trompa but he couldn't reach me.
      A: Why couldn't he reach you?
      Ch: Because I was [?] gates and he was somewhere up and the gates
were about that far and the elefante was about right there and I
saw an alligator and I saw patos y . . .
      A: ¿Víboras?
      Ch: Yeah. And I saw snakes and . . .

This observation is in accord with Swain and Wesche (1975), who found that language alternations in their subject's speech at about ages 3 years 5 months to 3 years 10 months consisted mostly of nouns. Lindholm and Padilla (1978) also noted that the most common type of language mixing found in their data involved nouns. It is of interest that Christopher does not necessarily switch simply because he does not possess the equivalent in the other language. This is apparent in (11), for example, where he produces "semillas" and then later within the same dialogue uses "seeds." He is flipping through a storybook on Sylvester and Tweety:

(11) Ch: . . . to eat it, that's why him flying, to eat papa and then he says I (3:5)
saw a puddy tat, I did! I did! Then got some pie [?] put semillas
and grandma put it on. Grandma says, "It ready," and . . .
      Then Sylvester put all pintura, and then, and then says, "Get
ready!" [?] and then throw a big clavado, then step on truck and
fall down, y luego, y luego got escalera off and he hit him así,
and then pa! got pie with pescado and seeds and then eat it, and
then . . .

Swain and Wesche and Lindholm and Padilla likewise frequently found within a single utterance a word and its equivalent in the other language.

Of primary interest in this report, however, are Christopher's bilingual utterances. The following examples were typical of his mixed-language utterances at the ages indicated:

(12a)	Ch:	I sudar 'cause I was running.	(3:4)
(b)		. . . y luego he baja de la escalera . . .	(4:5)
(c)		Me manchar myself with pintura.	(3:10)
(d)		I went a misa.	(4:5)

Several patterns in his bilingual speech are relevant to the question of linguistic interaction. The first and most apparent is his ability to switch from English to Spanish and vice versa at various grammatical points within a sentence. He frequently switches between the subject and the verb, a switching point not generally found in the bilingual speech of adults: (12a) and (12b), for example.

Another unit that is often broken up, again in a way not characteristic of adult speech, is the prepositional phrase. In (12c) the preposition is expressed in English, although the object of the preposition is in Spanish. This practice is also illustrated in the following examples:

(13a)	Ch:	. . . descompuzo by solo.	(3:6)
(b)		. . . throwing clock into afuera.	(3:5)

The constituents, or units, of adult bilingual speech, do not appear to operate the same way in Christopher's speech. He apparently does not yet possess any kind of code-switching grammar or any notion of what "goes together" and what does not; any word is subject to a switch. (See Aguirre, 1978, and Pfaff, 1979, for a discussion of code-switching grammars.)

In the following examples a predicate adjective, adjective, possessive adjective, part of a verb phrase, and a direct object are expressed in the alternative language:

(14a)	Ch:	. . . ball is ponchada, se ponchó.	(3:11)
(b)		The negro one.	(3:5)
(c)		En your libro.	(3:5)
(d)		The water is still choriando.	(4:5)
(e)		We trying find nueces.	(3:2)

An interesting sign of Christopher's bilingual competence appears in (14a). In this utterance the adjective "ponchada" agrees in gender with "pelota" (feminine), the Spanish equivalent of the English "ball," which the subject actually uses. This is a common occurrence, and it was observed in earlier stages of Christopher's speech. At 2 years 2 months, for instance, he produced the following:

(15a) Ota boot?
  (b) Oto piece?

Again there is gender agreement. The genders of the nouns "bota" and "ped-azo" are assigned to the English equivalents, as is evident from the child's use of "ota" ("otra," feminine) and "oto" ("otro," masculine) to modify them. These forms show that the subject has internalized these morphological features of Spanish—gender assignment and gender agreement—and, furthermore, is able to apply these rules cross-linguistically, not violating these language-specific rules even in mixed-language utterances.

Christopher has acquired the phonology, lexicon, and grammar of Spanish as well as English. His use of these components appears to be flexible. In a few cases he has transferred them across languages, using Spanish grammar without the corresponding sounds and vocabulary, for example. This type of linguistic alternation, the production of a sentence in Spanish that is actually modeled on the English version, is seen in the following examples:

(16a) Ch: ¿Con fea agua?   (3:10)
  (b)   ¿Qué se limpia las manos con?   (3:5)
  (c)   ¿Quién es esto pa?   (3:5)

Examples (16a)–(c) have the structure of English although the words are Spanish. That a transfer from English has occurred is readily apparent when one looks at the English translations:

  With ugly water?
  What are you cleaning your hands with?
  Who is this for?

Notice, however, that the Spanish article is correctly used in (16b) with body parts ("las manos"), instead of the possessive adjective that would be used in the English equivalent and that Christopher does in fact use in English utterances:

(17a) Ch: ... got to brush my teeth   (3:10)
  (b)   ... and my face look así ...

The subject has also correctly used the reflexive "limpiarse" in (16b), rather than the second person pronoun, which would be used in the English equivalent. Christopher is not, therefore, simply doing a word-by-word transfer in every case but is maintaining some structural features that occur only within one language, Spanish. He is clearly differentiating between languages here and correctly judging some rules to be not common to both but language-specific. This modeling of Spanish sentences on English versions is not unique to Christopher's speech and cannot, therefore, be attributed to the nonseparation of codes in his environment. Fantini (1974), for example, noted Spanish utterances in his son's speech that were directly transferred from English.

Ben Zeev (1977) has noted a tendency among bilingual children to be more analytical about their language than monolinguals. Sentence (16b) appears to reflect such an analytical process with regard to the subject's grammatical knowledge of English and Spanish, as do (12a) and (12c) and the following:

(18a) Ch: Me ver changos.   (4:6)
(b)   ... and then me venir a la casa ...   (4:5)

In these examples Christopher has simplified, or neutralized, the Spanish verbs by using the infinitive form instead of inflecting them to agree with correspond-ing subjects, probably because he does not yet possess the morphological knowledge to inflect these verbs correctly. Notice, however, that in all these utterances he has inserted subject pronouns, thereby providing information about person and number that he apparently recognizes as essential to the statements and that would otherwise be provided by the inflections of the Span-ish verbs. He clearly elects to avoid subject-verb conflict by using the neutral infinitive rather than risk using the wrong verb ending. This strategy of sim-plifying a structure within a language has also been noted in the speech of other bilingual children and is discussed in Ben Zeev (1977). Christopher thus seems to have analyzed the Spanish verb phrase and to be well aware that he can dispense with explicitly expressing the subject when he has the corresponding ending on the verb, as seen in the following:

(19a) Ch: ... y luego pasamos en frente de la gente ...   (4:5)
(b)   ... y luego fuimos sacando zacate.   (4:5)
(c)   We just stayed there and trabajamos.   (4:3)

He has used a Spanish verb with the correct inflection in all of these utterances and has, therefore, omitted the subjects, in accordance with the rule in Spanish. This rule, furthermore, is applied in most of his Spanish, but not his English, speech. See, for example, (8) and (10). Examples (16b), (17), (18), and (19) thus give us an indication of the analytical process this child is going through as he acquires Spanish and English simultaneously.

CONCLUSION

The principal question addressed in this study was whether the nonseparation of codes in a child's speech environment would negatively affect his or her pro-ductive skills in either or both languages. In an attempt to answer this question, I have described the language development of a child raised in a bilingual envi-ronment with no separation of codes and presented a qualitative analysis of his speech. Sociolinguistic and linguistic patterns in his speech demonstrated that the nonseparation of codes was not delaying or otherwise hindering his lan-guage development. He was indeed becoming bilingual, as evidenced by his ability to use Spanish, English, or both Spanish and English in a code-switching style of speech. Certain sociolinguistic patterns in his speech demonstrated that he was able to differentiate between the two languages; correct grammatical patterns in both English and Spanish showed his developing grammatical knowledge of both languages. The following can, therefore, be concluded from the findings presented in this preliminary study.

The subject has begun to separate his two codes much as bilingual children raised according to the one person–one language principle have done. This is true both sociolinguistically and linguistically. He was also less likely, at the stage covered here, to mix languages in his speech than he was prior to age 3 years 3 months, and was therefore producing longer all-English or all-Spanish dialogues.

Most of his language alternations now consist solely of nouns or noun phrases. These insertions, furthermore, are not always due to his not having the equivalent term in the other language. Christopher appears to have acquired a grammar of English as well as one of Spanish. He produces long, grammatically correct dialogues in either language, and he correctly applies language-specific rules in his speech. This was seen, for example, in the use of the definite article with body parts in a Spanish phrase, as opposed to the possessive adjective that he uses with body parts in English utterances. His knowledge and differentiation of the two grammatical systems is also shown in examples where he neutralizes a Spanish verb to an infinitive and inserts the subject pronoun rather than conjugate the Spanish verb and delete the subject. He does not delete the subject in sentences expressed in English.

In sum, the findings reported here show that a child raised in an environment without rigorous separation of codes has become bilingual. Nothing in the data supports the claim made by other researchers in child bilingualism that nonseparation of codes will delay the child's productive skills and differentiation of the two linguistic systems. This suggests that a linguistic environment where code switching occurs can be conducive to the acquisition of bilingualism in children. Such an environment may also permit the maintenance of a second language.

REFERENCES

Aguirre, A. *An experimental sociolinguistic study of Chicano bilingualism.* San Francisco: R & E Research Associates, 1978.

Ben Zeev, S. Mechanisms by which childhood bilingualism affects understanding of language and cognitive structures. In P. A. Hornby (Ed.), *Bilingualism: psychological, social and educational implications.* New York: Academic Press, 1977, pp. 29–56.

Bergman, C. R. Interference vs. independent development in infant bilingualism. In

G. D. Keller, R. V. Teschner, and S. Viera (Eds.), *Bilingualism in the bicentennial and beyond*. New York: Bilingual Press, 1976, pp. 87–96.

Burling, R. F. Language development of a Garo and English speaking child. In E. M. Hatch (Ed.), *Second language acquisition: a book of readings*. Rowley, Mass.: Newbury House, 1978, pp. 54–75.

Fantini, A. Language acquisition of a bilingual child: a sociolinguistic perspective. Doctoral dissertation, University of Texas, Austin, 1974.

Genishi, C. Rules for code-switching in young Spanish-English speakers: an exploratory study of language socialization. Doctoral dissertation, University of California, Berkeley, 1976.

Huerta, A. The acquisition of bilingualism: a code-switching approach. *Working papers in sociolinguistics*, no. 39. Austin, Tex.: Southwest Educational Development Lab, 1977.

Huerta, A. Code-switching among Spanish-English bilinguals: a sociolinguistic perspective. Doctoral dissertation, University of Texas, Austin, 1978.

Imedadze, N. V. On the psychological nature of child speech formation under condition of exposure to two languages. *International Journal of Psychology*, 1967, *2*, 129–132.

Leopold, W. F. A child's learning of two languages. In E. M. Hatch (Ed.), *Second language acquisition: a book of readings*. Rowley, Mass.: Newbury House, 1978, pp. 23–32.

Lindholm, K., and Padilla, A. Child bilingualism: report on language mixing, switching and translations. *Linguistics*, 1978, *211*, 12–44.

Pfaff, C. Constraints on language mixing: intrasentential code-switching and borrowing in Spanish/English. *Language*, 1979, *55*, 291–318.

Ronjat, J. Le développement du langage observé chez un enfant bilingue. In E. M. Hatch (Ed.), *Second language acquisition: a book of readings*. Rowley, Mass.: Newbury House, 1978, p. 465 (Abstract).

Swain, M., and Wesche, M. Linguistic interaction: case study of a bilingual child. *Language Sciences*, 1975, *37*, 17–22.

3 | Beto at the Sugar Table: Code Switching in a Bilingual Classroom

SARAH HUDELSON
Florida International University

In recent years, bilingual education programs have been inundated with language assessment instruments. For purposes of classroom placement and instruction, these tests are administered to numbers of elementary school children, most of whom are members of minority groups and native speakers of languages other than English. The tests purport to give an indication of a child's language ability in one or more languages. At least partly because of pressure from funding sources on schools to quantify the language abilities of children in their bilingual programs, these instruments receive wide use.

However, serious questions have been raised about what these tests tell teachers (Cazden, 1977; Dubois, 1974; Shuy, 1977). Of particular concern has been the generally contextless nature of the assessment tasks. Children are put into unnatural language situations and asked to produce language. Too often, the language the children produce in these unnatural settings is used to label them. From a minute piece of performance that frequently lacks any social or cultural context, a child's overall competence (or lack of it) is judged (Erickson, Florio, and Bremme, 1975), even though there is evidence that children's language performances vary with the kind of tasks they are asked to do (Cazden, 1970).

Even when a child has been found to function in two languages and has, therefore, been designated as bilingual, the label presents problems. What does it mean to call a child bilingual? Are bilingual children necessarily equally

This analysis was originally done for a seminar on Ethnographic Methods in Research in Bilingual Education taught by Frederick Erickson at the Linguistic Society of America Institute held at the University of Illinois in 1978. Thanks are due to Dr. Erickson for his helpful comments and to Blanca Rosa Rodriguez for permission to use one of her videotapes. Acknowledgments are also due to David Dillon, Judith Lindfors, and Carole Urzua, whose work in language functions has helped me grow in my understanding of children's language.

proficient in two languages? How does a bilingual child make use of his or her two languages, in the classroom and outside it? Do bilingual children use both languages in the same ways and for the same purposes? Can patterns of language be described for a bilingual child in a variety of social contexts? Can we analyze a child's sociolinguistic competence, rather than just his or her linguistic competence (Hymes, 1974)? No language-assessment instrument yet developed addresses these issues. Yet they are important questions for people working in the field of bilingual education. How might one begin to address them?

Perhaps a partial solution lies in the observation of bilingual children in more natural and less contrived settings and in the examination of what children do with the languages they speak in these contexts. If, for example, one wants to know more about a bilingual child's use of language in the school setting, one needs to examine his or her language across a variety of school occasions (Cazden in Erickson, Florio, and Bremme, 1975). In real life settings, with other children and with adults, a child may demonstrate a variety of language abilities that the label "bilingual" does not fully reflect.

One technique for collecting and examining spontaneous language samples is videotaping. Cameras may be trained on children or areas of a classroom for extended periods of time, and the tapes may then be studied. An advantage of videotape over audiotape is that the visual context is recorded, so that observations and analyses can include nonverbal as well as verbal behavior. The chapter that follows illustrates the discoveries that may be made about a bilingual child's language abilities through the examination of a twenty-minute segment of videotape.

ANALYSIS OF TAPES

The subject of our study is an eight-year-old bilingual Mexican American named Beto. He is enrolled in a bilingual classroom in California. A close examination of the videotape in which Beto interacts with Adrian (a Spanish-dominant child), two Anglo girls (both monolingual English-speakers), and other Chicanos (bilinguals) who enter and leave the scene reveals not only that he is bilingual but also that he is able to use both English and Spanish in a variety of ways.

Beto has been asked to help Adrian accomplish a task that involves constructing a design with sugar cubes that are pasted together and then mounted on paper. Beto explains the task to Adrian, after which they move to a work-table where two Anglo girls are seated. Most of the conversation takes place at this table.

On first viewing the videotape, it becomes obvious that Beto employs a strategy noted by several researchers of child bilingualism: When addressing someone, use the language your listener knows, or knows best (Genishi, 1976; Shultz, 1975). Beto consistently addresses Adrian (and the other Chicanos) in Spanish and the two Anglo girls in English. He does not make mistakes. He uses the language ability of the addressee to determine which language he himself will use. Every time Beto initiates a conversation, he initiates it in the language of the listener(s).

Beto's topics of conversation fall into the classes of task-related and non-task-related talk. The task-related items include getting the glue, commenting about the glue's consistency, and observations about the sugar-cube task. Non-task-related topics range from boy-girl relationships to classroom happenings to personal habits. Most often Beto's conversations with the girls are task-related; with Adrian and the other Chicanos he more frequently chats about something other than the task at hand. In addition, Beto at several points makes comments to himself in both English and Spanish. Some of these utterances will be seen in the selections from the transcripts that follow.

One's general impression of Beto, then, is that of a child with productive ability in both Spanish and English, who knows not only the grammars of both languages but when to use them (Hymes, 1974). Yet this overview does not describe adequately the variety of forms of English and Spanish that Beto uses and the uses that he makes of his languages. In order to get some feeling for the child's linguistic and sociolinguistic accomplishments, selected interactional sequences have been transcribed, and an attempt has been made to analyze them in terms not only of the language used and the form of the language, but also of the functions the various speech acts have. This tentative analysis is based on both the utterances themselves and the context of the utterances (the situation and the nonverbal behavior of the participants in the situation). Several of these transcriptions follow, with translation where needed and with notes on the context at the right. An analysis follows each transcribed section.

Segment 1

In this segment, Beto describes the sugar-cube project to Adrian.[1]

		Utterances	Context
(1)	B:	¿Qué? A ver, enséñame. (What? Let's see, show me.)	B and A are seated together on the floor. B is explaining to A what he
(2)	A:	Tienes que raller. (You have to write.)	has to do. Both are looking at the paper.
(3)	B:	Naah. Mira, tienes unos cuadros. Son así cuadrados. Y les pones aquí	

---

[1]*B* stands for Beto; *A* for Adrian; *C* for Chicano boy. A question mark [?] indicates inability to make out what was said. Ellipses mean that a portion of the tape was not transcribed.

como ya están así—uno aquí, dos
aquí, el otro aquí. (Naah. Look, you
have some squares. They are square
like this. And you put them here
like they are already here—one
here, two here, the other one here.)

(4) A: Yo sé. (I know.)

(5) B: Así después lo copias aquí con los
cuadros—la pegadura—y los haces
así. (This way after you copy it here
with the squares, you paste, and you
make them this way and this way.)

(6) A: Yo sé. (I know.)   B and A move to put paper in tote.

(7) A: ¿Ahora, por dónde voy a ir yo?
(Now where shall I go?)

(8) B: ¿Onde quieres ir? (Where do you
want to go?)

(9) A: Aquí. (Here.)   A joins a group that is in a lesson

(10) B: ¿Aquí? Teacher, teacher. (Here?   with a teacher. He is on the outer
Teacher, teacher.)   fringe of the group.

(11) B: Hey, Adrian—Adrian.   B leans in to talk to A.

(12) A: Eh? (Huh?)

(13) B: Tu querías jugar allá. (You wanted   B points to another section of the
to play over there.)   room.

(14) A: Vamos. ¿Ónde vas a jugar tú?   A turns around.
(Let's go. Where are you going to
play?)

(15) B: Onde tú vas. (Wherever you go.)   Boys get up and begin to walk
across the room.

(16) B: Mira, mira como lo está haciendo   B stops halfway across the room,
él. Mira le pone pegadura. (Look,   where a boy is working.
look at how he's doing it. Look at
how he puts glue on it.)

(17) B: ¿Qué es eso? ¿Tu nombre? (What's   B leans in to see the boy's paper.
that? Your name?)

(18) B: Parece un plato volador. (It looks   B looks away and leans on his chin
like a flying plate.)   as he says this.

(19) C: No es un platillo. Es un avión. (It's   Boy responds but keeps looking at
not a plate. It's an airplane.)   work.

(20) B: Avión—oh. Ahí está la pegadura.
(A plane, oh. There's the glue.)

(21) A: Vamos. (Let's go.)   A joins B, taps him on the shoul-

(22) B: ¿Eh? (Huh?)   der, and points toward another

(23) A: Vamos allá mejor. (It's better to go   area.
over there.)

(24)	B:	OK.
(25)	C:	[?]
(26)	B:	Esos no pegas con. . . (don't paste those with . . .)
(27)	A:	¿Eh? (Huh?)
(28)	B:	Mira—mira, mira ellas. Mira— OK, mira lo que voy a hacer. (Look—look, look at them. Look. OK, look at what I'm going to do.)
(29)	A:	Mira lo que voy a hacer. Mira lo que voy a hacer. (Look at what I'm going to do. Look at what I'm going to do.)
(30)	B:	Mira. Son siete. Mira. (Look. There are seven. Look.)
(31)	A:	Uno, dos, tres, cuatro, cinco, seis, siete. (One, two, three, four, five, six, seven.)

B and A walk away from the other boy and move to another table. They begin to work.

In this segment Beto demonstrates his ability to use Spanish in several ways. First, he employs the language to inform or explain, telling Adrian what his task with paper and sugar cubes is (1–6). He returns to this informing-explaining function as he and Adrian pass another child doing the sugar-cube task (16). He uses this child's work to show Adrian what Adrian must do. Still later (26–31), while watching what Adrian is doing, he asserts that what Adrian is doing is wrong and proceeds to explain the task again. This time he is even more specific; he tells Adrian to watch what he is doing as he counts the sugar cubes. (In the following segment he tells Adrian to get the glue.) Beto has explained and re-explained the task, but he has modified his strategies according to his interpretation of Adrian's lack of understanding (even though Adrian keeps saying that he knows what he is supposed to do). He explains in a general way (3), he gives an example (16), and he breaks the task down step by step (28, 30). Here Beto demonstrates that he is able to use language to inform and that he is able to adjust his informing strategies.

Beto also demonstrates some ability to use language to get others to do what he wants them to do. His task is to help Adrian with the sugar cubes, but Adrian joins a group working on another task (9). Beto gets him to move by using a suggestive form rather than a demand (13). This suggestion carries weight with Adrian because he agrees to move. A little later (17–20), he does a similar thing. He wants to know what the other child is making, but when he asks him (17), there is no response. Beto waits and then announces what he thinks it is (18). This statement brings a response from the child. Beto did not repeat his question or demand to know what the figure was; he even looked away from the boy as he commented on the object, feigning lack of interest. Yet he got an answer. Beto was able to use both language and body movements to achieve his ends.

We begin to get a hint of Beto's ability to code switch, when he turns from Adrian to summon the teacher (10). His previous phonology has been Spanish, but his "Teacher, teacher" is said with English phonology. When one listens to the tape, the phonological switch is pronounced. This is a hint of things to come.

Segment 2

Beto and Adrian have been joined at the table by two English-speaking Anglo girls.[2]

		Utterances	*Context*
(1)	G1:	Beto.	G1 leans across table to hand B something.
(2)	B:	What is it?	
(3)	G1:	Here [?].	
(4)	B:	Let's see—oh.	B looks at object in his hand.
(5)	G2:	Tammy, you should give it to Beto.	G2 talks to G1.
(6)	B:	Yeah, I want it.	
(7)	G1:	I'm gonna give it to my brother.	G1 shakes head no and reaches for object. B hands her object.
(8)	G2:	Beto knows him.	Children are bent over their work.
(9)	B:	I know.	
(10)	G1:	I've been to her house before.	
(11)	A:	Ya la hice, mira. (I made it, look.)	A looks at B as he talks.
(12)	G1:	[?]	
(13)	B:	OK, mira. Son siete. Después garras garras, después garras siete. (OK, look. There are seven. Afterward, grab, grab, afterward grab seven.)	B turns from his work to A.
(14)	G2:	This is good tacky glue.	G2 gets glue from glue pot.
(15)	A:	Uno, dos, tres, cuatro, cinco, seis, siete. (One, two, three, four, five, six, seven.)	B reaches for glue as A counts.
(16)	B:	OK. Garras la pegadura. (OK. Get the glue.) Is this tacky glue?	
(17)	G2:	Yes.	B grabs glue pot and hits it on table.
(18)	G1:	Boy.	
(19)	B:	Mira, aquí hay pegadura. (Look, here's the glue.)	B shows A the glue pot.

---

[2]*G1* stands for the first Anglo girl; *G2* for the second Anglo girl.

(20)	A:	Pero no tiene nada acá. (But it doesn't have any over here.)	Girls reach for pot and G1 passes pot to A.
(21)	B:	Que vida. (What a life.)	
(22)	B:	¿Cómo voy a hacer esto? (How am I going to do this?)	B looks straight ahead as he works and talks.
(23)	A:	¿Sabes qué? (You know what?)	A glances at B as he changes the topic.
(24)	B:	¿Qué? (What?)	B glances up at A and back at his work.
(25)	A:	Raul quiere a Aurelia. (Raul loves Aurelia.)	A glances at B as he talks, but mostly he gazes at his work.
(26)	B:	Ya sé. (I already know.)	
(27)	A:	Y a Marisol. (And also Marisol.)	Boys' eyes are focused on work.
(28)	B:	Ya sé. (I already know.) Glue. Yo ya sé todo. (I already know all that.)	B glances up as he says glue and then returns to work.
(29)	A:	¿Qué? (What?)	
(30)	B:	Yo, ya sé todo de ellos porque yo miro. (I already know everything about them because I watch.)	
(31)	A:	[?]	
(32)	B:	Los miro fuera en el lunch cuando comimos. Siéntate conmigo y allá te digo. (I see them outside at lunch when we eat. Sit with me and I'll tell you there.) . . . [The boys chat for two or three minutes.]	B looks away from work to A as he talks. He gestures with his hands.
(33)	B:	Give me glue.	B looks briefly in direction of girls and then looks away.
(34)	G1:	Tacky, want tacky. It's stuck	G1 moves glue toward B.
(35)	B:	So.	B has eyes on work.
(36)	G1:	to my finger. Ah, there.	
(37)	G2:	I can barely spread it.	Four-second pause here; then B starts to talk. He looks at G2 as he speaks in line 38.
(38)	B:	Wow, the glue sticks. The glue, ah.	
(39)	G1:	I need some tacky, I need some tacky.	G1 looks up at the group as she talks.
(40)	B:	Kakis? Kakis?	
(41)	A:	Caca. (Shit.)	
(42)	G1:	I mean I need a screwdriver—need a screwdriver.	G1 looks ahead at the group and glances at B.
(43)	B:	Glue, glue, glue, glue.	B has a fingerful of glue. He stretches out his finger, wiggles it, and repeats the word.
(44)	G2:	He has it.	G2 motions toward A.

(45) A: Acá. (Over here.)   A points to glue pot that he has
                                                      been using.
(46) B: Oh.   B looks at his cubes.
(47) G2: This kid was in my class last year
          and [?].
(48) B: O, lo hice mal, lo hice mal, lo hice   B crumples his paper and looks at
          mal. (Oh, I did it wrong, I did it   it.
          wrong, I did it wrong.)
(49) A: ¿Por qué?
(50) B: ¿Eh? (Huh?) No lo pegues aquí.   Beto looks at what A is doing,
          No lo pegues. (Don't paste it here.   reaches in to correct something,
          Don't paste it.)   and knocks some stuff onto the
                                                      floor.
(51) A: Mira lo que me hiciste, muchacho.   A looks at B as he talks.
          Mira no más. (Look at what you
          did to me, boy. Just look.)
(52) B: Mira. (Look.)
(53) G2: Tacky, tacky.   G2 looks at cubes as she makes
                                                      request.
(54) B: No lo pegues aquí, porque, porque   B looks at A and his creation.
          (Don't paste it here, because,
          because)
(55) G2: I need tacky glue.   Girl looks at B.
(56) B: van a sacar y ponerlo como allí.   B motions in another direction.
          (they are going to take and put it   Girl gets up and walks around to
          like over there.)   get glue.
(57) A: ¿Qué vamos a hacer—como?
          (What are we going to do—how?)
(58) C: Can I come to this table?   Chicano boy enters scene.
(59) B: Dile a la maestra. Oh no, porque y   B looks at Chicano as he talks.
          [?] llendas las sillas. Eh, ¿que era
          lo que agarrastes allí con la glue?
          (Ask the teacher. Oh no, because
          [?] the chairs taken. Hey, what
          was it that you took over there with
          the glue?)

The first thing that is obvious in this segment is Beto's ability to move
between Spanish and English, depending upon his addressee. He consistently
uses Spanish with Adrian and English with the two Anglo girls. But subtler
abilities also become obvious on closer examination. At the opening of this segment (1–10), Beto chats in English with the two girls about something unrelated to the gluing task. He is certainly able to maintain himself in the conversation, where each child inserts comments. Yet when Adrian summons him
in Spanish (11), he switches into Spanish, explaining Adrian's task in specific

terms (13–22). He explains again later (50, 54, 56). The use of language as well as the language itself changes.

When Adrian engages Beto in a non-task-related conversation (23–32), Beto uses Spanish both to chat and to put himself in a good light with Adrian. He emphasizes what *he* knows and what *he* sees, and he offers to let Adrian in on some of the information. As he talks, he is able to challenge Adrian for control of that part of the conversation. Indeed, he dominates that portion of the interaction (28–32). Thus, Beto uses Spanish for self-expression, for bragging, and for the manipulation of the conversation so that he dominates it. Beto also uses Spanish as a self-expressive vehicle when he is not necessarily expecting a response. He talks to himself in Spanish to figure out what he is to do (22) and to express lack of satisfaction with what he has done (48). When Adrian questions him after this second talking to himself, Beto is caught off guard ("Eh?"). Beto uses Spanish, then, to address himself.

Beto also evidences a use of Spanish to influence the language choice of another bilingual child. Another Chicano asks, in English, to join the group (58). Beto responds to him in Spanish. From that point on, this child's interactions at the sugar table are in Spanish. Possibly Beto's choice of Spanish influenced him. It should also be noted that Beto employs code switching at a lexical level in this interaction (59), when he uses the word "glue" instead of "pegadura," perhaps because this child is bilingual whereas Adrian is Spanish-dominant. (He consistently used "pegadura" with Adrian.)

Beto employs English in different ways. His chitchat in English has already been mentioned, but Beto uses English for purposes other than socializing. He employs English to establish and maintain task-relevant contact with the girls, and perhaps to maintain some minimal level of group feeling at the table. In (16), for example, Beto uses a question form to include the girls verbally in what is going on. Since one of the girls already has labeled the glue as tacky (14), Beto asks a question to which he already knows the answer. Beto does this again later when he comments on the glue (38). Earlier one of the girls had noted the stickiness of the glue. When Beto repeats this information, therefore, he is not using language to give new information but rather to acknowledge what has been said, to affirm the participation of the girls in the interaction. But his use of English excludes Adrian, and so Beto handles the inclusion-exclusion problem by moving back and forth between the two languages.

Additionally, Beto indicates that he is able to play with the sounds of English. When one of the girls asks for the glue (39), Beto responds, "Kakis, Kakis?" Since "tacky" has been used by all of them several times before this supposed question, the form is not really a question but rather a phonological commentary or playing around (which incidentally allows Adrian into the action with a Spanish word). This seems evident from the girl's response (42), which is to call for a screwdriver, thus continuing the fanciful use of language. Further on Beto produces the word "glue," holding out a finger covered with glue, wiggling the finger and repeating the word four times (43). One of the girls and Adrian respond by telling him where the glue is, but Beto does not stick his finger into the glue pot. Given the repetition of the single word and the elongation of the "-ue" each time, it seems plausible to interpret this production as playing or experimenting with the pronunciation of "glue," manipulating language for its own sake rather than actually requesting more glue.

Beto also uses English in this segment to request things. At the beginning of the segment, when he wants to examine what one of the girls has, he uses "What is it?" and "Let's see," both request forms (2, 4).

Segment 3

The children are still working at the sugar-cube task.

		Utterances	*Context*
(1)	B:	¿Tú miras las luchas? (Do you watch the fights?)	B and A have returned to the sugar table. B turns toward A.
(2)	A:	¿Tú?	A nods and looks at B.
(3)	B:	Sí.	B nods.
(4)	A:	¿Pues, dónde lo voy a pegar? (Well, where am I going to paste this?)	The boys are seated. A turns to B and indicates with his hand.
(5)	B:	¿Qué? (What?)	
(6)	A:	¿Ónde lo voy a pegar? ¿Cómo lo pego? (Where am I going to paste it? How do I paste it?)	A indicates with his hand what he needs help with.
(7)	B:	Give me tacky.	B looks at G2.
(8)	A:	Aquí hay, mira. (Here is some, look.)	A sticks hand in B's face.
(9)	G2:	Tacky, tacky glue over there.	
(10)	B:	Golly, it's, it dries fast so you better hurry up.	B and G2 are sharing the glue pot. They have turned toward each
(11)	G2:	I know. I forgot all about that.	other and glance at each other as
(12)	B:	It dries fast.	they talk and work.
(13)	G2:	I know.	B sits back and turns away from
(14)	A:	Mira, lo pegas aquí. Mira. (Look, you paste it here. Look.)	girl.
(15)	G2:	My thing's coming apart. I can't believe it's coming apart.	G2 is looking at her creation.
(16)	A:	[?] gringo.	A looks away from table as he talks to someone.
(17)	B:	Él no es gringo. Él no es gringo. Rickie sí es un gringo. Ella es una gringa, y ella es una gringa. (He's	B points to someone away from table and then points to the two girls.

not a gringo. He's not a gringo.
Rickie is a gringo. She's a gringa
and so is she.)

As in the previous segments, Beto is involved with the sugar-cube task. As before, he uses Spanish and English with different people. With Adrian he first uses Spanish in a conversation that is unrelated to the project (1). He is using the language in a social-interactive way. Later, when Adrian has referred to someone as a gringo, Beto uses his Spanish for informative purposes, to distinguish gringos from nongringos. Here he uses language to inform through classifying.

As in the previous sequence, he also uses English in more than one way, both to request (7) and to comment on the scene (10, 12). He may also be declaring what is already known to open up a conversation with the girls and keep the lines of communication open, since all parties are aware of the nature of tacky glue. The form of the declarative, then, does not necessarily correspond to its function.

Segment 4

In this part of the scene a Chicana[3] has entered the group and is standing between Beto and Adrian. She has in her hand a picture made by pasting beans on paper. All of Beto's interactions with her are in Spanish.

		Utterances	*Context*
(1)	B:	Mira. Así, porque si—mira Adrian—porque si lo pegas aquí, se pega aquí—y no lo puedes sacar—glue, tacky. (Look, this way, because if—look Adrian— because if you paste it here, it will get stuck and you can't remove it—glue, tacky.)	B and A are seated; one Chicana stands next to A. The two Anglo girls are also seated. B is helping A. B glances at one of the girls and holds out his hand for the glue.
(2)	G1:	We need it.	G1 glances at B.
(3)	B:	Well, we need it too.	G1 moves the glue toward B, stands between A and B.
(4)	A:	¿Qué es eso? Oh—los cacahuetitos (What is that? Oh, the little peanuts.)	A turns to Chicana and points toward what she is carrying.
(5)	B:	Son frijoles. (They are beans.)	
(6)	A:	¿Se los comen? (Do you eat them?)	
(7)	B:	No, son pitades—son pita—pinta-	

---

[3]*C* indicates Chicana.

		Utterances	Context
		dos (No, they are pain—pain—painted.)	
(8)	C:	Pitadas [laughs].	C points at B and then moves out of the scene.
(9)	B:	Yo no dije esto—¿no verdad?—pintados (I didn't say that—isn't that true?—painted.)	B looks at her as he replies, and then turns toward A and looks at him.
(10)	G2:	We need tacky.	
(11)	C:	[?]	C moves back into the scene and whispers to B.
(12)	B:	¿Qué? (What?)	
(13)	C:	[?]	
(14)	B:	Ni hablas bien. (You don't even talk right.)	B talks to girl's back as she departs.
(15)	A:	¿Qué dijo? (What did she say?)	
(16)	B:	Yo no sé. Ni habla bien. (I don't know. She doesn't even talk right.)	

The most interesting portion of this segment is Beto's revealing of a metalinguistic awareness of how Spanish should be pronounced. When he mispronounces "pintados," he goes back and says it correctly (7), monitoring his own speech. When the Chicana laughs at his mispronunciation, Beto denies that he has mispronounced the word and declares what he said. He later maintains, when he does not understand her, that she does not speak well, another comment on language as language.

In English, Beto requests the glue using an elliptical form, "Glue, tacky" (1). The intent of the words is evident not from the form, but from the context (the knowledge that the participants have about what is going on and Beto's nonverbal signals, including his glance at the girl and the extension of his hand). When one of the girls replies that the girls need the glue (2), Beto reasserts his claim in English (3). But more significant is what he does with his voice. As he says, "Well, we need it too," he pitches his voice higher, as if in imitation of the girls' voices. He elongates the word, making it "to-ooo," and instead of using the low fall appropriate for a declarative form, he uses a rise-fall. The effect is one of teasing.

Segment 5

At this point, one of the girls, Beto, Adrian, and another Chicano are at the table. Adrian has brought Beto a different pot of glue, and Beto is trying to open it. It will not open.

		Utterances	Context
(1)	A:	Ten, ábrela. (Here, open this.)	A hands B a glue pot with top on it.

		Utterances	Context
(2)	B:	Es que la pegadura—no se puede. (It's that the glue—it won't open.)	B tries to open the glue pot.
(3)	C:	Ya la pegates. (You already stuck it.)	
(4)	B:	Nah, yo no. (No, not me.)	
(5)	C:	¿No fuites que le dijites a la [?]? (Weren't you the one that told [?]?)	The Chicano makes a turning motion with his hands.
(6)	B:	Sí, pero no se pega bien pronto. (Yes, but it doesn't get stuck that fast.)	
(7)	C:	Aquí hay mas pegadura. (Here is more glue.)	The Chicano hands B another glue pot.
(8)	B:	Ten. No se abre. (Take this. It doesn't open.)	B hands the Chicano glue pot A had given him.
(9)	C:	Mira como lo dejates. (Look at how you left it.)	The Chicano indicates with his finger that there is glue around the top of the glue pot.
(10)	B:	Ves. Tu lo volteates también. Tu fuites asi. (You see. You turned it too. You went like this.)	B indicates with a gesture that the other child had also turned the pot.

In his talk with the other Chicano, Beto demonstrates that he is able to carry on an argument and return comment for comment in Spanish. He answers his opponent's arguments in a kind of verbal duel. Thus, he employs Spanish to assert himself, to argue, and to answer accusations.

Segment 6

Beto is still at the table, where he is finishing his sugar-cube picture.

		Utterances	*Context*
(1)	G1:	Beto, when you get finished just take it to [?].	Girl looks at B as she addresses him.
(2)	B:	Oh, good.	
(3)	B:	You stupid tacky glue.	B is rubbing his fingers together
(4)	A:	Mira. (Look.)	and looking at them. There is a
(5)	G1:	Oh, no.	five-second pause as everyone works.
(6)	A:	Mira, [?]. Te castiga si te comes uno, ¿verdad? (Look, [?]. You will get scolded if you eat one, won't you?)	A sticks a hand with a sugar cube in Beto's face.
(7)	B:	¿Quién? (Who?)	
(8)	A:	A uno. (One.)	The children look at their work as
(9)	B:	¿Quién te castiga? (Who will scold you?)	they talk.

(10) A: La maestra. (The teacher.)

(11) B: No te ca-sti-ga. (She won't scold   B looks at A.
          you.)

(12) A: Ga tiga. [Nonsense syllables.] [Six-
          second pause.]

(13) B: Frijoles. Yo no dije frifoles. Yo dije   B looks at A.
          frijoles. (Beans. I didn't say
          "beans" [mispronounced]. I said
          "beans" [correct pronunciation].)

(14) A: Frijoles. (Beans.)

(15) B: Frijoles. Verdad que. (Beans.
          Isn't it true that.)

The most interesting feature of this interaction is Beto's use of language to talk about language. As he and Adrian talk about whether the teacher will punish someone for eating a sugar cube, Beto asserts that she will not (11), elongating the syllables of "castiga" and articulating each one with exaggerated care to emphasize the point. Adrian, influenced by the exaggerated pronunciation, produces some nonsense syllables (12). Apparently this starts Beto thinking about language because after a pause he says the word "frijoles" (from segment 4). He then informs Adrian that he said "frijoles" rather than "frifoles." The syllables "jo" and "fo" receive exaggerated stress.

Segment 7

The children are still at the sugar table with their work almost completed.

		Utterances	*Context*
(1)	A:	¿Sabes qué es esto? (Do you know what this is?)	A points to the glue.
(2)	B:	¿Qué? (What?)	B glances up and then back to his work.
(3)	A:	Es cemento. (It's cement.)	
(4)	B:	[Laughs.]	The boys focus on their work and glance at each other.
(5)	A:	Sí. Es cemento. (Yes. It's cement.)	
(6)	B:	Es cemento. (It's cement.)	
(7)	A:	¿Tú no conoces cemento? (You don't know what cement is?)	
(8)	B:	Sí. (Yes.)	
(9)	A:	Que se pone en ladrillos. (That you put on bricks.)	
(10)	B:	Yo sí conozco cemento. (Yes, I know what cement is.)	After (10) the boys work silently for about a minute.
(11)	B:	Let him bite you. Hold his tail. Luchas. Está jugando box. (Fights. He's boxing.)	B looks out to the center of the room. There is a dog in the room. B calls out to someone who is not visible. B turns to A to make a comment to him in Spanish.

Although Adrian produces more language at the beginning of this exchange than Beto does, Beto's responses to his comments indicate his appreciation of Adrian's imaginative use of language. As the boys work with the glue and sugar cubes, Adrian compares the materials to cement and bricks. Beto obviously understands this allusion, as he first laughs appreciatively (4) and then repeats what Adrian has said (6), as if to affirm the idea. In this instance, Spanish is used figuratively rather than literally.

Later Beto's attention is drawn away from the table to the dog in the room. He switches to English and calls out to challenge someone (11). He then switches immediately back into Spanish with Adrian, appearing to feel that it is necessary to tell him what is occurring and, perhaps, offering an imaginative interpretation of the child's play with the dog, comparing it to boxing.

Segment 8

This segment immediately follows the preceding one.[4]

		Utterances	*Context*
(1)	B:	¿Tú tienes miedo de ese perro? (Are you afraid of that dog?)	B gestures toward dog.
(2)	A:	No. (No.)	A shakes head.
(3)	B:	Yo no. (Not me.)	
(4)	G1:	Ella (?). [The girl says something in Spanish, possibly the word "ella" ("she").]	G1 says something to B and gestures outward.
(5)	B:	What?	B leans forward and looks directly at the girl. This is the farthest forward he has leaned. G1 gestures out.
(6)	G1:	Ella (?). (She.)	B is still looking at G1 and leaning in. The girl gestures out.
(7)	B:	What?	
(8)	G1:	[?]	
(9)	B:	You don't know what I mean.	B leans back in his chair.
(10)	B:	Hey, that's for that table.	G3 enters the scene and takes the glue pot from table. Beto turns to face her as he talks to her.
(11)	G3:	Tacky glue's supposed to be over there.	Girl looks at B as she talks and leaves with the glue. Stretch of working. Beto and Adrian talk in Spanish. G2 has left table and now returns.
(12)	B:	What is that?	B turns to G2 and asks what is on her paper.
(13)	G2:	What is what?	G2 glances at B. Her head is down as she writes.

---

[4]*G3* indicates a third Anglo girl.

(14)	B:	That.	B gestures toward her paper.
(15)	G2:	[?]	
(16)	B:	Michelle, Michelle what?	B leans in and watches the girl write.
(17)	A:	Es azúcar, ¿verdad? (It's sugar, isn't it?)	A holds up a sugar cube in front of Beto.
(18)	B:	Sí es. (Yes, it is.)	The conversation continues in Spanish about not eating sugar with glue on it.
(19)	B:	Hey, lover boy.	B turns out from the table and makes this comment as a boy goes by.

This brief exchange provides a glimpse of another facet of Beto's linguistic repertoire. Beto has been conversing with one of the girls (12–16) when Adrian asks him if the cubes they are pasting are sugar. He confirms that they are and proceeds to talk to Adrian in Spanish. As someone walks by (from the tape it is not evident whether he is a Chicano or Anglo), Beto turns out and calls, "Hey, lover boy" (19). He has switched into English, but he has done more than simply switch languages. He has demonstrated knowledge of a particular English expression and applied it to a person. He is again playing with English and using the language in a figurative, creative way, to tease (perhaps) but also to express an "in-group" comment or joke. Beto raises the pitch of his voice during this utterance in a way that is reminiscent of a female pop singer.

Beto also seems to have an idea that certain people use certain languages. After he asks Adrian if he is afraid of the dog, one of the Anglo girls says something to him (4). Evidently he takes her remark as related to his comment to Adrian because he registers great surprise, both in the verbal form of a challenging "What?" and in leaning far forward and staring at the girl. In his challenge of the girl's use of Spanish (her comment sounded like Spanish, and this impression is confirmed by Beto's reaction), Beto asserts that the girl did not know what he meant, implying that only certain people use and know Spanish (5–9). Such a comment is not surprising in light of Beto's code-switching expertise.

Segment 9

		Utterances	*Context*
(1)	G1:	I need some tacky.	G1 leans in to get some glue.
(2)	A:	Ay.	A leans forward with a finger of glue and pokes some in girl's face.
(3)	B:	I didn't do that.	He gets glue on her nose. She backs away and touches her nose. B looks at her as he talks.
(4)	G1:	I know. Alejandro did.	

(5)	B:	It ain't Alejandro. It's A-dri-an.	B throws his arm out and waves his hand in A's direction as he pronounces his name.
(6)	G1:	I forgot.	A leans in to get glue pot. He picks it up.
(7)	A:	Thanks. Muchas thanks.	
(8)	B:	Muchas thanks [laughs].	
(9)	A:	Muchos thanks.	
(10)	G1:	I need ta-cky ta-cky.	G1 requests the glue and gets no response.
(11)	B:	Tacky, tacky.	G1 leans in to get glue. A won't let her have it.
(12)	A:	[?] bomba.	A picks up glue pot and pretends to throw it at G1. He lets the glue pot go. B's arm is raised, and the falling glue pot hits his arm and falls onto the table.
(13)	G1:	[Laughs.]	
(14)	B:	I saved your life.	
(15)	G1:	Thank you.	

In this final example, Beto provides more evidence of his versatility in English. Beto declares that he has saved the girl's life by intercepting the glue pot (14). He says this assertively but with tongue in cheek. He is again using English in a figurative way, experimenting with the language for effect and creating a momentary make-believe scene through this use of English.

Earlier, when the girl calls Adrian "Alejandro," Beto plays the role of language teacher pronouncing the correct name carefully, dividing the word into syllables (5). He switches to Spanish phonology. He also pitches the word higher, perhaps an indication that he associates higher pitch with a girl or with a teacher. In addition he gestures with his hand toward Adrian in what may be interpreted as a stereotypical female pose. The syllable "an" has the same rise-fall as the "oo" of "too" in segment 4. Here, then, Beto not only corrects the girl's utterance for truth value, but also indicates how he interprets female talk (or perhaps female teacher talk).

Finally, Beto's repetition of "muchas thanks" (8) and his amused chuckle at the expression may be seen as an appreciation of this creative mixing of languages and, simultaneously, an assertion that the expression is clever but not "correct."

CONCLUSION

This cursory examination of Beto's utterances in their social context reveals much about his sociolinguistic competence, to which the term "bilingual" does not do justice. Beto has emerged in this brief segment as a child with many sociolinguistic as well as linguistic capabilities.

1. He is able to use particular codes with particular people.
2. He is able to switch codes with ease.

3. He is able to speak in one code without inserting items from another code (unless he chooses to do so).
4. He is able to use both of his linguistic codes for a variety of language functions or aims: questioning, informing, persuading and controlling, playing with language, initiating and maintaining social interaction, and personal self-expression (Halliday, 1970, 1977; Kinneavy, 1971).
5. He is able to use many forms of his codes to accomplish his aims.

Certainly this slice of life does not provide a complete sociolinguistic portrait of Beto, but it offers a more complete sketch than a traditional language assessment instrument does.

It is not the purpose of this paper to suggest that videotapes of *all* children in bilingual programs should replace presently used language assessment instruments. This is not feasible. What it demonstrates is that children in bilingual classrooms possess sociolinguistic skills not evidenced by test scores. Therefore, tapes similar to the one analyzed here should be used both to illustrate children's sociolinguistic repertoires for teachers and to train teachers, as they work in their own classrooms, to tune in, listen for, and watch what children are doing and saying (Carrasco and Vera, 1977). In this way, teachers may acquire more realistic pictures of their pupils' abilities and provide opportunities for children to demonstrate and increase them.

REFERENCES

Carrasco, R., and Vera, A. Aspects of bilingual students' sociolinguistic performance in a classroom. Unpublished manuscript, Harvard Graduate School of Education, 1977.

Cazden, C. The situation: a neglected source of social class differences in language use. *Journal of Social Issues,* 1970, *26*(2), 35–60.

Cazden, C. Language assessment: where, what and how. *Anthropology and Education,* 1977, *8*(2), 83–90.

Dubois, B. Cultural and social factors in the assessment of language capabilities. *Elementary English,* 1974, *51,* 257–261.

Erickson, F., Florio, S., and Bremme, D. Children's sociolinguistic performance and teachers' judgements of children's competence. Paper delivered at the American Educational Research Association, Washington, D.C., April, 1975.

Genishi, C. Rules for code-switching in young Spanish-English speakers: an exploratory study of language socialization. Doctoral dissertation, University of California, Berkeley, 1976.

Halliday, M. A. K. Language structure and language function. In J. Lyons (Ed.), *New horizons in linguistics.* Baltimore: Penguin, 1970.

Halliday, M. A. K. *Explorations in the functions of language.* New York: Elsevier, 1977.

Hymes, D. *Foundations in sociolinguistics: an ethnographic approach.* Philadelphia: University of Pennsylvania Press, 1974.

Kinneavy, J. *A theory of discourse.* Englewood Cliffs, N.J.: Prentice-Hall, 1971.

Shultz, J. Language use in bilingual classrooms. Unpublished manuscript, Harvard Graduate School of Education, 1975.

Shuy, R. Quantitative language data: a case for and some warnings against. *Anthropology and Education,* 1977, *8*(2), 73–82.

4 | Private Speech Production During Task Performance by Bilingual and Monolingual Children

LUIZA B. AMODEO and MANUEL CÁRDENAS
New Mexico State University

Spontaneous private speech and its relationship to child development have recently become the focus of interest for educators and researchers. Private speech is communication with self; the child talks about objects, events, tasks, and so forth to no one in particular. Piaget (1926) referred to the nonsocial verbal communications of the child as "egocentric" speech: that is, speech not addressed to any auditor or listener, other than the child. More recent theories (Kohlberg, Yaeger, and Hjertham, 1968) suggest that the label "egocentric" may apply only in terms of Piaget's interpretation of the phenomenon and that "private speech" may be a more adequate label for nonsocial speech forms with self-communicative functions. Vygotsky (1962) defined spontaneous private speech as that speech not addressed to or adapted to a listener that occurs naturally during a child's activity and is most often observed in three- to-five-year-old children.

Reports of studies on the functions of spontaneous private speech in relation to problem solving and self-control have recently begun to appear (Kanfer, 1970; Meichenbaum and Goodman, 1976). These studies strongly support the role of private speech as a mediator of cognitive activities. For example, Meichenbaum and Goodman (1976) find that children assessed as impulsive by teacher nominations and performance on the Matching Familiar Figures Test (Kagan, 1966) produce private speech that may be largely considered immature and self-stimulatory, regardless of the situation that caused the child to produce it.

Other researchers replicate Luria's (1961) studies and support his hypothesis that overt private speech exerts functional control over motor behavior and serves as a mediator for behavior (Beaudichon, 1973; Flavell, Beach, and Chinsky, 1966; Kohlberg, Yaeger and Hjertham, 1968). Kohlberg et al. particularly stress the increase of "private speech with demands for cognitive activity" (1968, p. 733). Findings from these studies appear to support the notion that private speech has a critical role in the development of self-directed and self-controlled behavior and may form the roots of thinking or problem solving. Other studies (Dickie, 1973; Flavell, Beach, and Chinsky, 1966; Meichenbaum and Goodman, 1976; Vygotsky, 1962) look at the correlates of private speech and present evidence that situational and interpersonal variables affect both the quality and the quantity of private speech production.

As far as can be determined, all research on private speech has been carried out with monolingual children and has not addressed the issue of bilingualism. This study focuses on an aspect of language development that may be related to the success or failure of monolingual and bilingual children in problem-solving situations. The information presented is important to individuals in the areas of early childhood and bilingual education, where the development of language is of prime importance. The particular aspect that we will be investigating is the amount of language a child uses when communicating with himself or herself. The evidence is drawn from studies that examine the cognitive and affective functions of a child's nonsocial verbalization and studies of dual-language acquisition. The interpersonal variable of special significance here is the child's ethnicity or cultural background.

The discussion is organized into three sections. The first reviews the variables that may influence private speech: culture, sex, IQ measures, socioeconomic status, and task. The second part reports the procedures and results of a study that compared the private and social speech production of three ethnic groups. The summary section discusses the implications of these findings.

VARIABLES INFLUENCING PRIVATE SPEECH

Culture

Kohlberg, Yaeger, and Hjertham (1968), in their studies of private speech, examined the influence of culture and cultural sex roles upon the incidence of private speech. Their findings indicate that "national" and sex roles do not seem to affect the amount of private speech produced, but that the ability of a situation to elicit private speech is determined by the transcultural dimensions of the task. The children surveyed in their study were Anglo Americans and Norwegians in Norway.

Age

In all relevant studies of the production of private speech, the variable receiving the most attention appeared to be age. Vygotsky (1962) suggested a curvilinear relationship between age and the incidence of private speech, and Flavell, Beach, and Chinsky (1966) supported that position. On the other hand, Dickie

(1973) found that different categories of private speech have different developmental trends and that the relationship between cognitive development and private speech is dependent on the form of private speech. The age range found most significant generally ran from three to seven, whether the subjects were observed in groups or alone. Dickie recorded more social speech for older children than younger ones. Social speech for the older children was clearly distinct, whereas it was much harder to distinguish between private and social speech among younger children.

Sex, IQ, and Socioeconomic Status

Sex, IQ, and socioeconomic status have also been investigated in relation to private speech. Few of the studies surveyed suggest sex differences in the amount of private speech production. Davis (1937) discussed the possibility that young females might be more verbal than young males, but Martin (1975) found that males produce more total vocalizations as well as a greater absolute number of utterances than females.

Kohlberg, Yaeger, and Hjertham (1968) hypothesized that children with higher IQ's would have an earlier peak in private speech and that overt private speech would begin to decrease after this peak. IQ, according to Dickie (1973), affects some types of private speech but not others.

Kohlberg, Yaeger, and Hjertham (1968) have also implied that there are differences in the use of private speech among classes. Their observation that "middle-class children use more private speech than do culturally disadvantaged children" has not been addressed by other studies. The children investigated in this study are of lower- to middle-class socioeconomic status.

Task

Studies that examined the role of task-relevant speech clearly demonstrate the importance of the task used to elicit private speech (Deutsch and Stein, 1972; Kohlberg, Yaeger, and Hjertham, 1968; Meichenbaum and Goodman, 1976). The amount of private speech appears to increase with the difficulty of the task and with a situation of personal failure but to decrease with success. In this context, Deutsch and Stein attribute the greater incidence of private speech to aroused "achievement motivation" (1972). Similarly, Dickie (1973), Klein (1963), and Kohlberg, Yaeger, and Hjertham (1968) survey the connection between the complexity of the task and private speech. Their research also reveals evidence that increased difficulty leads to an increase in private speech.

METHODOLOGY

The present study of monolingual and bilingual children concerns itself with three ethnic groups: Anglo Americans, Asian Americans, and Hispanic American children. It addresses the possibility (suggested in a personal communication, Meichenbaum, May 1976) that children who are exposed to dual language codes may show functional differences in their production of private and social speech and that these differences may be affected by task performance, sex, culture, and age.

Subjects

The eighty children used in this study ranged in age from 2 years 5 months to 5 years 11 months. They were drawn from two preschools located within the greater Los Angeles area (Los Angeles Unified School District, 1974).

At the onset of school activities, children enrolled in preschools within the Los Angeles Early Childhood Program are routinely assessed in various areas. One of these areas is the child's intellectual performance, as measured by an Inventory of Development Tasks profile. This rating and teachers' recommendations determined the assignment of children to a high or low group and the difficulty of the task they were subsequently asked to perform for this study.

The designation of some children as bilingual was based on information supplied by the teachers about the children's language preferences in the classroom, on the playground, and in the home. Bilingual potential was also attributed to children who were found to have a home language different from the language predominantly used in the classroom and on the playground—in this case, English; two-thirds of the Asian and Hispanic American children surveyed were in this category. A summary of the distribution of subjects is presented in table 1.

Table 1: Distribution of Subjects by Age, Sex, Ethnicity, IQ, and Language

| | ETHNICITY | | | | | | IQ | | LANGUAGE | |
| | Hispanic | | Asian | | Anglo | | | | | |
AGE[a]	F[b]	M[c]	F	M	F	M	High	Low	Bilingual	Monolingual
2:0–2:5					1		1			1
2:6–2:11										
3:0–3:5		1	3			1	1	4	4	1
3:6–3:11	1	5	3	1	3	3	5	11	8	8
4:0–4:5	1	3	3	4	1		7	5	7	5
4:6–4:11	4	3	2	3	2		7	7	7	7
5:0–5:5	5	2	3	6	2	1	8	11	11	8
5:6–5:11	2	3	1	1	3	3	7	6	3	10
Total	13	17	15	15	12	8	36	44	40	40

[a]In year and months.
[b]Female.
[c]Male.

Materials and Observation Procedures

The choice of stimulus materials for this study was influenced by the studies of Kohlberg, Yaeger, and Hjertham (1968) and Vygotsky (1962). The materials used had to meet the following critical criteria:

1. The task should be of interest to the child.
2. It should require sequential steps leading to completion.
3. The child should be able to attain proficiency in the task over a period of time so that changes in private speech could be observed along with the development of skills.
4. The task should be one that could be made more or less difficult, and it should be possible to add or remove distractions and support.

Puzzles fit these criteria and were appropriate to the educational setting of the study.

During the summer months preceding this study, a pilot study was conducted at a daycare center. To determine the likelihood of obtaining spontaneous private speech productions in a naturalistic setting and the appropriateness of puzzles, children were chosen who were similar in age and ethnicity to those used in the later study. From the pilot sample's performance, we selected two sets of puzzles for the major study.

Ten factory-obtained puzzles were used. They were ordered into two sets, one of a high and one of a low level of difficulty. Each set was selected according to the following criteria:

1. The indicated level of difficulty, as determined and labeled by the manufacturer
2. The time needed for the completion of all the puzzles within each set, as determined from the pilot study
3. The amount of interest and concentration evidenced in the pilot study during the children's work period with the puzzles

The first set (high difficulty) comprised five puzzles judged by the manufacturer to be suitable for children two to six years old; each puzzle had 14 to 21 pieces. The second set (low difficulty) consisted of five puzzles with a similar age range but 7 to 13 pieces.

To record incidents of private speech as well as ongoing behavior, an observation scale was developed during the pilot study for use by trained observers. This scale was based on Meichenbaum (1976), whose work distinguished social speech from private speech by establishing both verbal and nonverbal behaviors. Social speech (category I here) included utterances addressed to the experimenter that were cued by the child's looking at the experimenter and establishing eye contact. If the child made reference to the experimenter in the context of a statement or repeated the statement when the examiner gave no response, Meichenbaum recorded the behavior as social speech. The presence of an observer in the room was required to distinguish between social speech and private speech. We found that this distinction could readily be made by having the observer move away from the child and sit in a corner working on the observation sheet; the distance between child and observer allowed for minimum interference in the child's activity.

All verbalizations not considered social speech were classified as private speech (category II) and assigned to various subcategories. The observation sheet used in this study was structured to include a modified version of Meichenbaum and Goodman's (1976) categories of private speech. The subcategories were:

1. Word play
2. Labeling or describing activity
3. Comments addressed to absent or nonhuman others
4. Questions asked and answered by self
5. Verbalizations relating to cognitive activity that precede the performance of the task.
6. Expletives expressing feelings about the task performance

Speech units were defined by natural phrasing and sentence structure, as well as a careful analysis of pauses. If a two-second or longer pause occurred between the verbalizations, then they were classified as separate units, regardless of sentence structure. The observers would tally the incidence of private speech at the end of each session.

The observation sheet also provided for an assessment of task performance based on the number of puzzles completed during three sessions. If the child completed all five puzzles during the three sessions, the observer rated his or her performance as level 1. Completing three out of five puzzles resulted in a rating of 2, and completing two puzzles or less a rating of 3. No session was allowed to extend past five minutes, and so the time needed to complete the task was not considered an important variable in this study.

The observers were matched to the children on the basis of ethnicity in order to reduce bias in the recording of the children's behavior. They were trained as a group through observation of videotapes of the children in the pilot study. These videotapes were used as independent measures to establish interobserver reliability. At the end of the data collection for session 2, another check on interrater reliability was taken. Each observer rated and scored a transcription of 50 utterances. All raters agreed on the same category for 48 of the 50 utterances.

Data Collection

Various methods of recording the spontaneous private speech of children have been used in other studies. This study was conducted in a naturalistic setting, where laboratory equipment was unavailable. A high-fidelity tape recorder with a built-in microphone was used during two sessions. The child's behavior was recorded by the observer, who was also able to observe the types of speech while the child was speaking. The third and final session was videotaped so that the record of speech and behavior could be transcribed and coded by the observer later.

The three sessions were designed to achieve specific purposes. The first and second were to familiarize the child with the procedures and allow him or her to explore the setting and examine the equipment. Each child was individually accompanied by the observer to the recording area. After a few moments of exploration and explanation, the child was seated at a table, where the disassembled puzzle had been deposited earlier. Another disassembled puzzle was placed on the corner of the table. The observer told the child that they were going to play with some puzzles. The child was asked to put the puzzles together while either the tape recorder or the video camera recorded his or her words and actions.

The observer then started the tape recorder and moved to the other side of the room. If the child showed any sign of not understanding the task or appeared uncomfortable or ill at ease, the session was stopped. Children were given instructions in their preferred languages, as determined by the observer's judgment or information from the staff. In some cases, the instructions were given in both the home language and English.

The last session was videotaped by an observer. The child was allowed several minutes for examining the equipment and asking questions. When the observer felt that the child was comfortable with the situation and the equipment, the instructions were given.

ANALYSIS AND RESULTS

Proportion and Incidence of Private Speech

An analysis was carried out to determine if the proportion of subjects using private speech was the same for the five ethnicity categories: Anglo English monolinguals, Asian English monolinguals, Asian bilinguals, Hispanic English monolinguals, and Hispanic bilinguals. The data and chi-square value for this analysis are presented in table 2. Because this analysis indicated significant differences ($p < .01$) among the five groups, further analyses were conducted to determine where these differences occurred.

Table 2: Proportion of Children Using Private Speech
in Five Ethnicity-Language Categories

	USE OF PRIVATE SPEECH		
ETHNICITY	Yes	No	Total
Anglo Monolingual[a]	13	7	20
Asian Monolingual	9	2	11
Asian Bilingual	4	15	19
Hispanic Monolingual	6	3	9
Hispanic Bilingual	8	13	21
Total	40	40	80

[a]Monolingual indicates native language
$chi^2 = 14.813$, p $<$ .01

Several comparisons between ethnic groups were made, in particular
between Anglo English monolinguals and non-Anglo English monolinguals,
Asian monolinguals and Hispanic monlinguals, and Asian bilinguals and Hispanic bilinguals. As shown in table 3, none of these comparisons resulted in a
significant difference (p $>$ .05).
A comparison was then made between bilinguals and monolinguals. This

Table 3: Ethnicity and Private Speech

	USE OF PRIVATE SPEECH		
ETHNICITY	Yes	No	Total
Anglo	13	7	20
Non-Anglo	15	5	20
Total	28	12	40
$chi^2 = .476NS^a$			
Asian Monolingual	9	2	11
Hispanic Monolingual	6	3	9
Total	15	5	20
$chi^2 = .613NS^a$			
Asian Bilingual	4	15	19
Hispanic Bilingual	8	13	21
Total	12	28	40
$chi^2 = 1.30NS^a$			

[a]p $>$ .05

comparison indicated a significant difference (p < .01) in the proportion of subjects using private speech (table 4). The percentages of monolinguals and bilinguals using private speech were 70 percent and 30 percent respectively, with a 99 percent confidence interval on the difference in the percentage using private speech being between the values 13.67 percent and 66.33 percent.

Table 4:   Language and Private Speech

Use of private speech	Monolingual	Bilingual	Total
Yes	28	12	40
No	12	28	40

chi^2 = 12.80, p < .01

The frequency with which private speech was used by each particular child was recorded and subjected to a covariate analysis using task and age as covariates and IQ, ethnicity, language, and sex arranged in a factorial structure. Significant differences were found in IQ [F(1,66) = 5.49, p < .05] and task [F(1,66) = 8.93, p < .01]. The subjects with high IQ used more private speech than those of low IQ. The significance in the task variable implied that the subjects who completed a greater portion of the task had a higher incidence of private speech.

There was no other significant difference in main effects. There was, however, a significant interaction between language and ethnicity for non-Anglos [F(1,66) = 8.26, p < .01]. The effect of the interaction is presented in table 5.

Table 5:   Incidence of Private Speech Among Asian and Hispanic Monolinguals and Bilinguals

Ethnicity	Bilingual	Monolingual	Average
Spanish	4.27(N = 11)	10.00(N = 19)	7.90
Asian	17.55(N = 9)	3.43(N = 21)	7.67
Average	10.25	6.55	

Proportion and Incidence of Social Speech

The proportion of subjects using social speech was not analyzed, since very few children from any category used it. The incidence of social speech was analyzed just as the incidence of private speech was. Significant differences were found for sex [F(1,66) = 4.03, p < .05] and age [F(1,66) = 8.00, p < .01]. Males used more social speech than females, and the older the subject the lower the incidence of social speech. No other main effect or interaction was significant when the data for the entire sample were employed in the analysis. However, the comparison between Hispanic bilinguals and Asian bilinguals just missed significance: $F(1,66) = 3.67$ and $p = .0599$.

An additional analysis was performed on data limited to the subjects who actually used social speech. Age continued to be significant ($p < .05$). Sex was no longer significant ($p > .05$), and this result, combined with that obtained using data from the entire sample, indicates that while males and females using social speech use it with the same frequency, the proportion of females using social speech is smaller than that of males. This analysis also revealed a significant interaction between IQ and sex [$F(1,23) = 5.76$, $p < .05$]. The interaction indicated that among children who use social speech, males with high IQs use more social speech than females with high IQs and, conversely, males with low IQs use less social speech than females with low IQs. The comparison between Anglos and the combined average of the four other groups was significant [$F(1,23) = 4.75$, $p < .05$]. Since this comparison was not significant when all of the data were used, we can conclude that on the average Anglos who used social speech used it more than the other groups; the proportion of Anglos using social speech, however, was smaller than that for the other groups.

Task was once again a significant variable when total speech was considered, and it exhibited the same trend as it had in the analysis of private speech. The only other comparison showing a significant difference was between Asian monolinguals and Hispanic monlinguals [$F(1,66) = 6.19$, $p < .05$], which showed that Hispanic monolinguals used more total speech than Asian monolinguals.

DISCUSSION

Differences in quantity of verbalization were found between bilingual and monolingual children during task performance. According to our interpretation of the data, these differences may be attributed to social and developmental variables as well as to the children's language backgrounds. We found that children responded to the study's setting by either talking English, the language of the setting, or not talking at all. Vygotsky (1962) noted a similar response when he placed children speaking one language in a room with children who spoke a different language. During our recording sessions, only four of the eighty children utilized actually used a language other than English. Two of the four children spoke solely their native language, while the other two mixed their native language with English.

Thus, the study supports the contention that functional differences in production of private speech occur when a bilingual child is placed in a culturally different environment. Regardless of the ethnicity of the observers, the children recognized that English was the language to be used in the task setting. Vygotsky (1962) observed that the use of overt private speech reflects the fact that the child is in a period when a new function of speech is beginning to split off from its social function. At this point in its development, therefore, private speech is particularly sensitive to the social milieu in which it appears.

For bilingual children, this sensitivity is complicated by their developmental level in second language acquisition. Bilingual children may be absorbing the sounds of the new language before attempting to put them together in spoken form. They may be experiencing a linguistic and cultural conflict (Saville-Troike, 1973) that involves language choice. Other researchers have suggested that teachers, staff, and other children can influence this choice. The stressing of English acquisition by school personnel signals to the child the minority status he or she occupies within society. The child's learning English depends not only on exposure and practice, but also on the attitude of his or her group toward itself and other groups and the attitudes of teachers towards the child and his or her language (Boyd, 1975; Saville-Troike, 1973; Slovin, 1973).

Dickie (1973) found social speech to be affected by activity in combination with other factors: It increased during free play and decreased when the child was involved in a task. As in the present findings, the task had the greatest effect on social speech among older children. In contrast to Davis's (1937) findings, the males in this study used more social speech than the females. This may be attributed to sex role socialization practices in the home and school, where girls are encouraged to work quietly and independently.

Our findings that the brighter children used more private speech during tasks than average children and that they more often completed the tasks are supported by various studies (Deutsch and Stein, 1972; Dickie, 1973; Kohlberg, Yaeger, and Hjertham, 1968). Interestingly, no significant differences were found between the task performance of the monolingual children and that of the bilingual children. Of the 40 monolingual children, 18 assembled all five puzzles, 18 assembled three or four, and 4 completed two or fewer; of the 40 bilingual children, 14 finished all five puzzles, 19 three or four, and 7 two or fewer.

Many bilingual kindergartens are highly structured, with a great many teacher-directed activities. This arrangement offers children few opportunities to explore, discover, and, in general, become involved in activities that would encourage private speech. Teachers who feel they must teach language to children through audiolingual methods, which are highly dependent on drill and repetition, leave little time for creative and innovative approaches to language learning. Bilingual kindergartens must provide challenging environments and accepting, supportive personnel who allow bilingual children to interact, discover, and solve problems in the language of their choice.

Further research on the relationship of private speech to conceptual language development is needed. As this study suggests, however, environmental factors play an important role in the private speech of bilingual preschoolers and these too deserve attention.

REFERENCES

Beaudichon, J. Nature and instrumental function of private speech in problem solving situations. *Merrill-Palmer Quarterly,* 1973, *19,* 117–131.

Boyd, Patricia. The development of grammar categories in Spanish by Anglo children learning a second language. *TESOL Quarterly,* 1975, *9*(2), 125–135.

Davis, E. A. The mental and linguistic superiority of only girls. *Child Development,* 1937, *8,* 139–143.

Deutsch, F., and Stein, A. The effects of personal responsibility and task interruption on the private speech of preschoolers. *Human Development,* 1972, *15,* 310–324.

Dickie, J. Private speech: the effect of presence of others, task, and intrapersonal variables. Doctoral dissertation, Michigan State University, 1973.

Flavell, J., Beach, D. R., and Chinsky, J. M. Spontaneous verbal rehearsal in a memory task as a function of age. *Child Development,* 1966, *37,* 283–299.

Kagan, J. Reflection-Impulsivity: the generality and dynamics of conceptual tempo. *Journal of Abnormal Psychology,* 1966, *71,* 17–24.

Kanfer, F. H. Self-regulation: research, issues and speculations. In C. Neuringer and J. L. Michael (Eds.), *Behavior modification in clinical psychology.* New York: Appleton-Century-Crofts, 1970.

Klein, W. An investigation of the spontaneous speech of children. Doctoral dissertation, University of Rochester, 1963.

Kohlberg, L., Yaeger, J., and Hjertham, E. The development of private speech: four studies and a review of theories. *Child Development,* 1968, *39,* 691–736.

Los Angeles Unified School District Census Data, 1974.

Luria, A. R. *The role of speech in the regulation of normal and abnormal behavior.* New York: Liveright, 1961.

Martin, R. Spontaneous private speech and the mediation of behavior in a resistance-to-temptation paradigm. Doctoral dissertation, University of Rochester, 1975.

Meichenbaum, D. Toward a cognitive theory of self-control. In G. Schwartz and D. Shapiro (Eds.), *Consciousness and self-regulation: advances in research.* New York: Plenum Press, 1976.

Meichenbaum, D., and Goodman, S. Critical questions and methodological problems in studying private speech. In Gail Zwin (Ed.), *Development of self-regulation through speech.* Wiley, 1976.

Piaget, J. *The language and thought of the child.* New York: Harcourt Brace, 1926.

Saville-Troike, M. *Bilingual Children.* Arlington, Va.: Center for Applied Linguistics, 1973.

Slovin, D. Cognitive prerequisites for the development of grammar. In E. E. Dingwell (Ed.), *A survey of linguistic science.* College Park, Md.: University of Maryland Linguistic Program, 1973.

Vygotsky, L. *Thought and language.* Cambridge, Mass.: MIT Press, 1962 (originally 1935).

II | Culture

5 | Cultural Antecedents of Cognitive-Style Variables in Mexican American Children

STEPHAN L. JACKSON
Intercultural Development Research Association, San Antonio, Texas

LINDA ESPINO
Southwest Educational Development Laboratory, Austin, Texas

Recent federal initiatives to provide equal educational opportunity for linguistic minority children (Title VI guidelines, the *Lau* v. *Nichols* decision by the Supreme Court, and the subsequent "Lau remedies") have specified that school districts must seriously consider the special educational needs of these children. Aside from language differences, these and other policy recommendations have focused on the concept of "learning style," as evidenced in the following excerpt from the Lau remedies:

> The second part of a plan must describe the diagnostic/prescriptive measures to be used to identify the nature and extent of each student's educational needs and then prescribe an educational program utilizing the most effective teaching style to satisfy the diagnosed educational needs. The determination of which teaching style(s) are to be used should be based on a careful review of both the cognitive and affective domains and should include an assessment of the responsiveness of students to different types of cognitive learning styles and incentive motivational styles. (Section II, p. 5)

Educators have pointed out, however, that substantial research needs to be done before school districts can be expected to comply with this section of the mandate (Cazden and Leggett, 1976). They particularly stress the need for studies of instrumentation reliability and validity with linguistic minority

This study was conducted in the third year of a three-year study, funded by the National Institute of Education, entitled "Cognitive Styles of Minority Children." The study was funded through the Southwest Educational Development Laboratory, in Austin, Texas (Grant no. NIE-G-78-0208).

65

groups and investigations of the relationship between cognitive-style variables, ethnicity, and education.

In order to address this specific need, the present study examines the life histories of ten third-grade Mexican American children to explore the relationship between cultural antecedent variables (socialization, child-rearing practices, interaction styles, schooling, and so forth) and the constructs of field dependence/independence and conceptual tempo. The primary goal of the study is to gain insights into why children respond to the different measures the way they do, focusing in particular on each child's experiences in his or her home, school, and community.

A "predictive ethnography" approach is used in this research. The life history of each child is analyzed, and patterns of cultural experience or behavior are used to predict test scores. The predicted scores are then compared to actual test results. Our research has produced the following results:

1. Experimentally testable hypotheses about the relationship between cultural variables and tested psychological constructs
2. Documentation of the intracultural diversity found in the lives of the children
3. A testing of the accuracy with which researchers can predict test scores using ethnographic data
4. A synthesis of the findings, with their implications for bilingual education, public policy regarding linguistic minorities, and further research

The first section of this chapter presents (1) a review of the literature on the relationship between cognitive style and cultural variables; (2) the concept of cultural "antecedents" as used in this study; and (3) the research questions. The second section presents a brief description of predictive ethnography and the instrumentation, data collection methods, and analysis applied. The third section presents examples of the case studies and the cultural patterns and predictions derived from them. A final summary discusses the findings in relation to previous research, general patterns applicable to all the children studied, certain theoretical constructs, the usefulness of ethnographic method in predicting test results, and the implications of the findings.

COGNITIVE STYLE AND CULTURAL VARIABLES

Field Dependence/Independence

The field dependence/independence construct (FD/I), the most thoroughly researched of the cognitive-style dimensions, has particular relevance to this study as a result of recent findings that Mexican American children tend to be more field-dependent than Anglo children (Buriel, 1975; Ramírez and Price-Williams, 1974b; Sanders, Scholz, and Kagan, 1976). In order to examine possible explanations for these observed differences, we will examine research related to the role of community type and child-rearing practices in the development of cognitive style. School-related variables, age, and sex are then explored as possible variables affecting results on FD/I measures.

COMMUNITY TYPE

Researchers have consistently found that children in more "traditional" communities are, as a group, more field-dependent than children in more "dualistic" or "atraditional" communities (Buriel, 1975; Laosa, 1978; Ramírez, Castañeda, and Herold, 1974; Ramírez and Price-Williams, 1974a). When Buriel (1975) examined children one or more generation removed from Mexico within a traditional community, he found only third-generation Mexican Americans to be significantly more field-dependent than Anglo children. In two studies controlling for the socioeconomic status of children within different communities (Ramírez, Castañeda, and Herold, 1974; Ramírez and Price-Williams, 1974b), no significant effect was found for SES, indicating that the culture of poverty has little or no impact on FD/I.

CHILD-REARING PRACTICES

Three types of variables relating the FD/I construct to the parent-child relationship have been identified: (1) characteristics of parents, (2) their child-rearing practices and beliefs, and (3) parent-child interaction styles. Ramírez and Price-Williams (1974b) describe the parental characteristics that distinguish the less traditional from the more traditional community, including paternal absence and maternal mobility. Holtzman, Diaz-Guerrero, and Swartz (1975) also identify two related variables—paternal noninvolvement in family life and maternal passivity—as commonly shared traits among Mexican and Mexican American families; the researchers presume that these traits help to explain the relative field dependence of Mexican and Mexican American children versus the field independence of Anglo children.

The second type of variable, parents' child-rearing practices and beliefs, has been a central concern of investigators studying the hypothesized relationship of "social sensitivity" to field dependence (Canavan, 1969; Holtzman, Diaz-Guerrero, and Swartz, 1975; Irving, 1970; Kagan, 1977; Ramírez and Castañeda, 1974; Ramírez and Price-Williams, 1974b; Sanders, Scholz, and Kagan, 1976; and Witkin, Dyk, et al., 1974). This relationship remains tentative, since the above-mentioned attempts to show a direct relationship have had mixed results. Generally, the results show that Mexican American children are more socially oriented, with parents stressing socially integrative values. However, comparisons between parents' responses to a socialization questionnaire and their children's FD/I scores indicate no correlations (Holtzman, Diaz-Guerrero, and Swartz, 1975; Sanders, Scholz, and Kagan, 1976), very low correlations (Canavan, 1969), or mixed ones (Ramírez and Price-Williams, 1974a). The one parental factor found by Sanders, Scholz, and Kagan (1976) to correlate significantly with field dependence in children was the need for personally defined achievement.

Other child-rearing practices and related beliefs suggested by Ramírez and Price-Williams (1974a) to explain the FD/I results of Mexican American children included parents' emphasis on respect for authority, strong family ties, sex-role identification, Mexican Catholic ideology, and child mobility. Holtzman, Diaz-Guerrero, and Swartz (1975) add to this list the intrusiveness and authoritarianism of parents, an emphasis on obedience, and the inhibition of initiative and independence.

A third type of variable may also relate parent-child interaction style to FD/I measures. Dyk and Witkin (1965) found that mothers of field-independent children introduced new situations with careful description and explanation, while mothers of field-dependent children used more vague verbal instructions. Laosa (1977) points out, however, that the less verbal style of interaction characteristic of Mexican American mothers is often coupled with more nonverbal guidance of the child's problem solving, and that there is therefore no difference in the total number of teaching behaviors between Mexican American and Anglo mothers.

SCHOOL-RELATED VARIABLES

The relationship between FD/I tendencies and such school-related variables as academic skills, the FD/I orientations of educators, and amount of schooling has been researched in various studies. Investigators have found significant positive correlations between field independence and (1) verbal and mathematical skills (Crandall and Sinkeldam, 1964), (2) mathematical ability (Bieri, Bradburn, and Galinsky, 1958), and (3) spatial ability (Gardner, Jackson, and Messick, 1960; Podell and Phillips, 1959). A number of researchers (DiStefano, 1969; Jarner, 1973; and Witkin, et al., 1977) have consistently found that when students are matched with teachers of similar FD/I tendencies, there is much greater interpersonal attraction, the teachers give higher grades, and teachers and students judge each other more positively, on both personal and cognitive attributes. The same researchers found that FD/I mismatches between teachers and students produce exactly the opposite effect. Studies that identify possible factors in such FD/I match-mismatch results include Freedman, et al. (1972), Marcus (1970), and Shows (1967), all of which suggest that the greater interpersonal attraction between persons of matched FD/I orientation may be due to similarity in modes of communication. Witkin, Dyk, et al. (1974) and Witkin, et al. (1972) attribute this attraction to shared personality characteristics.

Wober (1969) found a significant relationship between years of schooling and degree of field independence in Nigerian men. Thus, there is some evidence that the typical "Western" educational process itself fosters field independence and generally favors the field-independent child (Ramírez and Castañeda, 1974).

AGE AND SEX

Many researchers have studied the effects of age and sex on FD/I orientation. Children have consistently been found to become increasingly more field-independent with age (Holtzman, Diaz-Guerrero, & Swartz, 1975; Kagan and Zahn, 1975; Ramírez, Castañeda, and Herold, 1974; and Ramírez and Price-Williams, 1974a). Females are characteristically found to be more field-dependent in the studies reviewed (Ramírez, Castañeda, and Herold, 1974; Ramirez and Price-Williams, 1974a; and Witkin, et al., 1977). Witkin and Berry (1975) found, however, that sex differences in FD/I orientation were less prevalent among mobile hunting societies than in sedentary agricultural ones.

The interaction of age and culture, as studied by Kagan and Zahn (1975), produced cultural differences that increased with age. Holtzman, Diaz-Guerrero, and Swartz (1975), and Ramírez and Price-Williams (1974a), on the other hand, found that cultural differences tended to decrease with age.

Conceptual Tempo

In sharp contrast to the FD/I construct, little research has been done on possible links between conceptual tempo and cultural variables. In the only study found tying impulsivity/reflectivity to child-rearing practices, Campbell (1973) found that that mothers of impulsive children had lower academic expectations than mothers of reflective children and did not structure learning situations as much.

Kogan (1971) found a progressive increase in response time and a corresponding decrease in errors in children from five to eleven years of age. Yando and Kagan (1968), studying the effects of teachers' conceptual tempo on the tempo of first graders, found that only experienced reflective teachers had an effect on impulsive children, and that effect was an increase in response time with no corresponding decrease in errors. Experienced impulsive teachers had little impact on their pupils' conceptual tempo. Kagan, Pearson, and Welch (1966) found that impulsive children tended to respond more quickly and make more errors on inductive reasoning tasks, and this tendency remained statistically significant even when verbal ability (as measured by the Wechsler Intelligence Scale for Children—WISC) was controlled.

Thus, the variables that have been investigated in relation to conceptual tempo include mothers' academic expectations, the degree to which mothers structure learning situations, age, teachers' conceptual tempo, and performance on inductive reasoning tasks. It appears that a wide range of cultural variables are yet to be explored in this connection.

Cultural Antecedents

Antecedent conditions provide the primary set of variables affecting both cognitive styles (field dependence/independence, conceptual tempo) and interactive variables (cognitive development and language proficiency), which in turn are associated with academic achievement (see figure 1). These antecedent conditions include the socialization process, parental child-rearing practices, and the cultural practices of the child's social milieu (De Avila and Duncan, 1979).

Previous research had produced test scores for children from diverse cultural groups on each of the constructs of interest, including language proficiency, FD/I orientation, conceptual tempo, cognitive development, and achievement (see De Avila, et al., 1978; Duncan and De Avila, 1979; and De Avila and Duncan, 1979). While a study of the cultural antecedents of the cognitive-style constructs was beyond the scope of the first two years of this research (1977–1978), the third year was considered an appropriate time to conduct such a study.

Research Questions

The following research questions present both the general and the more specific goals of this study:

What are the cultural antecedents of FD/I orientation and conceptual tempo in Mexican American children with various degrees of proficiency in English and Spanish?

What conditions are evident in the children's life histories?[1]

What distinguishing patterns of conditions, evident in the children's life histories, substantiate or explain their FD/I orientation?

What distinguishing patterns of conditions, evident in the children's life histories, substantiate or explain their conceptual tempo?

---

[1]Life histories, as defined by this study, are distinct from those traditionally used in anthropological research (Kluckhohn, 1945; Pelto and Pelto, 1978). Here a life history is a reconstruction of the events in a child's life focusing on variables related to the constructs of interest and using the perspectives of relatives, educators, and peers.

Figure 1:   Cultural Antecedents and Cognitive Style

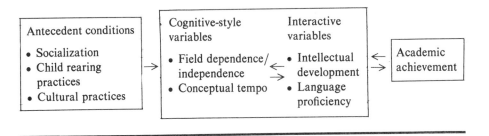

PROCEDURE

Predictive Ethnography

For the purpose of this study, "predictive ethnography" is defined as a procedure for predicting children's test scores on the basis of an ethnographic study of their cultural experience. The first step involves the extensive study of a small number of individual children, relying on the eclectic nature of ethnography to allow a wide range of cultural variables to be included (Pelto and Pelto, 1978). Next, ethnographers predict how each child will perform on measures of each construct and substantiate their ratings with patterns of observed or reported cultural experience and behavior. Once predictions and substantiations have been made, test scores are opened and compared to the predicted outcomes.

Ethnographic methods were chosen for two reasons:

1. The relevance of cultural factors to linguistic/psychological constructs was to be investigated rather than assumed in this study. Ethnographic methods not only allowed us to explore this question, but also broadened the range of cultural factors under consideration.

2. Ethnographic methods force the continual reformulation of the researchers' underlying hypotheses, as well as those suggested by previous researchers, regarding links between cultural variables and cognitive-style constructs.

The seven rather broad overlapping categories of ethnographic variables summarized in table 1 have been the primary focus of this study's data-collection effort, which included both focused interviews and observation. These areas of cultural experience were those suggested or implied in the literature on the links between the various linguistic/psychological variables and culture. Taken together, they may be seen as representing a means of reconstructing

Table 1: Summary of Cultural Antecedent Variables

Variable	Description
Language usage	Patterns of language usage (Spanish and English) across domains (home, school, and community) by child, family members, and others associated with the child; child's language background and language training; attitudes of parents toward language and bilingualism
Kinship patterns	Family geneological structure; child and sibling birth placement; nuclear and extended family residential patterns; household composition; interaction patterns; language usage patterns; educational, occupational, and re'igious characteristics of family members
Early childhood experiences	Language acquisition; educational patterns; significant persons and experiences in the life of the child since birth; residential and travel mobility
Child-rearing patterns	Child-rearing attitudes and practices, including family and peer-group interaction
Interaction patterns	Association and interaction of child and family with peers, neighbors, friends, school personnel, and others across settings (home, school, community, and outside of community)
Values and beliefs	Religious and Mexican cultural value system (this information derived indirectly, through interviews and observations focused on other variables)
Socioeconomic status	Education and occupation of family members contributing to income; size and condition of house and furnishings; number of people in household

the life history of each child, including cultural experiences as well as behavior patterns.

Instruments

Cognitive-style constructs depend heavily on the instruments used to measure them. The instruments used in this study were field-tested in the earlier phases of the research project (see De Avila, et al., 1978). In each case, the test instructions were translated and modified as necessary to ensure that the child could understand what was expected of him or her. The basic tasks remained the same, as did the scoring procedures.

The FD/I construct was measured with the Children's Embedded Figures Test (CEFT). The CEFT is a simplified version of the Embedded Figures Test, which was developed by H. A. Witkin, et al. (1971) to measure a person's ability to visually disembed a given figure from a complex drawing. In both the original EFT and the CEFT, the task presented to the subject involves looking first at a simple figure (such as triangle), and then trying to find and outline the same figure in a complex drawing without referring back to the isolated figure. The CEFT consists of twenty-five such items: eleven involve finding a "triangle" and fourteen involve finding a "house" form (a rectangle with a trianglar "roof" on one side). Respondents get credit for each item only if they find the embedded figure without seeking help from the test administrator or seeing the isolated figure again. The test is individually administered.

The Matching Familiar Figures Test (MFFT), developed by J. Kagan (1965), was the measure of conceptual tempo used in this study. The MFFT is a timed test in which the subject is shown two pages. One illustrates a single drawing, and the other shows six drawings, each of which looks much like the isolated drawing, but only one of which is exactly the same. The subject is timed to see how long it takes him or her to give the first response, with each incorrect choice scored as an error. Testers produce two scores, for time and errors, by summing the response times and the errors for the twelve items on the test.

Data Collection and Analysis

The following list summarizes the flow of events in the selection of the ten children chosen for the sample and the data-collection and -analysis process. The latter was in reality one interdependent process rather than two distinct steps in the research:

Site selection. The selection of sites was based on the presence of an adequate number of Mexican American children in third grade and the willingness of school officials and teachers to participate.

Identification of subjects. The choice of subjects was based on language test results in English and Spanish. The testing was not done by the ethnographers, so that we would be blind to test scores. Potential subjects' names were given to the ethnographers, who contacted parents to ask for their approval before beginning observations and interviews.

Observations and interviews. Observations were made, kinship charts developed, interviews conducted, and questionnaires completed over seven months, from December 1978 to June 1979.

Transcription of interviews. Some interviews were transcribed as the study progressed, though most were transcribed after the interviews were completed.

Summary of transcripts and field notes. Transcripts and field notes were analyzed for predominating patterns of cultural experience or behavior, resulting in concise summaries in which key quotations, incidents, and behaviors were noted.

Testing. Children were tested on each construct by members of the research team other than the ethnographers in May 1979.

Development of case studies. A case study was developed for each child, consisting of a short introduction followed by predictions of test results and substantiations of predictions based on ethnographic data. The predictions were made by the two ethnographers independently.

"Opening" of test scores. Actual test results were compared to predicted scores.

Post-hoc analyses. (1) The pattern of results and predictions was summarized for each child, and a section was added at the end of each case study. (2) The pattern of cultural variables linked to constructs was summarized for all ten children (tables 2 and 3). (3) A comparison of predictions and test results was summarized for all ten children (table 4).

Interpretation of results. Results were interpreted in the light of the goals of the study.

The existing theory and research linking culture and the tested constructs provided a basis for this study. However, no specific categories of cultural experience were tied to specific constructs before the ethnographic data were collected. On the contrary, predictions and substantiations were based on our own judgment; we examined cultural experiences and behavior patterns as they were expressed, without preconceived categories. No doubt some existing categories, particularly those included in the review of literature, were present in our minds and influenced our judgment, but seeing the individual children as perceived by themselves and by those who know or had known them remained the primary goal.

FINDINGS

The development of case studies for each child is a key step in the predictive-ethnography approach. Based on the ethnographic field notes, transcripts of interviews, and questionnaire results, patterns of cultural experience and behavior were used to substantiate predicted scores for each construct. After the predicted scores were recorded and substantiated, actual test results were entered for comparison, and a discussion and summary were then written for each child. Ten case studies were developed for the final report on the research

(Jackson and Espino, 1979); the following three case studies are presented here to illustrate this step in the analysis process. These three cases represent the spectrum of children sampled, especially in regard to language proficiency: Nancy is fully fluent in English and is a nonspeaker of Spanish; Gabriel is limited in English and fluent in Spanish; and Carmen is fluent in both English and Spanish.

The format for each case study follows this six-part sequence: (1) discussion of the child's general personality and background; (2) presentation of the predicted and actual scores on the CEFT test of FD/I orientation; (3) substantiation of the predicted score, citing cultural antecedents with data from field notes; (4) presentation of predicted and actual test results on the MFFT test of conceptual tempo for both time (impulsivity) and errors (accuracy); (5) substantiation, based on our cultural-antecedent notes, of predictions on the conceptual tempo measure; and (6) post-hoc analysis reflecting on possible reasons for the pattern of results in each case.

A nine-point scale was used in the predictions and test results for both FD/I orientation and conceptual tempo. In the FD/I measure, the higher the number the more field-independent the predicted outcome; the comparable CEFT results are based on students' scores converted into stanines, with the same direction in the scale. The predicted time and error scores are also on nine-point scales, with higher numbers representing a more reflective style and more errors respectively. Test results, again based on stanines, represent the same directionality. In many of the predictions cited, there are two numbers; these represent the opinions of the two ethnographers, made independently. Where only one number is entered as the predicted outcome, we were in agreement.

Three Case Studies

NANCY

Nancy is a very friendly, outgoing nine-year-old. Her parents and teachers and Nancy herself say that she usually gets her way, especially at home. She is the youngest of four children in her household, with three older half-brothers, her mother, and her father living at home. She is very close to her maternal grandparents and her two half-sisters, who live in a "lower-income" part of town, five miles away from where she presently lives, which is in a "middle-income" area. Nancy's FD/I scores were:

Predicted score: 6/8
Actual score: 4

Nancy was expected to score as field-independent. The relevant cultural antecedents in her case include the following:

Nancy's parents, particularly her mother, stress independence, autonomy, and responsibility for taking care of herself, her possessions, and her share of the household duties (washing dishes, vacuuming, cleaning the kitchen, keeping her room orderly). This emphasis on the part of parents is linked to field independence (FI).

Nancy evidently gets her own way with her parents, her grandparents, her siblings, and her friends. Everyone interviewed mentioned that Nancy was "spoiled." Her mother added that she was *agarrada* ("greedy"), bossy (with her friends), and *delicada* ("overly sensitive"). "Egocentric" is the word that best summarizes this aspect of the personality (FI).

Nancy tends to be a loner, even among her friends. She says she would rather have a lot of friends rather than a few close ones because then "if we fight, I'll still have some left" (FI).

Nancy is generally "external" in her motivation, rather than "internal," as a psychologically differentiated individual would be expected to be. This tendency is seen as related to field dependence (FD).

Nancy's conceptual tempo scores were:

Predicted time: 5/4
Predicted errors: 3/2
Actual time: 7
Actual errors: 3

Nancy was expected to score in the middle on impulsivity and to have fewer errors than the norm. She is quite impulsive in most social situations, but concentrates intently on school-related work, which is probably how she saw the MFFT. The relevant cultural antecedents include the following:

Nancy's interaction style with adults is primarily one of getting attention and gaining approval. Thus, we predicted that she would probably modify her impulsive tendency on the MFFT, as she would get negative feedback on errors and no feedback on speed of response. This would result in a more reflective response mode than would otherwise be predicted (R).

Her "external" orientation, mentioned earlier, would, we thought, strengthen her tendency to slow down and find the right answers. This external orientation may be seen as related to her materialistic value system, which was probably acquired from her parents (R).

Nancy's parents give her attention for her outstanding accomplishments, but not so much for her everyday activities. This fact is seen as related to her impulsivity in social situations (I).

Nancy's home environment is very orderly; she takes an active role in keeping the house clean and neat, carrying out her assigned daily chores (R).

Her impulsivity in social situations may be seen as related to her parents' tendency to "give in" easily to her demands. Her maternal grandparents also have this tendency, and from all accounts (parents, siblings, teacher, and Nancy), they "spoil" her more than her parents do (I).

Nancy's father notices, reinforces, and highly approves of her competing (baseball, football, kickball, etc.). His pressure to perform and compete is seen as related to her relative impulsivity (I).

Nancy scored as slightly field-dependent (sensitive), in contrast to both raters' predictions of a field-independent score. It may be that her behavior ("greedy," "bossy," *"delicada"*) is in fact a better predictor of field dependence than of field independence.

She was expected to score in the middle (5/4) on conceptual tempo; yet her results showed her to be distinctly reflective (7). As was pointed out, she tends to behave impulsively in social situations; yet she concentrates on school-related work. Thus, it appears that she responded to the MFFT as she would to other school-related tasks, taking her time and making relatively few errors.

Nancy may be seen as conforming to the expectations of her teachers, as indicated by her reflective conceptual tempo. Her FD/I scores contradicted not only our predictions, but also previous research linking such variables as verbal skills and mathematical ability to field independence: Nancy had the highest achievement test scores in both reading and mathematics of the ten children involved in the study.

GABRIEL

Gabriel is a very dignified, self-assured child. Although he appears reserved at first, with time he reveals his personal warmth and sensitivity. He is the youngest of four children, including a twenty-year-old married half-sister and two brothers. He lives with his monolingual Spanish-speaking grandmother and mother and his two brothers in a small (population 150) agricultural community seven miles outside of town. His father lived with the family until his accidental death in October 1978 (two weeks before Gabriel became involved in the study). Gabriel's FD/I scores were:

Predicted score: 5/7
Actual score: 4

Gabriel was expected to score in the middle on FD/I orientation, neither strongly field-dependent nor strongly field-independent. Gabriel's social behavior is strongly sensitive (field-dependent); yet he concentrates on academic tasks, and his personality shows a high degree of psychological differentiation. Relevant cultural antecedents in Gabriel's case include the following:

> His mother stresses obedience and respect, an influence that various theorists have linked to field dependence (FD).

> His father was relatively uninvolved in Gabriel's upbringing, especially in the last months before his death in October 1978 (FD).

> While Gabriel's mother and grandmother have stressed socially integrative values (not fighting, not showing anger, having good friends as opposed to a lot of friends), features linked to FD style, his older sister has guided him more in his school work, stressing individual achievement (FI).

> Being the youngest of four children, Gabriel has received more individual attention than his siblings and is often protected by his maternal grandmother, who lives with the family (FI).

> Gabriel is relatively free from individual responsibility at home; he has few or no daily chores to do (FI).

> Gabriel's behavior toward his friends is socially integrative; he seldom pushes his leadership and tends to be conciliatory in disputes (FD).

Thus, Gabriel shows some behavior patterns that are highly individualistic, indicating field independence, and others that are socially integrative, indicating field dependence. Since we assumed that Gabriel would see the test measuring this construct as an academic task, we predicted that his field-independent tendencies would manifest themselves, counterbalancing his generally field-sensitive interaction style and producing a "middle" score.

Gabriel's conceptual tempo scores were:

> Predicted time: 7
> Predicted errors: 3
> Actual time: 8
> Actual errors: 5

Gabriel was expected to score as reflective and to produce relatively few errors. The relevant cultural antecedents included the following:

> Gabriel is seldom pressured to perform or respond at home; he is given an abundance of individual attention. Both factors are seen as linked to reflectivity (R).

> As the "baby" of the family, he is often left to play with his friends, do his homework, or watch television with few interruptions. This experience is seen as leading to his typically total absorption in whatever he does (R).

> Gabriel's home environment is very orderly; he has a relatively limited range of possible daily activities and a fairly predictable daily and

weekly schedule. This fact is seen as related to his habit of taking his time and finishing whatever task he has undertaken, particularly at school (R).

His mother has observed that Gabriel will often consider a situation, particularly a social situation, for a minute before he gets involved in it (R).

Gabriel's teacher says that he will ask questions if he is not sure of what to do and will sometimes hesitate when speaking English. She attributes his hesitation to his thinking of the word or words he wants to use (R).

Gabriel's predicted scores generally corresponded closely to his test results. He was expected to be more field-independent and to make fewer errors and take less time on the MFFT. The general pattern of the predictions for the two constructs was accurate, however, indicating that Gabriel is slightly field-dependent (sensitive) and quite reflective.

CARMEN

Carmen is a very bright and personable nine-year-old. She appears to be mature for her age psychologically, showing a high degree of self-reliance as well as a consistently deep concern for others who are close to her. She lives with her paternal grandmother, her step-grandfather, and a seven-year-old sister in a garage apartment surrounded by an extremely rich and apparently chaotic environment: old cars, furniture, soda machines, rabbit hutches, pigeon cages, chickens, numerous dogs and cats, and a vegetable garden. Carmen's mother, who had two children from a second marriage in addition to Carmen and her sister, died in an automobile accident when Carmen was seven. Her father remarried and now lives in another town a hundred miles away with his second family. Her stepfather lives about thirty miles away and visits weekly, bringing his two daughters (three and five), Carmen's half-sisters, whom she helped raise (as the oldest child) when she lived with them, up until two years ago.

Carmen's FD/I scores were:

Predicted score: 7/5
Actual score: 8

She was expected to score as strongly field-independent on the CEFT. Her high degree of social sensitivity might indicate a field-dependent cognitive style, though she was expected to have the cognitive ability to disembed figures and is quite independent. Thus, she is seen as "bicognitive," in accordance with the description (and cultural antecedents) presented by Ramírez and Castañeda (1974). The relevant cultural antecedents in her case are the following:

Carmen's grandparents stress social sensitivity (FD), but also believe that she will discover her own capabilities through experience (FI). They approve of her involvement in competitive sports (track, karate, etc.) (FI).

She takes on responsibilities around the house and at school, but does not push herself (FI). She is seen as more of a follower than a leader at school (FD).

Carmen's grandparents allow her to choose her own friends (within limits). She has a relatively small group of close friends, and has one very close friend at school and another in her neighborhood (FD).

She is very "internal" in her motivation; she avoids attracting attention to herself but applies herself intensely to any task she undertakes (schoolwork, care of animals, babysitting, sewing, running track, or making kites) (FI).

Her interaction style with her peers is generally conciliatory (FD), but she will assert her authority when it is called for; for example, with her younger siblings or with students when she is teacher's helper (FI).

Carmen sets high standards for herself, enjoys competing in sports, and seeks out intellectually challenging tasks (FI).

She generally avoids personal conflicts and will concentrate on her work even when those around her are noisy or distracting (FI).

Carmen expresses her feelings openly, is very much aware of others' feelings, and expresses concern for others regularly (FD).

Carmen's conceptual tempo scores were:

Predicted time: 6/8
Predicted errors: 2/1
Actual time: 5
Actual errors: 3

She was expected to score as slightly reflective and to produce few errors. The relevant cultural antecedents here were the following:

Carmen's grandparents accept her as she is and respect her right to choose her own activities and set her own goals. Thus, she is allowed a high degree of autonomy (R).

Her grandparents are very much aware of her daily activities and willingly provide transportation to enable her to visit friends, go to the park, or practice running; thus, Carmen does not have to do anything special or annoying to attract their attention (R).

Carmen is allowed ample time to finish activities once she has begun (R).

She is somewhat reticent at first in new social situations but becomes fully involved once she enters into social interactions (R).

Carmen will ask for clarification in school if she is not sure of instructions, but she usually understands them the first time they are given (R).

The predicted scores for Carmen match her test results fairly closely. Thus, she is very field-independent (though possibly bicognitive) and neither impulsive nor reflective, but accurate, on the MFFT. Carmen is an example of what Ramírez and Castañeda (1974) would call a bicognitive child, with an enhanced capacity for flexible and abstract thought. Without a measure on which field dependence (or sensitivity) is favored, however, there is no way of knowing whether Carmen has the capacity to be as field-dependent as she is field-independent.

Cultural Patterns, Predictions, and Results

Tables 2–4 present the cultural patterns that emerged for all ten children in the study as well as the predicted outcomes and test results for each construct. Tables 2 and 3 include the cultural experiences and behavior patterns linked to FD/I orientation and conceptual tempo respectively. Table 4 presents the predicted scores, actual scores, and discrepancies between the two for each of the constructs.

Tables 2 and 3 summarize the cultural experiences and behavior patterns of the ten children for each measure. The case studies provided the source for these data: a category of experience or behavior was checked off only if substantiated by the enthnographic data. Children's results are rank-ordered for each construct measured, with the "highest-scoring" child on the left and the "lowest scoring" on the right. Patterns of xs across the page can thus be examined to find which cultural variables seem to discriminate or predict the children's scores.

The most striking thing about the pattern of FD/I results in table 2 is the lack of any definite pattern at all. Two of the cultural variables—"parents stress obedience and respect" and "parents absent or uninvolved with raising child"—show some power to discriminate between field-dependent and field-independent children. Three children out of seven in each case, however, scored as decidedly field-dependent, even though the category was not indicated as applying to them. Parents who allow their child a high degree of autonomy in the home were predicted to have children who scored as field-independent. The results show that all but one of the children with this category checked actually scored as more field-dependent (the exception was Christian [Chr.]). "Parents recognize and approve of competition by child" and "parents believe in internal motivation" would have been powerful predictors of field independence, except that the most field-dependent of the ten children, Jasmín (Jas.), fell into both categories. The remainder of the patterns serve to illustrate the high degree of diversity observed in the cultural experiences and behavior patterns of the children involved in the study.

The pattern of results documented in table 3 indicates that two opposing

Table 2: Cultural Antecedents Linked to Field Dependence/Independence

	Carm (8)[b]	Chr (7)	Joh (5)	Nan (4)	Gab (4)	Lou (4)	Fran (3)	Liz (3)	Carl (3)	Jas (3)
CULTURAL EXPERIENCES										
Parents stress obedience and respect (FD)[a]			X		X	X	X	X	X	
Parents absent or uninvolved with raising child (FD)			X		X	X	X	X	X	
Parents stress social sensitivity (FD)	X[c]	X	X		X	X	X	X	X	X
Parents prefer lasting friends for child (FD)	X				X		X		X	X
Parents stress individual achievement (FI)	X			X				X		
Parents allow child high degree of autonomy (FI)		X		X	X	X	X	X	X	X
Parents assign daily chores (FI)		X		X				X		X
Parents emphasize individualism and independence (FI)		X		X						X
Parents recognize and approve of competition by child (FI)	X	X	X	X					X	X
Parents believe in internal motivation (FI)	X	X	X							X

82

Behavior Pattern	1	2	3	4	5	6	7	8	9
Child seeks attention from adults (FD)	X			X	X		X	X	X
Child has close, lasting friendships (FD)		X		X	X	X	X	X	X
Child is "external" in his/her motivation (FD)			X	X		X	X		X
Child expresses feelings openly (FD)	X		X	X	X				X
Child is concilliatory with peers (FD)	X		X	X	X				
Child regularly takes care of others (FD)	X		X	X	X	X			
Child enjoys competition (FI)	X	X	X				X	X	X
Child likes intellectual challenges (FI)	X	X		X				X	X
Child works for personal goals, not rewards (FI)	X	X		X					X
Child shows high need for achievement (FI)	X		X		X	X		X	X
Child is task-oriented in school (FI)	X		X	X	X	X		X	X
Child avoids personal conflicts (FI)	X		X	X				X	X
Child concentrates despite distractions (FI)	X	X		X	X				X

[a] *FD* indicates experiences and behavior linked to field dependence; *FI*, those linked to field independence.

[b] Figures in parenthesis give test results. Scores are rank-ordered from left to right. They are expressed as stanine equivalents, based on norms for nine- and ten-year-olds published in the Children's Embedded Figure Test manual (Witkin, et al., 1971). A score of 1 indicates field dependence; a score of 9, field independence.

[c] An X indicates the presence of a cultural variable.

Table 3: Cultural Antecedents Linked to Conceptual Tempo

	Gab (8/5)[b]	Jas (8/4)	Nan (7/3)	Carl (6/6)	Chri (6/6)	Joh (5/2)	Carm (5/3)	Lou (3/7)	Liz (3/7)	Fra (3/5)
CULTURAL EXPERIENCES										
Parents seldom pay attention to child (I)[a]								X	X	X
Parents pressure child to perform, compete (I)			X						X	
Parents give in easily to child's demands (I)			X			X			X	
Parents notice child primarily when he/she behaves "well" or "badly" (I)			X			X			X	X
Parents pay attention to child's routine, everyday activities (R)	X[c]	X		X	X	X	X	X		
Parents give child abundant individual attention (R)	X	X	X	X	X					
Parents accept child as he/she is (R)	X	X		X	X		X	X		
Parents allow child time alone to finish tasks or games (R)	X	X	X	X	X		X	X		X
Home environment is very orderly (R)	X	X	X	X	X			X		X
Child's daily schedule is fairly predictable (R)	X	X	X	X				X		X
BEHAVIOR PATTERNS										
Child interrupts conversations (I)			X			X				
Child tries to attract attention (I)			X			X				
Child has "external" orientation, attends to social cues, especially from adults (R)			X			X		X	X	X
Child hesitates in new social situations (R)	X	X		X	X		X	X		
Child will ask for help if not sure of instructions in school (R)	X	X		X	X		X	X	X	X
Child will hesitate when talking if unsure of wording (R)	X			X				X		

[a] *I* indicates experiences and behavior linked to impulsivity; *R*, those linked to reflectivity.

[b] Figures in parentheses give test results, with time score first, followed by error score on MFFT. Scores are rank ordered from left to right. They are expressed in stanines; "8/2" indicates a reflective, accurate response. Stanine cutoffs were derived from unpublished data on third-grade Mexican American children collected for a study of the cognitive styles of minority children in 1978 (NIE Project #G-78-0208).

[c] An *X* indicates the presence of a cultural variable.

categories of cultural experience discriminate between impulsive and reflective children: "parents seldom pay attention to child (I)" and "parents give child abundant individual attention (R)." The pattern may thus be said to indicate that the degree of parental attention to the individual child predicts conceptual tempo. Other, similar variables—"Parents pay attention to child's routine, everyday activities" and "Parents accept child as he/she is"—also appear to predict reflectivity to some degree, but anomalies in the patterns prevent these results from being definite. There is some evidence that children raised in an orderly home environment with fairly predictable schedules tend to be reflective; yet Louisa (Lou.), who scored as distinctly impulsive, falls into both of these categories of cultural experience.

An examination of behavioral variables indicates that the only behavior shown to be even remotely predictive of conceptual tempo is the tendency to "attend to social cues, especially from adults," indicating an "external" orientation. This behavior was originally linked to reflectivity in making predictions; yet it seems here to be related fairly strongly to impulsivity. The lack of clear relationships between observed behavior and conceptual tempo is enigmatic, especially since the impulsivity/reflectivity dimension might be expected to reveal itself clearly in everyday activities. One plausible explanation for this phenomenon is that the MFFT measures a very test-specific type of impulsivity/reflectivity, and not impulsivity/reflectivity as generally manifested in school or home settings.

Table 4 summarizes the predictions, test results, and discrepancies between predicted and actual outcomes for the ten children for both constructs. Where the two raters' predictions differed, Jackson's prediction is shown to the left of the slash and Espino's to the right. Where we agreed, only one score is given. Stanine equivalents are used for both the FD/I and the conceptual tempo scores.

The predicted scores for FD/I orientation vary considerably from the test results. This may be due in part to differences between what the test measures and what the ethnographers were basing their judgments on: behavior and experiences in the home as well as at school. Nevertheless, if accuracy is defined as plus or minus one stanine, then 70 percent of Jackson's and 50 percent of Espino's predictions correspond with test results, indicating that their data do predict test performance to a reasonable degree. Although the degree of interjudge reliability appears to be low, raters' predictions are consistently within 2 points of each other and are always on the same side of the mean. Seven out of ten predictions by both researchers correspond to test results, if one considers only whether a subject's score falls above or below the mean.

Table 4 also shows a striking amount of disagreement between the raters. Many predictions differ by two stanines, and one set differs by five stanines. The most plausible explanation for these discrepancies is that Jackson gener-

Table 4: Predicted and Actual Field Dependence/Independence and Conceptual Tempo Test Results

| | PREDICTED SCORE[a] | | | TEST RESULTS | | | DISCREPANCY | | |
| | FD/I | Conceptual Tempo | | FD/I | Conceptual Tempo | | FD/I | Conceptual Tempo | |
		Time	Errors		Time	Errors		Time	Errors
Nancy	6/8	5/4	3/2	4	7	3	+2/+4	−2/−3	0/−1
Gabriel	5/7	7/8	3	4	8	5	+1/+3	−1/0	−2
Carmen	7/5	6/8	2/1	8	5	3	+1/+3	+1/+3	−1/−2
Liz	4/2	3/2	6/4	3	3	7	+1/−1	0/−1	−1/−3
Johnny	4/3	3/5	5/3	5	5	2	−1/−2	−2/0	+3/+1
Christian	7/8	7/8	3/2	6	6	6	+1/+2	+1/+2	−3/−4
Jasmin	5/3	6/8	4/1	3	8	4	+2/0	−2/0	0/−3
Carlos	3/4	6/8	6/3	3	6	6	0/+1	0/+2	0/−3
Louisa	2/3	7/2	7/4	4	3	5	−2/−1	+4/−1	+2/−1
Frank	4/3	4/7	6/4	3	3	7	+1/0	+1/+4	−1/−3

[a]FD/I scores are based on the Children's Embedded Figures Test. Test results are expressed as stanine scores, with stanine cutoffs derived from published norms for nine- and ten-year-olds (Witkin, et al., 1971). Conceptual tempo scores are based on the Matching Familiar Figures Test. Results are expressed as stanines, derived from unpublished data on rural third-grade Mexican Americans, collected for a study of the cognitive styles of minority children in 1978 (NIE Project #G-78-0208).

ally collected his data in the school, and Espino collected hers in the children's homes. There is no apparent pattern in these differences or in the degree to which one rater's predictions were more or less accurate than the other's, though Jackson's predictions were somewhat more on target. If plus or minus one stanine is considered accurate, then, for time, Jackson was on target 60 percent of the time, and Espino 50 percent. For errors, Jackson was right 60 percent of the time, and Espino 30 percent.

SUMMARY

Our first goal was to analyze the findings of this study in light of previous research and theory tying cultural variables to field dependence/independence and conceptual tempo. The second was to document the degree of intracultural diversity and analyze it by re-examining tables 2 and 3. A judgment of the power of ethnography to predict test scores, our third goal, involves summarizing the percentage of accurate predictions for the two constructs measured. We then present the implications of our findings for educators and discuss further research suggested by this study.

Findings in Relation to Previous Research

The FD/I construct is the one cognitive-style variable with a well-developed theory relating cultural experience to test performance (Dyk and Witkin, 1965; Witkin, Dyk, et al., 1974; Witkin, et al., 1977). Thus, one would expect certain cultural experiences to discriminate between field-dependent and field-independent children.

The findings of this study do not generally support this expectation, however, as only three cultural variables show even weak predictive power (all predict field dependence):

1. Parents stress obedience and respect
2. Parents absent or uninvolved with raising child
3. Parents allow child high degree of autonomy

The first two of these variables have been suggested by Witkin and others (Holtzman, Diaz-Guerrero, and Swartz, 1975; Ramírez and Price-Williams, 1974a) to explain the more field-dependent scores of some groups. The third was found in this study to relate to field dependence, although Witkin et al. (1962) has proposed "encouragement of autonomous functioning" as a child-rearing practice related to field independence.

As we noted above, the lack of any definite pattern relating cultural antecedents to FD/I orientation was our most striking finding in this area. Only three of the twenty-three cultural and behavioral variables examined in table 2 show even weak predictive power. Though this study is admittedly limited by its small sample, there is apparently little support for most of the child-rearing and socialization practices that have been cited in previous research to explain differences in FD/I orientation between groups of children. As Holtzman, Diaz-Guerrero, and Swartz (1975) and Sanders, Scholz, and Kagan (1976) found in their studies of socialization practices and the FD/I construct, differences between groups may be significant, but correlations between parents' socialization patterns and children's scores are generally not significant.

The only category of cultural experience found to relate clearly to any construct is parental attention, which was found to predict conceptual tempo. Children whose parents give them abundant individual attention score as reflective; children whose parents seldom pay attention to them score as impulsive. Other cultural variables that are very similar but are not such powerful predictors of reflectivity are related to whether (1) parents pay attention to the child's routine, everyday activities, and (2) parents accept child as he/she is. One behavior pattern predicted impulsivity fairly well, though it was thought originally to be associated with reflectivity; this was the child's tendency to pay attention to social cues, especially from adults.

The link between parental attention and reflectivity supports to some degree findings of Campbell (1973) that parents of reflective children intervened or structured learning situations for their children more than parents of impulsive children did. Thus, it appears that parents who are willing to spend time with their children and get involved with teaching them are more likely to have children who are reflective.

General Patterns Across Children and Constructs

An examination of the patterns of results for all the children and all the constructs reveals the following:

> The one child who scored as fully fluent in both English and Spanish (Carmen) also scored as field-independent, fast and accurate in her conceptual tempo, and high in both reading and mathematical achievement. The main cultural factor distinguishing Carmen from her peers has been her ongoing close involvement with her monolingual Spanish-speaking grandmother. Their activities together include daily lessons in Spanish, watching and discussing Spanish television programs, and shopping. (On shopping trips Carmen translates for her grandmother.) All the other children in this study have Spanish-dominant grandparents, but Carmen is the only child who is so close to her grandmother and maintains a strong relationship involving the use of Spanish with her.

> All the parents interviewed valued bilingualism highly and expressed a desire for their children to learn to read and write Spanish as well as understand and speak it. Those who knew about or mentioned bilingual education, however, were generally opposed to their children's involvement, seeing it primarily as a "remedial" program in which placement was based on the child's "limited English proficiency."

> The tests used to measure each construct in this study met psychometric criteria for reliability and validity, based on the testing of large numbers of children. When individual children's scores and their relationship to observed behavior were examined, however, test performance often did not appear generalizable to behavior in other settings.

These three general patterns are based on too few cases to warrant any conclusions, but they do suggest that further research might be useful.

A high degree of intracultural diversity was found among the ten children, all Mexican American third graders attending the same school. Of the more than one hundred cultural experiences and behavior patterns evidenced in the life history data, only three were found to characterize all ten children: "Spanish-dominant grandparents," "parents value bilingualism," and "child prefers active, outdoor activities." The significance of this result is limited by the small number of children and the uniqueness of the community in which they were raised.[2] It indicates, however, that researchers and educators need to exercise caution in ascribing characteristics to Mexican American culture. They should realize that differences in socialization practices, patterns of language use, kinship systems, values and beliefs, and interaction styles probably exist within any cultural group, even within a single community.

The Ethnographic Method

The accuracy of our predictions for the tested constructs can be summarized from results displayed earlier in table 4. The percentages given below indicate the number of accurate (within one stanine) predictions out of the total number of predictions made in each case. The percentage of accurate predictions for Jackson is shown first; that for Espino follows:

FD/I orientation: 70 percent/50 percent
Conceptual tempo (time): 60 percent/50 percent
Conceptual tempo (errors): 60 percent/30 percent

Implications of Findings

The findings of this study, we believe, have implications for educational policy and practice.

The ethnographic procedures used in this research may be adapted to train teachers and other educators to conduct similar studies in their local communities as a means of cultural sensitization. Many of the teachers interviewed in this study expressed an interest in knowing more about their students' home life, and the parents who were asked expressed their desire to have teachers know more about their child's background.

Educational policy and practice that assume that Mexican American children are homogeneous in terms of language background, home experiences, interaction styles, or any other variable are bound for trouble. The degree of intracultural diversity documented in this study indicates that Mexican American students, like students of any cultural group, must be seen as individuals.

When psychological constructs such as those examined in this study are used for educational diagnosis and prescription for *individual* children,

---

[2]The community in which this study was conducted is a rural town in central Texas, with a population of 6,000, over half of whom are Mexican American. For extensive information on this town and history, see the final project report to the National Institute of Education (Jackson and Espino, 1979).

extreme caution is warranted. Performance on tests, especially measures of cognitive style, needs to be balanced with systematically observed behavior before any decision, such as placement in a special program, can be considered valid.

Possibilities for Future Research

The following research possibilities are suggested by the results of this study:

Testing the degree to which the relationships between cultural variables and test performance, described earlier in this section, also are found with larger numbers of children and different ethnic groups

Replicating this study with different ethnic groups or in different locales, particularly an urban center

Re-examining the ethnographic data from this study using pre-existing categories based on others' theory and research, and contrasting the results with those found here, which were based primarily on the ethnographers' judgments

Looking at the impact—on teachers, students, and parents—of a teacher-training program that used ethnography for cultural sensitization, after first developing and field-testing such a program

REFERENCES

Bieri, J., Bradburn, W. M., and Galinsky, M. D. Sex differences in perceptual behavior. *Journal of Personality*, 1958, *26*, 1–12.

Buriel, R. Cognitive styles among three generations of Mexican-American children. *Journal of Cross-Cultural Psychology*, 1975, *6*, 417–429.

Campbell, S. B. Mother-child interaction in reflective, impulsive, and hyperactive children. *Developmental Psychology*, 1973, *8*, 341–349.

Canavan, D. Field dependence in children as a function of grade, sex, and ethnic group membership. Paper read at the meeting of the American Psychological Association, Washington, D.C., 1969.

Cazden, C. B., and Leggett, E. L. Culturally responsible education: a response to Lau Guidelines II. Paper presented at the conference on Research and Policy Implications of the Task Force Report of the U.S. Office of Civil Rights: Findings specifying remedies for eliminating past educational practices ruled unlawful under *Lau* v. *Nichols*. Austin, Tex.: Southwest Educational Development Laboratory, 1976.

Crandall, V. J., and Sinkeldam, C. Children's dependent and achievement behaviors in social situations and their perceptual field dependence. *Journal of Personality*, 1964, *32*, 1–22.

De Avila, E. A., and Duncan, S. E. Cognitive styles of minority children. Proposal to

National Institute of Education from Southwest Educational Development Laboratory, 1979, p. 21.

De Avila, E. A., Duncan, S. E., Fleming, J. S., Cervantes, R. A., and Laosa, L. M. Cognitive styles of language minority children: some preliminary results. Paper presented at the conference of the National Association for Bilingual Education, San Juan, Puerto Rico, 1978.

DiStefano, J. J. Interpersonal perceptions of field independent and field dependent teachers and students. Doctoral dissertation, Cornell University, 1969.

Duncan, S. E., and De Avila, E. A. Relative linguistic proficiency and field dependence/independence: some findings on the linguistic heterogeneity and cognitive style of bilingual children. Paper presented at the annual meeting of Teachers of English to Speakers of Other Languages (TESOL), Boston, Mass., 27–28 February 1979.

Dyk, R. B., and Witkin, H. A. Family experiences related to the development of differentiation in children. *Child Development,* 1965, *36,* 21–55.

Freedman, N., O'Hanlon, J., Oltman, P., and Witkin, H. A. The imprint of psychological differentiation on kinetic behavior in varying communicative contexts. *Journal of Abnormal Psychology,* 1972, *79,* 239–258.

Gardner, R. W., Jackson, D. N., and Messick, S. J. Personality organization in cognitive controls and intellectual abilities. *Psychological Issues,* 1960, *2* (monograph 8).

Holtzman, W. H., Diaz-Guerrero, R., and Swartz, S. D. *Personality development in two cultures.* Austin and London: University of Texas Press, 1975.

Irving, D. The field dependence hypothesis in cross-cultural perspective. Doctoral dissertation, Rice University, 1970.

Jackson, S. L., and Espino, L. Final report: cultural antecedents of language proficiency, cognitive style, intellectual development and achievement in Mexican American children. Austin, Tex.: Southwest Educational Development Laboratory, 1979.

Jarner, C. D. R. A cognitive style approach to teacher-pupil interaction and the academic performance of black children. Master's thesis, Rutgers University, 1973.

Kagan, J., Pearson, L., and Welch, L. Conceptual impulsivity and inductive reasoning. *Child Development,* 1966, *37,* 583–594.

Kagan, S. Social motives and behaviors of Mexican American and Anglo American children. In J. L. Martinez (Ed.), *Chicano psychology.* New York: Academic Press, 1977.

Kagan, S., and Zahn, G. L. Field dependence and the school achievement gap between Anglo-American and Mexican-American children. *Journal of Educational Psychology,* 1975, *67,* 643–650.

Kluckhohn, C. The personal document in anthropological science. Social Science Research Council, bulletin 53, 1945.

Kogan, N. Educational implications of cognitive style. In G. Lesser (Ed.), *Psychology and educational practice.* Glenview, Ill.: Scott, Foresman, 1971, pp. 242–292.

Laosa, L. M. Cognitive styles and learning strategies research: some of the areas in which psychology can contribute to personalized instruction in multicultural education. *Journal of Teacher Education,* 1977, *28*(3), 26–30.

Laosa, L. M. Development of cognitive styles among Chicanos in traditional and dualistic communities. Paper prepared for the Cognitive Styles of Minority Children project, contract #400-65-0051, National Institute of Education and Southwest Educational Development Laboratory, 1978.

Marcus, E. S. The relationship of psychological differentiation to the congruence of temporal patterns of speech. Doctoral dissertation, New York University, 1970.

Pelto, P. J., and Pelto, G. H. *Anthropological research*. New York: Cambridge University Press, 1978.

Podell, J. E., and Phillips, L. A developmental analysis of cognition as observed in dimensions of Rorschach and objective test performance. *Journal of Personality*, 1959, *27*, 439–463.

Ramírez, M. and Castañeda, A. *Cultural democracy, bicognitive development and education*. New York: Academic Press, 1974.

Ramírez, M., Castañeda, A., and Herold, P. L. The relationship of acculturation to cognitive style among Mexican Americans. *Journal of Cross-Cultural Psychology*, 1974, *5*, 425–433.

Ramírez, M., and Price-Williams, D. R. Cognitive styles in children: two Mexican communities. *Interamerican Journal of Psychology*, 1974a, *8*, 93–100.

Ramírez, M., and Price-Williams, D. R. Cognitive styles of children of three ethnic groups in the United States. *Journal of Cross-Cultural Psychology*, 1974b, *5*, 212–219.

Sanders, M., Scholz, J. P., and Kagan, S. Three social motives and field-independence-dependence in Anglo American and Mexican American children. *Journal of Cross-Cultural Psychology*, 1976, *7*, 451–462.

Shows, W. D. Psychological differentiation and the A-B dimension: a dyadic interaction hypothesis. Doctoral dissertation, Duke University, 1967.

Witkin, H. A., and Berry, J. W. Psychological differentiation in cross-cultural perspective. *Journal of Cross-Cultural Psychology*, 1975, *6*, 4–87.

Witkin, H. A., Dyk, R. B., Fatherson, H. F., Goodenough, D. R., and Karp, S. A. *Psychological differentiation*. New York: Wiley, 1962.

Witkin, H. A., Dyk, R. B., Fatherson, H. F., Goodenough, D. R., and Karp, S. A. *Psychological differentiation*. Potomac, Md.: Erlbaum, 1974.

Witkin, H. A., Lewis, H. B., Hertzman, M., Machover, K., Meissner, P. B., and Wapner, S. *Personality through perception*. Westport, Conn.: Greenwood Press, 1972.

Witkin, H. A., Moore, C. A., Goodenough, D. R., and Cox, P. W. Field-dependent and field-independent cognitive styles and their educational implications. *Review of Educational Research*, 1977, *47*(1), 1–64.

Witkin, H. A., Oltman, P. K., Raskin, E., and Karp, S. A. *A manual for the embedded figures test*. Palo Alto: Consulting Psychologists Press, 1971.

Wober, M. Distinguishing centri-cultural from cross-cultural tests and research. *Perceptual and Motor Skills*, 1969, *28*, 488.

Yando, R. M., and Kagan, J. The effects of teacher tempo on the child. *Child Development*, 1968, *39*, 27–34.

6 | Reinforcing Culture in Three Bilingual Education Programs

FRANK GONZALES
Texas Tech University

Prior to the civil rights movement, biculturalism and multiculturalism were not associated with the educational process. A person who chose to maintain more than one cultural identity did it of his or her own will and often at the cost of being socially and educationally ostracized by the majority group. The Bilingual Education Act of 1968, Title VII, Elementary and Secondary Education Act (ESEA), the first legislation of its type in American educational history, attempted to redress the miseducation of ethnic minority children whose home language was other than English and whose culture was other than Anglo Saxon. The home and socialization experiences of many children are based on a language, heritage, values, and a style of teaching not represented in the classrooms of most public schools. Culturally different children are confronted with learning the complexities of a culture and a code of behavior alien to them.

Historically the education process has been monocultural or culturally exclusive. Castañeda, Harold, and Ramírez (1974a) accuse the schools of failing to make systematic provision for the language, heritage, values, and learning styles of cultural, racial, or social minority groups. Carter (1971), Cortés (1974), Holt (1973), Medina (1972), and Nava (1966) all express the same concern and agree that Chicano children starting school cannot help but sense a rejection of nearly everything they have learned during their first five years in their family environments. Their personality and self-esteem are affected. González (1974) reaffirms that self-concept is a determining factor in a child's cognitive development. Mazón and Arciniega (1974) urge implementation of a competency-based education program for the culturally different, while Carlisle (1971) and Gaarder (1965) support cultural understanding as a priority of bilingual education (Carlisle, 1971; Castaneda et al., 1974b; Gaarder, 1965).

Bilingual educators, from the inception of bilingual education, have stressed the importance of bicultural reinforcement. González (1974) concluded that culture and personality are intrinsically united and that healthy self-concept,

93

motivation, and positive cognitive behavior are grounded in childhood experiences that are basically ethnocentric. He assembled a model of culture for Mexican American children that focuses specifically on the educational implications of that culture. The model consists of six major categories: formal culture, deep culture, situational culture, language and communications, humanistic values, and miscellaneous historical and heritage areas. González favors incorporating cultural content into all subject areas and urges that instruction be approached from the children's perspective, providing cultural referents with which they can formulate hypotheses of reality that can be tested later.

The plea to integrate culture into all phases of language instruction has been reiterated by such writers as Brooks (1969), Christian (1970), Fishman and Lovas (1970), Lambert (1975), and Walsh (1973). Strategies for doing this with various subjects have been developed by the U.S. Department of Health, Education and Welfare (1976), Brooks and Marino (1976), Casso (1976), and John-Stein and Cooper (1976); yet only thirteen states have legislation supporting bicultural-bilingual education (Peña, 1975). Of the five southwestern states, only Texas has made provisions for mandatory transitional bilingual programs for schools with twenty or more children of limited English-speaking ability (LESA) per grade level. Moreover, even where state laws exist, in the final analysis individual school districts decide whether bilingual-bicultural programs are necessary, as the U.S. Commission on Civil Rights observed (1974). The commission also concluded that many programs in the Southwest are labeled bilingual-bicultural even though they actually focus on teaching English and have no cultural component or course content presented in two languages. The commission's investigation revealed "a systematic failure of the educational process which not only ignores the educational needs of the Chicano students but also suppresses their culture and stifles their hopes and ambitions" (1974).

In 1972 the Commission on Multicultural Education of the American Association of Colleges for Teacher Education (AACTE) called for incorporation of minority cultures into classroom work, emphasizing multicultural education as a means of reorganizing cultural diversity as a valuable resource of American society. (The AACTE adopted the commission's statement in its assembly.) The statement also suggested that multicultural education should go beyond cultural awareness and cultural understanding to a recognition of the right of different cultures to exist (American Association of Colleges for Teacher Education, 1972).

This paper will first present a brief overview of definitions of culture and then a report of a study implemented in a public school setting to determine what elements of minority culture were evident in bilingual classrooms. The final section presents a discussion of the findings and implications of this study.

CULTURE

The first definition of culture to appear in print was that of E. B. Tyler. Tyler, in 1871, used "culture" and "civilization" as synonymous terms representing the sum total of human behavior: "Culture, or civilization, . . . is that complex whole which includes knowledge, belief, art, law, morals, custom, and any other capabilities and habits acquired by man as a member of society" (Kroeber and Kluckhohn, 1952). Seelye's (1976) definition, "culture is seen to include everything that people learn to do" (p. 10), emphasizes the acquisition or learning process. Brooks (1973) defines culture as "the distinctive life-way of a people, whether tribesmen, townsmen or urbanites, who are united by a common language" (p. 3). Thus, culture is a learned habit of a distinctive life-way (Seelye, 1972).

Brooks (1966) divided culture into two categories: "formal culture" and "deep culture." (A more recent term, "surface culture," has become associated with "formal culture," and for the purpose of this study, "surface culture" and "formal culture" are used interchangeably.) Brooks refers to "formal culture" as consisting of "the products of artistic endeavor, achievements of intellectual and artistic genius, deeds of heroic valor, concepts of lofty spirit, and various modes of significant thought, genteel living, and racial vigor" (p. 4). "Deep culture," on the other hand, refers to "the thoughts and beliefs and actions, the concerns and hopes and worries, the personal values, the minor vanities and the half serious superstitions, the subtle gradations of interpersonal relationships as expressed in actions and words, the day-by-day details of life as it is lived" (p. 4).

At the risk of oversimplification, this study considers the tangible elements of the Mexican American culture as surface culture and the intangible elements as deep culture. Surface culture elements are to some extent concrete and can be presented in a classroom situation. This category includes such items as language, songs, dances, arts and crafts, foods, holidays, and history. Feelings and attitudes toward various matters, however, are deep culture elements.

CULTURAL ELEMENTS IN THE BILINGUAL CLASSROOM

Procedure

A questionnaire was developed to establish which elements of Mexican American culture were reinforced or taught in a bilingual-bicultural classroom. The questionnaire was answered on a voluntary basis by 180 teachers and instructional aides in grades one through three at three sites in Texas.

Site 1 was located in the Llano Estacado (Staked Plains) region of North Texas; Mexican Americans made up 38 percent of the student population there. Site 2, located in South Central Texas, had a 68 percent Mexican American student population. Site 3 was located in the semitropical Rio Grande Valley and had an 86 percent Mexican American student population. The three sites illustrate the variations in bilingual education programs in the state.

On-site visits were made to each district. Data were gathered in nine schools, selected with the help of the bilingual education directors of each district. The questionnaire took approximately thirty minutes to administer. Tape recordings were made to record the attitudes and feelings of the instructional staff toward the topic, Mexican American culture, as well as toward the questionnaire itself.

Surface Culture Reinforcement

The questionnaire grouped surface culture or tangible elements into four categories: music, language arts, art and culinary activities, and discussion. These in turn were further subdivided to facilitate the indentification of elements.

Classroom musical activities covered three areas: songs, *rondas,* and dances. Traditional songs in Spanish were taught by 83 percent of the respondents. They included *"La Cucaracha," "Las Mañanitas,"* Christmas songs, *"Cielito Lindo,"* and *"El Rancho Grande."* Two-thirds of the teachers (66 percent) used contemporary songs in their classes. *De Colores,* popular *corridos,* and record albums of Carol Perkins, Eddy Cano, and Hap Palmer were used for instruction. *Rondas,* such as *"Doña Blanca," "Tin Marin,"* and the *"Para Chiquitines"* series, were used by less than half of the teachers (48 percent). Mexican dances—*"La Raspa," "El Jarabe Tapatio," "La Bamba," "Las Chiapanecas,"* and *"El Huapango"*—were taught by 31 percent. Students from two of the sites performed at public functions or celebrations every year. The least reinforced musical category at all three sites was contemporary Chicano songs and music, which were introduced by only 11 percent of the teachers.

Language arts activities were separated into six areas: Spanish-language children's stories, Spanish-language folktales, *dichos* and *refranes, adivinanzas, versos* or Spanish poetry, and drama or role playing in Spanish. Stories in Spanish were used by 68 percent of the teachers, who devoted less than 50 minutes per week to this activity. These low figures for exposure to Spanish literature are due to the fact that 45 percent of the teachers at site 1 were monolingual English-speakers and did not incorporate Spanish reading into the bilingual program at all. A similar situation existed at Site 3, where 10 percent of the teachers were unable to read Spanish. This failure to emphasize reading instruction in the children's home language is typical of many bilingual education programs in Texas.

Spanish-language folktales were incorporated into the instruction by only 49 percent of the respondents, and many of these teachers considered *"Caperucita Roja"* or *"Los Tres Ojos"* usable folktales for the bilingual classroom. I had hoped that this item on the questionnaire would elicit the names of folktales representative of Mexican American culture, but such was not the case. Teachers and aides from sites 1 and 2 listed only translated fairytales from the English language. Site 3 listed the school's curriculum guide and the *Stories That Must Not Die* series as resources.

Only 31 percent of the respondents incorporated *dichos* and *refranes* into their learning activities. Methods of presentation varied, the most common being to incorporate them into a reading or writing lesson. *Adivinanzas,* or riddles, were used on all three grade levels at all sites. The sources listed included textbooks and magazines. *Versos* or poems, were used by 61 percent of the teachers. Poetry was included in reading, mathematics, and oral language development lessons. Drama and role playing in Spanish were used at all of the sites and incorporated into reading, oral language development, and social studies lessons. A teacher at site 1 indicated that songs and *cuentos* were often role-played as well.

Traditional Mexican crafts were taught by 31 percent of the teachers, and only 18 percent chose class art projects that incorporated Mexican American culture. Weaving, pottery, tissue paper flowers, *ojo de dios,* and papier-mâché masks were common individual projects. Class art projects included making *piñatas,* a relief map of Mexico, and a mosaic. Contemporary Chicano art and artists were not discussed or displayed by any of the teachers. Art and craft activities that reinforce Mexican American culture were obviously a low priority in all nine schools. This could have been due to the fact that some of the schools had full-time art teachers who were unfamiliar with the culture of the Mexican American student body. Obviously, the bilingual classroom teachers in these schools had delegated all art activities to those teachers.

Culinary activities received a better response. Thirty-one percent of the teachers used the television program *Villa Alegre* to teach the origin of *tortillas, guacamole, buñuelos,* and chocolate. Almost half (44 percent) of the classrooms prepared ethnic foods sometime during the year, and a vast array of foods traditionally considered Mexican were reportedly prepared by instructional aides or the children's mothers.

The questionnaire contained three sections on class discussions. Teachers were asked about their treatment of Mexican American holidays, historical contributions, and personalities. Two patriotic holidays of Mexico, *el 16 de septiembre* and *el 5 de mayo,* were discussed by 51 percent of the teachers. Religious holidays, such as *la Semana Santa, la Pascua Florida, el Día de los Santos, el Día de los Difuntos, el Día de la Virgen de Guadalupe, las posadas, la Nochebuena, la Navidad,* and *el Día de los Reyes Magos,* were incorporated into lessons by the same number of teachers. Personal holidays were given less emphasis; only 37 percent discussed *el día de santo, el cumpleaños, bodas, bautismos,* and *quinceañeras.*

The historical contributions of the Spanish-speaking people of the Southwest received less emphasis than any other category. Only 5 percent of the respondents discussed the contributions of Spanish-speakers during the discovery period (1492–1750), and contributions during the colonization period (1750–1910) were discussed by only 2 percent. None of the teachers discussed the immigration period (1910–1950) or the Chicano movement from 1960 to the present. Either teachers are unaware of this history or they are not encouraged by curriculum directors to share it with their pupils.

Historical Mexican personalities were discussed by 30 percent of the teachers. Miguel Hidalgo, General Santa Anna, Benito Juárez, and Pancho Villa were the historical figures most often mentioned. Contemporary Mexican American personalities—Efrén Herrera, César Chávez, Freddy Fender, José Feliciano, Vicki Carr, Lee Treviño, Ruben Torres, and Kika de la Garza— were discussed by 35 percent. Such local Mexican American personalities as school administrators, firemen, and police officers were discussed by only 21 percent.

Deep Culture Reinforcement

Within the category of deep culture, I selected for the questionnaire twenty dimensions from those identified by Brooks (1973). The respondents were asked if they discussed these topics from a Mexican American cultural perspective. If the response was affirmative, they indicated whether the activity was presented in an organized lesson or handled on an impromptu basis. The responses indicated that approximately two-thirds (67 percent) of the bilingual education classes studied received no reinforcement or minimal reinforcement in ten of the dimensions. The following list briefly defines these dimensions and gives the percentage of teachers who conducted organized discussions of each topic:

> Courtship and marriage (attitudes toward dating, marriage, and raising a family): 1 percent
>
> Space and proxemics (ideas about acceptable distances between individuals and one's relationship to the land): 3 percent
>
> Ceremony (what a person says and does at weddings, funerals, religious services, celebrations, etc.): 5 percent
>
> Health and medicine (how a person reacts to sickness, death, soundness of mind and body, medicine, etc.): 11 percent
>
> Gesture and kinesics (forms of communication or reinforced speech, such as the use of the eyes, the hands, and the body): 16 percent

Ownership (attitudes toward ownership of property, individual rights, loyalties): 17 percent

Tabus (attitudes toward violations of cultural prohibitions): 17 percent

Religion (attitudes toward the divine and the supernatural and their effects on thoughts and actions): 19 percent

Sex roles (how one views, understands, and relates to the opposite sex and what deviations are allowed and expected): 19 percent

Rights and duties (personal obligations, voting, taxes, military service, legal rights, personal demands, etc.): 28 percent

Dimensions that were reinforced in organized discussions by fewer than 30 percent of the teachers were:

Precedence (accepted behavior toward older persons, peers, and younger persons): 28 percent

Ethics (how a person learns and practices honesty, fair play, moral principles): 22 percent

Aesthetics (the beautiful things in Mexican American culture—literature, music, dance, art, architecture—and their enjoyment): 21 percent

Rewards and privileges (attitudes toward motivation, merit, achievement, service, social position, etc.): 14 percent

The dimensions of culture receiving the most reinforcement were:

Time (attitudes toward being early, on time, or late): 53 percent

Folk myths (attitudes toward heroes, traditional stories, legendary characters, superstitions, etc.): 46 percent

Subsistence (attitudes toward providing for oneself, the young, and the old; responsibility to protect others): 40 percent

Family ties (feelings toward family, friends, classmates, roommates and others): 39 percent

Grooming and presence (cultural differences in personal behavior and appearance, such as laughter, smiling, voice quality, gait, poise, hair style, cosmetics, dress): 34 percent

Values (attitudes toward freedom, education, cleanliness, cruelty, crime, etc.): 31 percent

DISCUSSION AND IMPLICATIONS

Although culture is learned, culture in its totality cannot be taught in the classroom. Yet cultural elements can and should be transmitted and reinforced in the bilingual classroom if national, state, and local efforts supporting bilingual education are to achieve their goals. Children spend a good part of their time interacting with the teacher and the other students of the classroom of which they are a part, and the teacher is thus in a unique position to support or inhibit minority culture. This study has identified the specific elements of Mexican American culture that are reinforced or transmitted by the teachers in three bilingual education programs in Texas.

The findings indicate that the promotion of this culture remains one of the most misinterpreted and inadequately achieved goals of bilingual education instruction. The following recommendations regarding teachers, curriculum, and further studies are based on these findings.

Training and Retraining Bicultural Teachers

Bilingual classroom teachers need not be members of the target minority population, but the entire staff should be bilingual and bicultural whenever possible. Just as having a Spanish surname does not ensure that a person speaks Spanish, neither does being a Mexican American ensure that a person is bicultural. A substantial number of the Mexican American adults who have gone through the Anglo educational process have rejected many elements of Mexican American culture for numerous reasons, survival being one of the most common. The challenge of preparing teachers who are bicultural rests upon the same institutions of higher learning that for so many years produced teachers who exemplified an educational theory aimed at assimilation into the Anglo middle class. Higher education must meet this challenge by:

Incorporating cultural elements into pedagogical courses

Incorporating culturally oriented books and materials into reading requirements

Requiring competencies in cultural areas

Requiring a high degree of competence in the target language through practical language courses, pedagogical courses taught in the target language, and field experiences in the community or study abroad

Designing programs that correct the inadequacies shown by this study in the areas of Mexican American history, cultural and historical contributions of the Spanish-speaking people, Spanish language arts, and the intangible elements of Mexican American culture

With the advent of mandatory bilingual education in Texas, school districts were faced with the problem of providing teachers proficient in the Spanish language. Few such teachers existed. The tendency to certify any teacher with two years of college Spanish on his or her transcript brought many unqualified teachers into bilingual classrooms. School districts throughout the state must determine the cultural inadequacies of the teaching staffs within their bilingual programs and take steps to alleviate them—for example, by:

Setting up in-service training programs with bicultural emphasis

Revising teaching manuals and guides to include cultural topics in all subject areas

Encouraging teacher participation in relevant cultural activities in the school or community

Involving the culture of the home in the school's teaching activities

Compiling reading lists of pertinent books, articles, and pamphlets for teachers and aides

Using the target language as much as possible for everyday school communication by faculty, staff, and administrators, since language is an integral part of culture

Curriculum Changes

In recent years educational publishers have flooded the market with bilingual instructional materials. Often these items have proved to be less than desirable instruments for instructional use. Because Spanish-speaking children are not homogeneous, materials developed in one area of the United States often have little or no cultural relevance in another area; in fact, this can sometimes be said of districts within a single state. Curriculum personnel need to determine the significant factors of the bilingual child's culture and incorporate those elements into the curriculum of the district. A bicultural or multicultural curriculum for any school district can be achieved by:

Involving the ethnic community in the establishment of cultural goals and priorities

Adapting present curricula to reflect cultural differences and similarities

Sequencing cultural materials through grade levels

Further Study

One cannot draw definite conclusions from a sample of three school districts in a state the size of Texas. The following questions are proposed so that other studies can examine the reinforcement of Mexican American culture in the bilingual education classroom on a statewide or nationwide basis. They are relevant to other target cultures as well.

Would replication of this study in other areas of Texas produce similar results?

Would replication of study with other cultural groups in other areas of the United States produce similar results?

Are the cultural elements reinforced in prekindergarten and kindergarten bilingual classrooms the same as those reinforced in grades 1–3?

Is cultural content represented in the various disciplines? If so, which elements receive the most emphasis? If not, why not?

Is cultural content conveyed in a planned and structured sequence from grade to grade?

What are the dimensions of Mexican American or other target cultures?

Which of the elements presented in schools are positive and accurate representations of the culture and which are negative and inaccurate stereotypes?

CONCLUSION

This study sought reassurance that bilingual-bicultural education programs in Texas presented the Anglo and Mexican American cultures as equally valued and that students in bilingual education classes were being instructed in two languages with reinforcement of both cultures. This was not the case in the majority of the classrooms involved in this study. If they are typical of the bilingual education classrooms in the state of Texas, then further substantive changes must occur. Mandatory bilingual education has improved the educational situation of the Mexican American of Texas, but it has not yet incorporated Mexican American cultural elements into classroom work to the extent needed to bring about mutual respect and bicultural understanding.

REFERENCES

American Association of Colleges for Teacher Education, Commission on Multicultural Education. No one model American. Adopted by AACTE Board of Directors, November, 1972.

Brooks, B. D., and Marino, S. Strategies for teaching within a bicultural setting. *Reading Improvement,* 1976, *13,* 86–91.

Brooks, N. Culture and language instruction. In *Teacher's notebook in modern foreign languages.* New York: Harcourt, Brace & World School Department, 1966.

Brooks, N. Teaching culture in the foreign language classroom. *Florida Foreign Language Reporter,* 1969, *7,* 20–28.

Brooks, N. Parameters of culture. *Foreign language news exchange* (Connecticut State Department of Education), 1973, *1,* 8–13.

Carlisle, J. Needs in bilingual education. *Hispania,* 1971, *54,* 322–326.

Carter, T. P. Culture content for linguistically-different learners. In Thomas D. Horn (Ed.), *Research basis for oral language instruction.* Urbana, Ill.: National Council of Teachers of English, 1971.

Casso, H. J. Bilingual/bicultural education and teacher training. NEA Professional Studies Series. Washington, D.C.: National Education Association, 1976. (U.S., Educational Resources Information Center, ERIC Document ED 181-050).

Castañeda, A. P. Harold, L., and Ramírez, M. A new philosophy of education. In

New approaches to bilingual, bicultural education. Austin, Tex.: Dissemination and Assessment Center for Bilingual Education, Education Service Center, Region XIII, 1974a.

Castañeda, A. P., Harold, L., and Ramírez, M. Persisting ideological issues of assimilation in America: implications for assessment practices in psychology and education. In E. G. Epps (Ed.), *Cultural pluralism: series on contemporary educational issues.* National Society for the Study of Education. Berkeley: McCutchan, 1974b. pp. 56–70.

Christian, C. C. The analysis of linguistic and cultural differences: A proposed model. In James E. Alatis (Ed.), *Twenty-first annual round table meeting on linguistics and language studies.* Washington. D.C.: Georgetown University Press, 1970.

Cortés, C. E. Concepts and strategies for teaching the Mexican American experience. In *New approaches to bilingual, bicultural education.* Austin, Tex. Dissemination and Assessment Center for Bilingual Education, Education Service Center, Region XIII, 1974.

Fishman, J. A., and Lovas, J. Bilingual education in a sociolinguistic perspective. *TESOL Quarterly,* 1970, *4,* 215–222.

Gaarder, A. B. Teaching the bilingual child: research, development and policy. *Modern Language Journal,* 1965, *49,* 165–175.

González, J. M. A developmental and sociological rationale for culture-based curricula and cultural context teaching in early instruction of Mexican American children. Doctoral dissertation, University of Massachusetts at Amherst, 1974.

Holt, J. *How children learn, how children fail.* New York: Dell, 1973.

John-Stein, V., and Cooper, E. Recent trends in bilingual education. (U.S., Educational Resources Information Center, ERIC Document ED 128–504), 1976.

Kroeber, A. L., and Kluckhohn, C. *Culture: a critical review of concepts and definitions.* Cambridge, Mass.: Peabody Museum Press, 1952.

Lambert, W. E. The changing role of language programs and teachers. *Cross cultural communication: implications for language and ethnic studies.* (U.S., Educational Resources Information Center, ERIC Document ED 130–547), 1975.

Mazón, M. R., and Arciniega. T. A. Competency based education and the culturally different: a ray of hope or more of the same? (U.S., Educational Resources Information Center, ERIC Document ED 092 523), 1974.

Medina, R. Building on backgrounds. *Instructor,* 1972, *81,* 39–52.

Nava, J. Cultural backgrounds and barriers that affect learning by Spanish speaking children. In J. H. Burma (Ed.), *Mexican Americans in the United States: a reader.* Cambridge, Mass.: Schenkman, 1966, 123–133.

Peña, A. A. An overview on bilingual education. *Today's Education,* 1975, *64,* 70–84.

Seelye, H. N. Teaching cultural concepts in Spanish classes. (U.S., Educational Resources Information Center, ERIC Document ED 108–454), 1972.

Seelye, H. N. *Teaching culture: strategies for foreign language education.* Skokie, Ill.: National Textbook Company, 1976.

United States Commission on Civil Rights. *Toward quality education for Mexican Americans. Report VI, Mexican American education study.* Washington, D.C.: Office of Education, 1974.

United States Department of Health, Education and Welfare. Multicultural planning conferences: summary. Washington, D.C.: National Institute of Education, Multicultural/Bilingual Division, 1976 (U.S., Educational Resources Information Center, ERIC Document ED 130–918).

Walsh, J. E. Thought and expression in culture learning. *Culture and Language Learning Newsletter,* 1973, *2* (1), 1–10.

7 | Irrelevance and Bias in Multicultural Curricula: Toward an Authentic Curriculum

GLORIA CONTRERAS
The University of Texas at Austin

The concept of multicultural education that evolved from the first minority studies programs of higher education in the 1960s eventually filtered down to early childhood instruction during the succeeding decade of curriculum reform and experimentation. Today, an early childhood education program that is multicultural in nature should be compatible with a child's home language and traditions. It should satisfy the psychological needs for belongingness and self-esteem (Maslow, 1954) and help bilingual children better adjust to the school environment. The sense of trust (Erikson, 1964) that the home has begun should extend into the classroom, school, and community of young children. Then, teachers should proceed with the task of planning and teaching a multicultural curriculum in accordance with the principle that children's learning is dependent on sensory information, as Castaneda observes elsewhere in this volume.

The desired outcome of education is an individual who is economically self-sufficient and a contributing citizen of the community. However, the goal of achieving socioeconomic and political equality (Ochoa, 1980) for diverse American ethnic groups and other special populations is unattainable as long as many so-called multicultural education programs continue to operate in a nonintegrated fashion and to focus on minority participants who study only their own particular cultural heritage in a superficial manner. Other multicultural programs that are designed to include the Anglo majority are frequently confined to affective-based intergroup relations, which only develop another form of superficial awareness. All programs need to emphasize more future-directed education that is designed to increase socioeconomic equity in society. Therefore, the purpose of this paper is twofold: (1) to review some weaknesses associated with multicultural education programs in general, and (2) to recommend basic tenets for producing a more authentic multicultural curriculum in early childhood education programs.

Because the concept of multicultural education is an evolving pedagogy, some of the more common biases associated with existing multicultural education programs will be restated here. Alternative structures are suggested and discussed in greater detail in the second part of this paper.

IRRELEVANCE AND BIAS IN MULTICULTURAL CURRICULA

Multicultural education continues to develop. As a result, it is only natural that some of yesterday's model programs, unless they have undergone continuous evaluation and modification, inadequately address the needs of an increasing number of special populations clamoring for educational equity in today's schools. Table 1 summarizes some of the deficiencies found in multicultural programs that need refinement. Each bias or limitation depicted in the table is discussed below.

Multicultural Education Versus Ethnic Studies

There is need to understand better the nature of ethnic studies and multicultural education and the relationship of these two distinct approaches in program and curriculum development. The difference between ethnic studies and

Table 1:   Bias in Multicultural Education Programs

Multicultural Education IS NOT:	Multicultural Education IS:
Synonymous with ethnic studies	The positive study of American diversity of life-style, custom, age, religion, race, ethnicity, national origin, language, physical makeup, socioeconomic class, occupation, and other differences
Intended solely for the benefit of minorities in the form of a separate program	A comprehensive educational reform for attaining social, political, and economic equity for special groups who have been denied equal educational opportunity
Limited to affective-based race-relations activities	Cognitive-based interdisciplinary instruction that also affects the attitudes of people toward diversity
Confined to developing only a superficial awareness of bias in American society	*Action* that is designed to promote equity and the value of diversity

multicultural education is stated below. Ethnic studies is the study of the histories, cultures, and experiences of the ethnic groups within a society. The term refers primarily to the objectives, concepts, methods, and materials that make up the courses of study within schools, colleges, and universities (Banks, 1979). Some of the Title IX ethnic heritage projects of the 1970s were the Chinese American Heritage Project; California Ethnic Heritage Program; Minneapolis Multi-Ethnic Curriculum Project; and Summer Institute on Folklore and Traditions of Mexican Americans, Black, and Appalachian People (Haley, 1981; McCormick, 1980). Thus, ethnic studies is concerned exclusively with ethnic groups and is more limited in scope than multicultural education.

In view of the evolving nature of multicultural education, ethnic studies programs were, indeed, a good beginning. However, today ethnic studies programs are an integral component of the more comprehensive venture that multicultural education entails. At one time the major goal of multicultural education was to change the total educational environment so that it promoted respect for a wide range of cultural groups and enabled all culture groups to experience equal educational opportunity (Banks, 1979). More recently, multicultural education is based on the belief that other differences of lifestyle, religion, age, and physical makeup also contribute positively to the American identity. Thus, stereotypes associated with sex, religion, physical handicaps, age, language, occupation, family lifestyle, socioeconomic class, and national origin are to be combated alongside racial and ethnic bias in the schooling process and in society (June, 1971; Newman, 1977; Ochoa, 1980).

In the broadest sense, multicultural education is defined as a pedagogical process for total educational reform of instructional strategies, structural organization of the school, and its institutional values (Gay, 1979). While a more detailed discussion of multicultural education follows in the second part of this paper, it is important to note again that multicultural education is a process. As Gay indicates, "to view it as a process provides the flexibility, the elasticity, and the adaptability needed to embrace the new data, new analyses, new interpretations, and new experiments which are bound to occur before it reaches pedagogic maturity" (p. 27).

A recent meeting with a group of graduating student teachers illustrates the type of multicultural diversity that has become standard across this nation's public school classrooms. These preservice teachers were critical of their training program, which they felt failed to prepare them adequately to work effectively with the many kinds of "special" populations they encountered in the so-called "regular" classroom. Some of the "special" kinds of students they found in their teaching situations were:

Special education students being forced into the mainstream
Recent refugees from Vietnam and other Asian countries

Nonimmigrant students from foreign countries, especially from countries
in the Middle East and Asia

Students representing non-Christian religious backgrounds

Students from extremes in socioeconomic backgrounds and different kinds
of family units

Students with limited English-language proficiency

American minority students, especially blacks and Chicanos

This demonstrates that the so-called "regular" classroom is rich with diversity. To view it as a problem *is* the problem; to see it as an opportunity for implementing multicultural education is what teaching is all about today!

Short-Term Versus On-Going Multicultural Instruction

Some multicultural education programs are still intended only for minority student populations of schools or school districts where they study their own particular ethnic heritage. On the other hand, those designed for a student body at large frequently operate as a one- or two-week unit or program that falls outside of the general school curriculum. For example, I recently witnessed such a case in one elementary school where a "dosage" of multicultural instruction is administered to all students in the school for a two-week period. The program developer, a dynamic, resourceful, and knowledgeable Filipino teacher, originally designed this multicultural program for her own self-contained first-grade class made up of Chicanos, blacks, Filipinos, Anglos, and Vietnamese children. Pictures and articles from *National Geographic Magazine* form the basis of her curriculum and instruction. For example, she might select an article on Alaska's wilderness and plan an interdisciplinary unit around this subject. The accompanying photographs, which are always colorful and attractive, would be used to stimulate children's interest and inquiry in the subject. Language arts and reading instruction might consist of a selection rewritten to fit the children's interest and/or reading level. A social studies lesson might follow in which concepts from the social sciences, particularly cultural geography and anthropology, would be systematically explored. Maps and globes, in continuous display, would be used to introduce such basic concepts as size, shape, and location. Math instruction might be creatively taught within the context of the Arctic environment just as science, health, and art instruction would also fall under the same theme.

Students compile giant-sized books filled with pictures from *National Geographic,* which are classified according to such cultural universals as food, dance, marriage, clothing, shelter, bodily adornment, family life, special celebrations, and so on. Affective, cognitive, and skill-based instruction is imparted through a comparative reference to previously studied environments, cultures, and peoples of the United States and the world. It becomes apparent that one of this teacher's main goals is the development of human understanding in which affective gains are achieved through a cognitive-based curriculum.

Soon after learning about this teacher's successful experience in curriculum development, the school principal modified the school schedule so that each class within the school could benefit from this "multicultural laboratory" for a period of at least two weeks. The decision of this well-intentioned administrator rendered this effort an end in itself rather than an on-going process and means for achieving a much broader and more effective multicultural school program.

Cognitive-Based Versus Affective-Based Activities

Another weakness associated with existing multicultural education programs surfaces when the curriculum centers around so-called "touchy-feely" activities that lack substantive content. Frech's (1973) study of fourth graders showed a reduction of extreme ethnocentrism when teachers used cognitive-based material not written specifically to moderate ethnocentrism. That such moderation occurred indicates that cognitive training may be used to achieve affective goals of instruction.

Similar results occurred in a study by Knight (1979) on the relationship between geography curricula and international understanding. This study showed that a lack of student knowledge produces a negative attitude toward the people of Latin America. Students in the most distant countries of this study, such as New Zealand and Scotland, where the role of geography in the curriculum is more prominent than in the United States, knew more about the Americas and were less prone to stereotyping than their counterparts from the United States, Mexico, and Canada. In particular, the students from the United States, where geography is not as highly valued, are geo-illiterate and therefore subject to forming stereotyped images.

My study (1979), which focused on a comparison of the Mexican and Texas geographic curricula, showed more international understanding in the Mexican sample. The difference could be attributed to the Mexican's systematic study of world geography from the primary grades through high school, as mandated by the Mexican Ministry of Education.

Two conclusions are implied here. First, these studies show that knowledge required for cultural understanding among people is not learned from incidental sources such as the news media, television, movies, and so on. Second, while affective instruction can foster respect for the worth and dignity of every individual, as the intercultural and human relations movements of the past have shown (Cole and Cole, 1954), the affective domain is only a part of today's more sophisticated multicultural education programs.

Awareness Versus Equity

A fourth limitation of some programs, as shown in table 1, occurs when student awareness of bias is viewed as a final goal of a multicultural program. Awareness is only one side of the multicultural coin. As Newman (1977) suggests, in evaluating multicultural programs one should look for indicators that show that learners have not only increased their awareness of the value of diversity, but have also (1) demonstrated behavior intended to promote equity, and (2) demonstrated behavior intended to increase others' awareness of bias and/or the value of diversity. Some questions for teachers to ask themselves are:

What have I done as a follow-up to awareness development?
What were my most successful activities in reducing the incidence of bias?
What else can I do to promote equity in my classroom?

In order to help carry out the *action* phase of table 1, the American Association for Colleges of Teacher Education through its Commission on Multicultural Education and the insightful leadership of Klassen and Gollnick (1977) has prepared four documents to assist teacher education institutions in the process of designing multicultural programs. The first, Multicultural Teacher Education: Preparing Educators to Provide Educational Equity, recommends strategies for implementation of multicultural education and examines related issues. The second volume, *Multicultural Teacher Education: Case Studies of Thirteen Programs,* presents thirteen alternative strategies for implementing multicultural teacher education programs.

Multicultural Teacher Education: The Annotated Bibliography of Selected Resources is another valuable document for teachers and *Multicultural Teacher Education: Guidelines for Implementation* provides guidelines that go beyond the minimum requirements of the National Council for Accreditation of Teacher Education (NCATE) standards toward designing exemplary teacher education programs that reflect a commitment to multicultural education and the provision for educational equity.

The first part of this paper examined deficiencies of existing multicultural education programs. The next section discusses in more detail the need for bilingual teachers to provide young children with a more relevant multicultural curriculum.

TOWARD AN AUTHENTIC CURRICULUM

Nowhere is the importance of multicultural education more critical than in the earliest years of formal education. During this young age many minority children leave home to be confronted by an environment where much of what they know, including language, is absent. Often this creates discontinuity (Laosa,

1977) or incompatibilities (Cardenas and Cardenas, 1977) that may affect learning.

All children should enter a learning environment that embraces them as contributing members of a diverse situation in which their own differences, as well as all other children's, will be appreciated, respected, and systematically studied. To achieve this sense of trust and respect, one important goal of early childhood instruction should be to foster the understanding that people have different group identities, experiences, interests, and needs. Evidence shows that the concepts of group identity and ethnicity, for example, can be used in early childhood instruction. Proshansky and Newton (1975) showed that black children between the ages of three and seven become increasingly aware of racial differences and emotional responses associated with various ethnic groups, including their own.

An earlier study by Goodman (1964) also revealed that young children are aware of physical racial characteristics and favorably inclined toward attributes of the white majority. During these critical formative years minority children learn to be ashamed of their identity and linguistic differences and majority children learn to be racially prejudiced (Allport, 1954; Jahoda, 1963). In order to combat these negative ethnic-related values that begin to manifest themselves early in one's years, multicultural education must begin in early childhood and be a part of every child's formal instruction.

Multicultural education poses a particular challenge to bilingual educators. As Gonzales suggests elsewhere in this volume, extrinsic aspects of the Mexican American culture have dominated bilingual instruction. The superficial study of famous people, fiestas, and foods begs enrichment with the inclusion of more varied extrinsic as well as intrinsic cultural traits (González, 1974). Thus, beyond the study of the Mexican American heritage, other cross-cultural groups and social consciousness raising issues need to be addressed. This more inclusive approach might entail highlighting the following kinds of multicultural understandings which are reflected in children's literature.

1. There are many Mexican Americans who, like their Jewish, Polish, black, Asian, or other counterparts, maintain an ethnic identity at the same time that they share a common American culture (Tate, 1980; Politi, 1978; Purdy, 1972; Reit, 1971; Steele, 1976; Simon, 1976).
2. There are productive men and women leading traditional as well as nontraditional roles and occupations across all socioeconomic levels of society (Goldreich, 1981; Merriam, 1972; Alexander, 1981; Kline, 1975).
3. There are equally productive older Americans willing to share life experiences that no formal education can equal (Wittman, 1978; Sonneborn, 1971; Gerson, 1979; Bourne, 1968; De Paola, 1973).

4. There are "nuclear families" as well as extended family models, single-parent families, and families with adopted or foster children (Vigna, 1980; Grand and Grand, 1972; Zolotow, 1971; Caines, 1977).
5. There are handicapped children and adults able and eager to become productive wage earners (Arthur, 1979; Doorly, 1967; Litchfield, 1976; Smith, 1979; Wolf, 1974).
6. There are many languages other than English spoken in the United States as well as many forms of religion practiced alongside of Christianity (Marcus, 1981; Densmore and Schoolcraft, 1974; Feelings and Feelings, 1974).

While some may argue the appropriateness of these understandings for young children, the following should be noted. Piaget (1951) contended that students pass through stages of spatial decentration, perceiving themselves as belonging to progressively larger and more inclusive territorial units. An assumption of formal instruction is that decentration is highly related to school learning. Thus, children will not perceive themselves as part of a diverse multicultural world unless they have adequate knowledge of that system. Considerations for implementing multicultural instruction in preschool situations follow.

An Inclusive Curriculum

It is imperative that all early childhood bilingual teachers be skilled in identifying materials that are free of bias and stereotypes. They need to know how to adapt existing materials to multicultural situations and how to develop materials appropriate to multicultural education. The seventies produced a variety of evaluation instruments to help teachers review curricula. Some notable reference works that are useful in evaluating materials or programs include:

Curriculum Guidelines for Multiethnic Education. Washington D.C.: National Council for the Social Studies, 1976.

Growing Free: Ways to Help Children Overcome Sex-Role Stereotypes. Washington, D.C.: Association for Childhood Education International, 1976.

Guidelines for Selecting Bias-Free Textbooks and Storybooks. New York: Council on Interracial Books for Children, n.d.

School Checklist for Racism and Sexism. New York: N.Y. Council on Interracial Books for Children, n.d.

Cornejo, Ricardo J. "Some Criteria to Assess Spanish Reading Instructional Materials," *Language Development in a Bilingual Setting.* Los Angeles: Dissemination and Assessment Center, 1979.

Ten Quick Ways to Analyze Children's Books for Racism and Sexism. New York: The Council on Interracial Books for Children, n.d.

While guidelines for eliminating racism and sexism in educational materials are more readily available, similar guidelines are needed to help teachers combat the other kinds of bias previously discussed. The most comprehensive yet are the *Guidelines for Selecting Bias-Free Textbooks and Storybooks* issued by the Council on Interracial Books for Children, a reference collection of criteria and checklists to help avoid stereotypes and bias against females, minorities, the disabled, and older people.

Human Relations Competence

The National Conference of Christians and Jews in 1978 issued a massive survey of racial attitudes from 1963 to 1978 that drew some optimistic conclusions. One key finding showed that there is much greater contact between blacks and whites, with nearly half of all whites now coming into regular contact with black coworkers. A second key finding indicated that fewer whites subscribe to stereotypes of blacks due to a reduction of white uneasiness in interracial situations. In the matter of race relations, this study shows that familiarity has improved human understanding. The study suggests that there is a need to address systematically social learning in programs of early childhood education in order to help children develop basic interpersonal competencies that will enable them to act as effective individuals and group members of a multicultural society.

Wyner's (1978) article on preschool children states that planning must respond to themes that will dominate future realities of these youngsters. Conflict is one of those recurring realities of life. Thus, examples of real conflict between individuals should be taken from the children's environments at school, at play, or at home. From the television programs that children view, teachers can develop lessons on how to resolve similar problems in the future by means of a strategy called conflict management. Because the very egocentric young will not learn as well from conflict resolution, it is suggested that conflict episodes be studied by other more effective means such as role playing, group discussions, simulations, and dramatic play. Children's literature also offers ample opportunity for discussing conflict episodes.

The Informal Curriculum

Educators are paying greater attention to the informal environments of children. The "societal" curriculum is gaining special attention due particularly to innovations in media and the profound effect that television has on learning. As Cremin (1975) notes: "The important fact is that family life does educate, religious life does educate, and work does educate; and, what is more, the education of all three realms is as intentional as the education of the school, though in different ways and in different measures" (p. 5).

Research of the use of television in the United States shows that the average child under twelve spends approximately twenty-five hours per week watching television. These same children spend 85 percent of their viewing time watching nonchildren's programs and only 15 percent watching programs designed for children (Nielsen, 1976). Mays and Pagano (1978) offer teachers a strategy for using television to promote the most desirable social outcomes of this widely influential technology. For example, when children viewed a segment on hair, they learned about the relationship between this particular subject and the biological differences of humans. The concept of prejudicial attitudes was also introduced. In another daycare center, a high interest level in *Roots* led to an introduction to African culture.

Youngsters must be taught the power and limitations of television and other media. They must learn that what they see and hear on their favorite television programs often is not realistic. At the same time, the concepts of racism, sexism, ageism, classism, and other social issues in society should be related to the programs children view.

Global Education

In their 1978 report, the Michigan Department of Education states:

> Global education is the lifelong growth in understanding, through study and participation, of the world community and the interdependency of its people and systems—social, cultural, economic, linguistic, technological, and ecological. Global Education requires an understanding of the values and priorities of the many cultures of the world as well as the acquisition of basic concepts and principles related to the world community.

Torney (1979) points out some of the psychological and institutional obstacles to a global perspective in education. She cites research data that make clear the urgency of beginning global education early in a child's life in school. Adding global dimensions to bilingual education programs is a natural linking process, for "foreign language is a vital connection in the interdependent relationships of the next century" (Phillips, 1977, p. 2).

Some inexpensive materials to help the bilingual teacher apply global perspectives to early childhood instruction are published and distributed by UNICEF (1981–82). These multicultural education materials describe the lives of children in other lands and include slide sets, teachers' kits, children's books, records, games, puzzles, posters, and musical instruments designed for preschool children. These materials are distributed according to topics such as arts and crafts, pen pals, or holidays, or by specific countries.

The cardboard, free-standing models of festival figures from around the world, for example, could easily be used to teach children the parts of the body, the names of various articles of clothing, or colors and numbers. Coloring activities are an important part of early childhood instruction and can also take on a global dimension as children color drawings portraying the realistic activities of children in many cultures. UNICEF's quality paper dolls of the Middle East are an excellent model for studying any other region and people of the world. Thus, as young children acquire the vocabulary to describe their own families, shelter, and clothing, they can learn the equivalent of their counterparts who live in other parts of the world.

Evaluation of Multicultural Education that Is Congruent with Tomorrow

Multicultural education is an evolving pedagogy requiring an on-going evaluation process to assess the effectiveness of programs and the degree to which changing social and world conditions are accurately reflected in the curricula. Because of a technological revolution, changes are rapidly occurring at all levels of society, and this transformation affects today's preschool children. The future of today's youngest children will include a radically new global economy dominated by transnational corporations; global communications systems by satellites and computers; and transnational groupings based on educational, scientific, and other interests (Toffler, 1980; Shane, 1974).

The twenty-first century will belong to those children under seven years of age today. For this reason a future-oriented evaluation approach to early childhood education is important. Shane observes, "Beginning very early, children need experiences that help them to understand the nature of change, to recognize that the future is at least partly malleable—that there are alternative futures among which they can choose . . ." (p. 183). Teachers will do well to remember that the younger the children, the longer their lives extend into tomorrow and the more future-oriented the curriculum should be.

Teachers of bilingual preschool children are challenged to proceed from a bicultural mode of instruction to a more encompassing multicultural approach to education. Nowhere is the importance of multicultural education more critical than at the earliest years of formal education. Negative ethnic-related attitudes begin early in life, and it behooves educators to make multicultural education a part of every young child's formal learning.

REFERENCES

Alexander, M. *Marty McGee's space lab, no girls allowed.* New York: Dial Press, 1981.
Allport, G. W. *The nature of prejudice.* Boston: Beacon Press, 1954.
Arthur, C. *My sister's silent world.* Chicago: Children's Press, 1979.

Banks, J. *Teaching strategies for ethnic studies.* 2nd ed. Boston: Allyn & Bacon, 1979.

Bourne, M. A. *Raccoons are for loving.* New York: Random House, 1968.

Caines, Jeanette. *Daddy.* Scranton, Pa.: Harper & Row, 1977.

Cardenas, J. A., and Cardenas, B. *Theory of incompatibilities.* San Antonio, Tex.: Intercultural Development Research Association, 1977.

Cole, S. G., and Cole, M. W. *Minorities and the American promise: the conflict of principle and practice.* New York: Harper & Row, 1954.

Contreras, G. *A study of the relationship between geography curricula and international understanding in Mexico and the United States.* Paper presented at the National Council for Geographic Education, Mexico City, November 1979.

Cremin, L. Public education and the education of the public. *Teachers College Record,* September 1975, *77,* 1.

Densmore, F., and Schoolcraft, H. R. (Eds.) *Songs of the Chippewa.* New York: Farrar, Straus & Giroux, 1974.

De Paola, T. A. *Nana upstairs and Nana downstairs.* New York: G. P. Putnam's Sons, 1973.

Doorly, R. *Our Jimmy.* Westwood, Mass.: Service Associates, 1967.

Erikson, E. Eight ages of man. In *Childhood and society.* 2nd ed. New York: W. W. Norton & Co., 1964.

Feelings, M., and Feelings, T. *Jambo means hello.* New York: Dial Press, 1974.

Frech, W. P. An analysis of the anthropology curriculum project materials. The concept of culture: in the ethnocentric attitudes of fourth grade students. Doctoral dissertation, University of Georgia, 1973.

Gay, G. Changing conceptions of multicultural education. In H. P. Baptiste and M. L. Baptiste (Eds.), *Developing the multicultural process in classroom instruction.* Washington, D.C.: University Press of America, 1979.

Gerson, C. *Tread softly.* New York: The Dial Press, 1979.

Goldreich, G. *What can she be?* New York: Holt, Rinehart & Winston, 1981.

Gonzales, F. Reinforcing culture in three bilingual programs. In T. H. Escobedo (Ed.), *Early childhood bilingual education.* New York: Teachers College Press, 1983.

González, J. M. A developmental and sociological rationale for culture-based curricula and cultural context teaching in early instruction of Mexican American children. Doctoral dissertation, University of Massachusetts, 1974.

Goodman, M. E. *Race awareness in young children.* New York: Collier Books, 1964.

Grand, S., and Grand, T. *The children of Israel.* New York: Twayne Publishers, Inc., 1972.

Haley, F. *Ethnic studies sampler: the oest of Title IX project materials.* Boulder, Colo.: Social Science Education Consortium, 1981.

Harris, L., and Associates. A study of attitudes toward racial and religious minorities and toward women. Study prepared for the National Conference of Christians and Jews, 1978.

Jahoda, G. The development of children's ideas about country and nationality. *British Journal of Educational Psychology,* 1963, *33,* 47–60, 143–153.

June, N. *Where do I fit in?* New York: Holt, Rinehart & Winston, 1981.

Klassen, F., and Gollnick, D. (Eds.) *Pluralism and the American teacher: issues and case studies.* Washington, D.C.: American Association of Colleges for Teacher Education, 1977.

Kline, N. *Good girls can be anything.* New York: E. P. Dutton, 1975.

Knight, C. L., et al. *Geography of the Americas: a study of the relationship between geography curricula and international understanding.* Paper presented at the National Council for Geographic Education, Mexico City, November, 1979.

Laosa, L. Socialization, education, and continuity: the importance of the socio-cultural context. *Young Children,* July 1977, *32* (5), 21–27.

Litchfield, A. *A button in her ear.* Chicago: Albert Whitman & Company, 1976.

Marcus, A. F. *But this night is different: a Seder experienced.* New York, N.Y.: Union of American Hebrew Congregations, 1981.

Maslow, A. H. *Motivation and personality.* New York: Harper & Row, 1954.

Mays, L., and Pagano, A. L. Children and media. In A. L. Pagano (Ed.), *Social Studies in Early Childhood: An Interactionist Point of View.* Council on Social Studies, bulletin 58, 1978, 70–81.

McCormick, R. *Ethnic heritage studies program catalog: 1974–1979.* Boulder, Colo.: Social Science Education Consortium, 1980.

Merriam, E. *Boys and girls, girls and boys.* New York: Holt, Rinehart & Winston, 1972.

Michigan Department of Education. *Guidelines for global education.* Lansing, Michigan: Michigan Department of Education, 1978.

Newman, J. A. *Guidelines for identifying and counteracting bias in instructional materials.* Olympia, Wash.: State of Washington Superintendent of Public Instruction, 1977.

Nielsen Co., A. C. *The television audience.* Chicago: A. C. Nielsen Co., 1976.

Ochoa, A. Policy issues on multicultural education: dymystification of multicultural education, a social contradiction of social benefit. Paper presented at the National Association for Bilingual Education, Anaheim, California, April 1980.

Phillips, J. K. (Ed.) Language is the link. *ACTRFL Foreign Series,* 1977, *9, 2.*

Piaget, J., and Weil, A. The development in children of the idea of the homeland and of relations with other countries. *International Social Science Bulletin,* 1951, *3,* 361–578.

Politi, L. *Mr. Fong's toy shop.* New York: Charles Scribner's Sons, 1978.

Proshansky, H., and Newton, P. Color: the nature and meaning of Negro self-identity. In P. Watson (Ed.), *Psychology and race.* Chicago: Aldine Publishing Company, 1975, pp. 176–212.

Purdy, S. C. *Jewish holidays.* Philadelphia: Lippincott, 1972.

Reit, Seymour. *Child of the Navajos.* New York: Dodd, Mead & Co., 1971.

Shane, H. G., and Shane, J. G. *Educating the youngest for tomorrow.* New York: Random House, 1974.

Simon, N. *Why am I different?* Chicago: Albert Whitman & Co., 1976.

Smith, L. *A special kind of sister.* New York: Holt, Rinehart & Winston, 1979.

Sonneborn, R. *I love Gram.* New York: Viking, 1971.

Steele, W. O. *The man with the silver eyes.* New York: Harcourt Brace Jovanovich, 1976.

Tate. E. E. *Just an overnight guest.* New York: Dial Press, 1980.

Toffler, A. *The third wave*. New York: Bantam Books, 1980.

Torney, J. Psychological and institutional abstracts to global perspectives in education. In James M. Becker (Ed.) *Schooling for a global age*. New York: McGraw-Hill, 1979.

UNICEF Publications and Educational Materials Catalog, 1981–1982. New York: U.S. Committee for UNICEF, 1981.

Vigna, J. *She's not my real mother*. Chicago: Whitman, 1980.

Wittman, S. *A special trade*. Scranton, Pa.: Harper & Row, 1978.

Wolf, B. *Don't feel sorry for Paul*. Philadelphia: Lippincott, 1974.

Wyner, N. Children becoming citizens. In A. L. Pagano (Ed.), *Social Studies in Early Childhood: an Interactionist Point of View*. Council on Social Studies, bulletin 58, 1978, 40–45.

Zolotow, C. *A father like that*. New York: Harper & Row, 1971.

8 | Field Dependence–Independence: A Theoretical Framework for Mexican American Cultural Variables?

THERESA H. ESCOBEDO and
JOHANNA H. HUGGANS
The University of Texas at Austin

The incorporation of a culture component as part of bilingual programs for Hispanic children has become a necessary element of bilingual education. First of all, culture and language have always been closely tied to the identification of cultural groups. Therefore, it is important to recognize how the culture of a particular language group will affect learning. Understanding a culture is as vital to communications as understanding a language. Culture acts as a selective screening device that admits some information, while filtering out the rest, so that individuals from different cultures perceive experiences differently, "inhabit different sensory worlds" (Hall, 1966, p. 2). This in itself has grave implications for the education of culturally different children; that culture may have an impact on children's cognitive style, or preferred way of learning, is of greater consequence to individuals in bilingual education programs. Previously, these cultural differences have often been overlooked or seen by many as deficiencies. Recent focus on culture has caused the deficiency theory to fall somewhat in disfavor, and the emphasis has become one of accommodating cultural as well as language differences.

Researchers and educators attempting to identify cultural elements that may influence practices of bilingual classrooms have been faced with a vast dilemma: arriving at a relevant definition of culture, identifying cultural variables that affect learning, and determining how these influence elements that make up a culturally relevant environment and curriculum (González, 1974; Murdock, 1945). One approach has been to stress the knowledge of history, geography, traditional customs and foods.[1] These outward manifestations have been labeled as evidence of the explicit, or surface component of culture. Implicit culture, the second, harder-to-discern component, is the internal, often subconscious manifestation of culture that shows up in values, social patterns,

---

[1]See F. Gonzales, this volume, for definitions of culture and integration of culture into the classroom.

interactive styles, and communicative behaviors (Rodriguez and Plank, 1981). The effect of the implicit cultural ingredients on cognitive functioning has drawn the interest of several education and psychology researchers in attempts to meet the educational needs of Mexican American children.

The search for implicit cultural elements pertinent to Mexican Americans and their education has been drawn mainly from two bodies of research. One has been that of descriptive studies based on anthropological and sociological methods. The earlier studies of Madsen (1964) and Heller (1968) and others posed several negative characteristics which are still often mistakenly associated with Mexican Americans. These have formed the basis for the stereotypic views of this group as generally unmotivated, passive, and having low self-concept and negative attitudes toward school. The second body of research related to cultural elements of Mexican Americans has been the psychological research, particularly in the area of cognitive style. The large number of dimensions attributed to field dependence-independence (FD-I) as well as its later emphasis on family socialization patterns have made this a useful tool for cross-cultural research. Some of the assumptions derived from research regarding Mexican American culture and FD-I cognitive style have closely paralleled some of the previous descriptions of Mexican Americans, furthering negative stereotypic views of this group as passive and unassertive. However, many of the available studies investigating the relationship of cognitive style and cultural differences of Mexican Americans have reported findings that are contradictory and inconclusive on various points.

The purpose of this paper is to present a review of the literature related to FD-I cognitive style and subsequent intrinsic cultural variables associated with FD-I and the Mexican American culture. The first part will briefly trace the stages of development of FD-I, interpretations attributed to FD-I measurements, and how these interpretations were related to Mexican Americans. The second part of this paper will focus on the social orientation dimension of field dependence and its relationship to Mexican American culture. Particular emphasis is given to interpersonal spacing as a function of Mexican American culture. The third part will draw implications about the usefulness of FD-I cognitive style as a theoretical framework from which to explore Mexican American culture and identify intrinsic cultural elements that can be incorporated into cultural components of bilingual programs. The information included here will be useful to individuals interested in bilingual and/or multicultural education as well as to researchers in these areas.

FIELD DEPENDENCE-INDEPENDENCE (FD-I)

The development of the field dependence-independence (FD-I) cognitive style, originally formulated by Witkin and associates, is described by Kagan and

Buriel (1977) as occurring in four stages: simple perception, personality through perception, psychological differentiation, and subsequent reconceptualization. Their review of the different meanings attached to results from measurements of cognitive style at each of these four stages explains why findings based on a simple perceptual measurement have been given so much importance and such broad generalizations have been made about personality and cognitive functioning. These generalizations are particularly important when they are related to cultural variables associated with Mexican Americans. This section presents a brief summary of the FD-I construct as presented by Kagan and Buriel (1977) and then details the relation of FD-I to Mexican Americans.

Stages of Development

Witkin and his associates first studied the influence of gravitational and visual factors in the perception of the upright when it was found that some pilots lost their sense of uprightness when flying with zero visibility. The two instruments devised for the earlier studies, the Body Adjustment Test (BAT) and the Rod and Frame Test (RFT) required adjustment of the body (BAT) or rod (RFT) to vertical position from initially tilted positions. Success meant that subjects made their determination on internal cues and not on reliance on the visual field. Correlation between the two tasks was taken to explain that differences were caused by the tendency to perceive the environment in either an analytic or a global fashion and reflected the ability to separate items from their surrounding, embedding contexts (simple perception). Based on the disembedding notion, various embedded figures tests (EFT) were later developed that required subjects to find simple geometric figures hidden within a larger complex picture. Correlations between the ability to find hidden figures and ability to set the rod or align one's body upright led to the conclusion that individuals were either "field independent," perceiving themselves and objects as independent of the surrounding field, or "field dependent," perceiving themselves and objects in relation to the field and thus having more difficulty in separating an item from its background. Work by Witkin and his coworkers that investigated the relation of FD-I to various personality variables formed the basis for the second stage of FD-I, personality through perception. The major conclusion was that the extent of activity spent in dealing with one's environment was the characteristic that most effectively discriminated individuals with different modes of perception. Activity, or assertiveness, was seen as characteristic of field-independent individuals; passivity was seen as characteristic of field-dependent individuals and included a view of them as having an absence of initiating activities, a low evaluation of themselves, and a poverty of inner life.

Further research by Witkin resulted in a major revision of the FD-I construct. The third stage, psychological differentiation, included claims that FD-I instruments retrieved information about individuals' problem-solving behavior, body image, sense of separate identity, and major psychological defenses. Findings leading to the expanded interpretation showed that field-independent children excelled on parts of intelligence tests requiring disembedding and restructuring abilities, while field-dependent children did best on the parts having to do with vocabulary, information, and comprehension and most poorly on those requiring restructuring and analytic abilities. Thus, cognitive abilities presumed to favor field independence became part of the interpretation. The new meaning attached to FD-I measures changed the central focus from activity versus passivity in relation to the environment to a focus that stressed the capacity to segregate the self throughout a broad range of psychological activities. The emphasis on segregation gave rise to the differentiation hypothesis that stressed field independence as the end point of development and, conversely, assumed that field dependence was the result of inhibited development. The fact that young children differed on FD-I measures led Witkin and associates to study socialization factors that might account for the differences. From global rating scales used to assess the behavior of mothers on variables thought either to facilitate or inhibit the development of differentiation, the researchers developed the "field dependence socialization cluster." Included were behaviors attributed to mothers of field-dependent children who stressed conformity and limited exploration and creativity. Mothers of field-dependent children were also thought to be submissive or indulgent toward their children and to lack self-assurance, thus hampering their children's ability to define their own role as separate persons.

Subsequent reconceptualization, the fourth stage of the FD-I construct, arose in response to research that provided much new information. Included were findings from cross-cultural research that indicated the effects of ecological environment and related socialization practices as well as from studies indicating that field-dependent individuals may have superior social skills. The resulting major revisions were a deemphasis on the value of field independence and an emphasis on social orientation as part of field dependence. The neutral view taken by Witkin and associates asserted that the FD-I dimension is a bipolar, stylistic dimension and not a unipolar, ability dimension; there are advantages and disadvantages to both.

Other researchers also used Witkin's work to further expand and reconstruct the FD-I construct. Ramírez and Castañeda (1974) took the FD-I bipolar dimension one step further and interpreted it to signify two separate cognitive styles and not two dimensions of one. More recently others have criticized the stressing of culturally related differences of Mexican Americans and, focusing on the role of experience and cognitive abilities, used Piagetian type measures to research FD-I (De Avila, Havassey, and Pascual-Leone, 1976).

Field Dependence and Mexican Americans

The hypothesis that FD-I is a function of the sociocultural environment and of child-rearing practices made the theory especially adaptable to the study of cultural variations (Berry, 1971; Witkin, 1967; Witkin and Berry, 1975). Cultures that were mainly rural, emphasized social conformity, and exhibited marked sex differences were thought to encourage development of field dependence. The Mexican American culture with its stress on parental authority, respect, and obedience to elders, and separation of sex roles seemed to coincide with these presumed socialization antecedents of field dependence (Holtzman, Diaz-Guerrero, and Swartz, 1975; Laosa, 1980; Ramírez and Castañeda, 1974). In efforts to develop a viable theory and identify factors that would provide guidance in dealing with cultural differences, several studies investigated field dependence as related to Mexican Americans.

The earlier works asserting that Mexican American children were more field dependent than Anglo Americans used rod-and-frame type measures, as did later studies reporting cultural differences (Kagan and Buriel, 1977). In two studies, Ramírez (1973) and Ramírez and Price-Williams (1974) used rod-and-frame type measures. The findings of both studies indicated that Mexican American children performed significantly more field dependently then Anglo American children. Buriel (1975) and Kagan and Romero (cited in Kagan and Buriel, 1977), using the PRFT, also reported significant FD-I differences between Mexican American and Anglo American children.

Other studies using the embedded figures tests have found no significant differences between Mexican American and Anglo American children on field independence. Results of three studies that compared Mexican American and Anglo American children on embedded figures test (CEFT) indicated that the cultural groups did not differ significantly (Knudsen and Kagan, 1977; Kagan, Zahn, and Gealy, 1977; Kagan and Buriel, 1977). Two studies compared embedded figures test scores (CEFT and PEFT) of Mexican American children to those of the Anglo middle class children used in standardization of the instruments. De Avila and Duncan (cited in Escobedo, 1981) using CEFT scores and Escobedo (1981) using PEFT scores found their Mexican American sample significantly more field independent than the Anglo population norms reported by the CEFT and PEFT manuals. A distinction made by Kagan and Buriel is that studies using the embedded figures measures reported no significant cultural differences on FD-I scores for Mexican American/Anglo American comparisons, while those studies using rod-and-frame type measures did. One explanation posited by the authors was that embedded figures tests may measure variables on which Mexican American and Anglo American children do not differ and rod-and-frame tests may tap a different set of variables on which they do; this is supported by Buriel's research (in Kagan and Buriel,

1977), which indicates that the embedded figures and rod-and-frame type measures "fail to correlate to a sufficient degree to meet the basic convergent validity requirements of a psychological construct" (p. 322).

The various meanings attributed to field dependence measures are of specific importance when related to Mexican Americans. The original focus of the FD-I construct on activity versus passivity, appeared to support previous stereotypic views of Mexican Americans as passive, cooperative, noncompetitive, and perhaps even lazy (Ramírez and Castañeda, 1974). Anglos, as field independent, were seen as active, assertive, and competitive to a point of irrationality (Nelson and Kagan, 1972; Ramírez and Castañeda, 1974). In addition, the differentiation hypothesis with its emphasis on field independence as an end point of development and association of less analytical cognitive ability with field dependence further cast a negative view of field dependent individuals (Kagan and Buriel, 1977). Thus, the identification of individuals from traditional and rural cultures, including Mexican Americans, as more field dependent tended to attach the same negative views to them: unassertive, less able to perform analytical tasks, and less receptive to abstract learning. For many Mexican American educators the negative interpretation of field dependence scores persisted even after the formulation of the theory that stressed the neutral value of FD-I. Therefore, they questioned the validity of the instruments, the interpretations, and the relationship of field dependence to Mexican culture. The research was seen as confirmation of the "damaging-culture" assumption (Ramírez and Castañeda, 1974) that had been pervasive in earlier studies of Mexican Americans in various fields (Edmonson, 1957; Garretson, 1928; Heller, 1968; Madsen, 1964; Tuck, 1946). Even the bicognitive approach formalized by Ramírez (1973) that emphasized the positive value of field dependence as related to culture was questioned. "To argue that Mexican-American children are field sensitive and consequently not receptive to learning abstract problem-solving strategies is superficially no different, at the practical level, than to argue that the intellectual capabilities of Mexican-Americans are limited to Level I type tasks because of genetic endowment" (De Avila, Havassey, and Pascual-Leone, 1976, p. 6).

FIELD DEPENDENCE SOCIAL ORIENTATION

The second influence that had an impact on the reconceptualization of the FD-I construct was a large body of research indicating that field dependent individuals are more interpersonally oriented and thus may possess superior social skills. Witkin and Goodenough (1977), after an extensive literature review, concluded:

> Field-dependent people are attentive to the views of others; they are sensitive to social cues; they have an interpersonal orientation, encompassing a strong inter-

est in people, a preference for being with others and even being physically close to them, emotional openness and, in some circumstances, facility in getting along with others. These characteristics add up to a set of social attributes and social skills that are less evident in field independent-people. (p. 682)

Thus, the scope of psychological differentiation theory was enlarged to encompass interpersonal interaction, and specific behaviors were identified as being manifestations of a more differentiated (FI) or less differentiated (FD) cognitive functioning.

Interpersonal Orientation

Witkin and Goodenough (1977) divided interpersonal orientation into four major categories: (1) use of social referents; (2) attention to social information; (3) interpersonal relations; and (4) interpersonal versus impersonal orientation. Generally, field-dependent individuals were found to make greater use of social referents, attend to social information, get along with others, and prefer interpersonal interaction to a greater degree than field-independent individuals. Most of the studies in the first category reported that field-dependent individuals showed greater reliance on external social referents in determining their own judgments and attitudes. They were particularly prone to make use of the opinions of other people with whom they were involved in group interaction, tended to rely more on others as sources of information when information was not very clear, and reflected greater need for external guidance. However, the two did not differ in their use of social referents when the situation was not ambiguous.

Various other studies investigating FD-I have reported differences in social behaviors. Field-dependent individuals used looking at others significantly more than field-independent ones as a means of gaining information, had greater extent of memory for previously encountered faces, better recall of social words versus neutral words, and better level of performance in learning situations in which social cues were used. Greater effectiveness of field-dependent individuals in interpersonal relations as a function of cognitive style is inferred from characteristics derived from personal attributes rating scales and from distinct ways of handling hostility. Field-dependent individuals were described as friendly, considerate, and warm. Field-independent individuals were seen as self-centered, rude, inconsiderate, manipulative, and power seeking. Also, field-independent individuals had a greater tendency to direct hostility against others and field-dependent individuals to avoid such expressions. Field-dependent individuals' preference for interpersonal interaction seems to emerge early in life. Nursery school field-dependent children spent significantly more time in social play and field-independent ones in solitary play (Coates, Lord, and Jakabovics, 1975). This is reflected in career choices. Relatively field-dependent persons are likely to favor educational-vocational domains that feature social content and require interpersonal relations for conduct but for which analytical functioning is not particularly important; conversely field-independent individuals are likely to prefer the opposite (Witkin, Moore, Goodenough, and Cox, 1977). There are no significant differences in overall achievement indicators such as grade point average, only in the courses for which similar averages are earned. Ratings have also provided descriptors showing that field-dependent individuals "have a strong interest in people, prefer to be physically close to others, are emotionally open, and favor real-life situations that will bring them into contact with people . . ." (Witkin and Goodenough, 1977, p. 672). Preference for physical closeness, interpersonal space, is also seen by Hall as an important variable on which cultures differ and is one often associated with Mexican American culture. Therefore, a more comprehensive discussion of interpersonal space is included in a separate section.

Social Orientation and Field Dependence of Mexican Americans

The superior social orientation of field dependence, also attributed to traditional Mexican American culture, has been the focus of various research efforts. Ramírez and Castañeda (1974), best known for their work of FD-I with Mexican American samples, have based their definition of this cognitive style on social orientation. The authors see the social orientation of Mexican Americans as characterized by openness, warmth, commitment to mutual dependence, cooperativeness, sensitivity to feelings of others, and respectfulness of adults and social convention. This orientation is a result of four value clusters identified as composing the Mexican American value system: (1) identification with family, community, and ethnic group, (2) personalization of interpersonal relationships, (3) status and role definition in family and community, and (4) Mexican Catholic ideology. In contrast, the values of mainstream Anglos are characterized by "(1) sense of separate identity; and (2) individual competitive achievement" (Ramírez and Castañeda, 1974, p. 56). Therefore, cultural values of Mexican Americans determine the type of socialization practices[2] that occur in Mexican American families: emphasis on obedience and conformity to family and cultural norms, which, in turn, influence the development of social orientation and cognitive styles.

The model developed by Ramírez and Castañeda differed from that of Witkin in that field dependence and field independence are seen as two distinct cognitive styles, and not two dimensions of one, each reflecting distinct cultural

---

[2]Socialization processes as part of the cultural antecedents of cognitive style of Mexican Americans are discussed in depth by Jackson and Espino elsewhere in this volume.

values and norms. The instruments developed to assess the cognitive style of children and teachers also differ from those developed by Witkin and are observation scales based on interpersonal behaviors. For these researchers, field-independent and field-sensitive (as they prefer to call field-dependent) cognitive styles are defined by specific sets of observable behaviors and not scores on perceptual orientation tests. This is a major deviation from the traditional FD-I construct as originally conceptualized. It is not known if the two are related and the degree of correlation between the observation scales and traditional FD-I measurements has not been established (Hernandez-Holtzman, Goldsmith, and Barrera, 1979). The four areas of behavior that compose the Ramírez and Castañeda cognitive style model are:

1. Communication style (the preferred language for communication)
2. Learning styles (the way people perceive, assimilate, and organize information)
3. Incentive-motivational style (manifested in competition or ways of seeking recognition)
4. Human-relational style (ways of relating to others)

Three of the four areas focus on social orientation and specific interpersonal behaviors that are also associated with later Witkin social interpretations. Research by Ramírez with Mexican American elementary school children has confirmed the developers' assumption that these children are field dependent or field sensitive and learn in distinct ways. Greater cooperativeness, desire to belong to a social group (affiliativeness) and to interact with others, and sensitivity in interpersonal relations were also related to their field-sensitive (FD) cognitive style. Implementation of learning environments based on cognitive style have also produced favorable results (Kagan and Buriel, 1977). Many other studies have also observed a greater cooperativeness and less competitiveness within the Mexican American culture (Kagan, 1977; Kagan and Madsen, 1972).

Research investigating the relationship of field dependence and social orientation of Mexican Americans utilized traditional FD-I instruments also. Ramírez and Castañeda (1974) used rod and frame (PRFT) measures and reported findings that indicated a relationship between field dependence and the more social orientation of Mexican American children. Cooperativeness and competitiveness as indicative of field-dependent social orientation have been investigated in relation to FD scores of Mexican American children. Several studies confirmed that Mexican Americans are more field dependent on traditional measures as well as more cooperative and less competitive. However, the differences tended not to be empirically related. In one study, the greater field dependence of Mexican American children showed no consistent relation to their more cooperative tendency (Kagan, Zahn, and Gealy, 1977);

another study reported that the less intense competitiveness of Mexican American children in comparison to Anglo American children in role playing mother-child conflict was not related to field dependence or independence (Hoppe, Kagan, and Zahn, 1977). Neither were affiliative measures of Mexican American children and field dependence scores significantly correlated (Sanders, Scholz, and Kagan, 1976). Thus, investigation of two major aspects of interpersonal interaction has failed to confirm that the more prosocial orientation of Mexican American children is related to their greater field dependence.

Interpersonal Space

An assumption about social orientation related to both field dependence and culture is that of preference for closeness in interpersonal interactions. The regulation of interpersonal spacing as a direct result of culture has been posited by Hall (1966) and supported by Ramírez and Castañeda (1974), who further relate this variable to cognitive style. Based on these authors' theories several bilingual educators have suggested interpersonal space as an important factor to be considered when identifying implicit culture variables of Mexican American children (Castillo and Cruz, 1974; McNicholas, 1976; Rodriguez and Plank, 1981).

The relationship of interpersonal spacing to FD-I has been the topic of various studies (Witkin and Goodenough, 1977), and differences in distances between persons have been reported by several that used adult samples. Justice (1967) reported that field-dependent students maintained close distances to the investigator regardless of level of topic intimacy of a required presentation. Holley (1972) asked subjects to position themselves relative to another person at distances that they felt were optimal or least desirable for conversation; field-dependent subjects distanced themselves closer to the other person than did field-independent subjects. In another study (Trego, 1971), subjects were asked to distance themselves in relation to a second person in a series of four halls differing in length. The distancing of field-dependent subjects remained constant for all four situations, but varied for field-independent subjects. This finding led Trego to conclude that field-dependent subjects used the other person in distancing while field-independent persons focused on other aspects of the situation. The relationship of FD-I and interpersonal spacing has been observed in young children also. Hulls, Melson, and Cohen (1980), in a study that investigated cognitive style, interpersonal orientation, and situational specificity of nursery school children, found a significant relationship between field dependence and personal space measures; field dependence correlated with closer personal space preference in the more ambiguous social interaction situation.

This finding supported classic field dependence theory of interpersonal orientation as affected by ambiguous situations.

Studies of interpersonal spacing among young children during actual interaction, though limited in number, have focused on possible confounding variables such as age, sex, and culture. In most studies, age and sex were mediating variables, with younger children maintaining closer spacing and females being more sensitive (Melson, 1977; Lomranz, Shapiro, Coresh, and Gilat, 1975). Aiello and Jones (1971), in a study that included different cultural groups, found that lower socioeconomic Puerto Rican and black children exhibited closer proxemic behaviors than did middle-class Anglos. In a later study, Jones and Aiello (1973) examined both cultural and sex differences in interpersonal spacing behaviors of elementary school–aged black and Anglo children. During a planned activity involving same-age and same-sex dyads, white females were observed to maintain the greatest distances, black females maintained the least, and both black and white males maintained moderate distances. Scherer (1974) reported differences between black and Anglo children that were indicative of socioeconomic class as opposed to culture; lower class children maintained closer distance. Baxter (1970) did find cultural differences in a sample that included Mexican Americans as one of three subcultures and three age levels: adult, adolescents, and children. Findings indicated that Mexican American children displayed a closer distance for interpersonal spacing behaviors than did Anglo and black children. However, none of the studies above investigated personal spacing in relation to cognitive styles.

The only study that investigated interpersonal spacing and FD-I of Mexican American children among cultures included Anglo, black and Mexican American preschool children in a sample of fifty-seven children (Escobedo and Huggans, in progress). Interpersonal space measures were obtained in two situations: once when the child was asked to sit next to a target child of the same culture and same sex, and once when the target child was from the same culture but opposite sex. A three-factor analysis of variance indicated ethnic group differences. Both Mexican American males and females made sex-role discriminations in interpersonal spacing. Significant differences were revealed between measurements of sitting next to a same-sex child as compared to opposite; same-sex dyads sat closer than opposite-sex dyads. Black females made similar discriminations; no significant differences were found for black males nor for Anglo males and females. Cognitive style was significantly correlated with interpersonal spacing for Anglo children only. Thus, even though Mexican American children made the most clear-cut distinction based on sex, their interpersonal spacing behavior was not related to cognitive style. The findings did, however, reflect the greater separation of sex roles attributed to Mexican American culture.

SUMMARY AND CONCLUSION

A review of the field-dependent–independent literature related to Mexican Americans raises several questions regarding the value of FD-I construct as a framework through which to explore and/or identify implicit cultural variables relevant to bilingual classrooms. The most pertinent to the purpose of this paper are:

1. Is there a cultural difference between Mexican American and Anglo children on FD-I scores?
2. Are social orientation differences between the two groups a function of the FD-I construct?
3. Based on current information, does the FD-I cognitive style provide a viable theoretical framework to aid incorporation of implicit cultural elements in bilingual classrooms?

The remaining discussion will address these questions, and briefly explore alternatives.

Comparison of Mexican American and Anglo children on FD-I scores has produced contradictory findings. Studies using rod-and-frame type FD-I instruments have established a reliable difference between Mexican American and Anglo children. However, a cultural difference between the two groups was not evident in studies using embedded figures tests. Therefore, a generalization proposing cultural difference in FD-I cannot be made. In addition, the low intercorrelations of the two measures indicate that these may tap two different variables, one on which Mexican American and Anglo children differ and one on which they do not. Therefore, indications appear to be that the FD-I construct may not be as reliable an indication of cultural differences as previously presumed.

The second major question that emerged was: Are social orientation differences between Mexican American and Anglo children a function of the FD-I construct? Various studies reported differences between Mexican American and Anglo children on assertiveness, competitiveness, and affiliativeness, the variables most often associated with a field-dependent social orientation. However, the differences were not related to field dependence. In another area associated with field dependence and Mexican Americans, one study reported that differences between Mexican American and Anglo children about preferences for close interpersonal spacing were not related to field dependence. Overall, studies conducted among Mexican American children did not support the FD-I theory that social orientation is related to a more field-dependent cognitive style. What did emerge was a rather reliable cultural difference in social behaviors that was not a function of cognitive style.

The utility of FD-I as a theoretical framework through which to view variables of Mexican American culture is not supported by research to date. In addition to lack of conclusive evidence on Mexican American and Anglo differences on FD-I measures and on the relationship of field dependence and the more prosocial orientation of Mexican Americans, other problems exist with the FD-I construct. A major one has been the overstated support for FD-I theory, especially in regard to the socialization antecedents of field dependence. Differences between Mexican Americans and Anglo Americans in socialization practices were also not related to field dependence scores (Kagan and Buriel, 1977). The ambiguity of the various FD-I measurement instruments has confused ability and style. Further, the low correlations between the instruments has failed to establish essential validity for the FD-I construct. Value judgments are inherent in the instruments as interpretations of data are based on the greater analytic abilities (perception of detail) associated with field independence. The social abilities of field-dependent individuals are seen as a compensation for lack of analytic abilities and not as representative of autonomous cultural value (Kagan and Buriel, 1977). Perhaps most potentially damaging for Mexican Americans is the overreliance on the results of very narrow psychological tests and the possibility of labeling children as one or the other, thus perpetuating stereotypes. Also, the broad dimensions of culture are not evident in the one process, cognitive style, even in its wide range of interpretations. Kagan and Buriel (1977) suggest that in view of the limits of FD-I measures, alternative explanations of cultural differences merit consideration in order to meet the needs of Mexican American children: efforts might proceed more efficiently if those needs "were directly assessed and addressed rather than inferred from presumed differences in field dependence as traditionally defined" (p. 323).

Ramírez and Castañeda proposed a much broader based model that could be considered an alternative theoretical framework. Comparison of the Ramírez and Castañeda model, which uses interactive behaviors, to that of Witkin, which uses perceptual orientation, indicates a substantially different approach and one that goes beyond the boundaries associated with cognitive style. Behaviors are assessed directly by observation scales and not inferred from a perceptual measurement, as in Witkin's model. Theoretically, a fundamental difference lies in Ramírez's claim that FD-I is not one but two distinct cognitive styles. The measures are different; one produces actual behaviors while the other produces a perceptual score on which behaviors are inferred. It is, therefore, more appropriate to view them as two separate theories. However, the Ramírez and Castañeda model also suffers from various problems, the major being its foundation on the presumed field dependence socialization cluster. The negative aspects of field dependence, lack of analytic cognitive abilities compensated by social abilities, is carried over to Ramírez's field sensitivity. The rating scale includes a wide range of behaviors but still relies on the classification of children into two groups, and, even though it is considered possible to be bicognitive, there is still the potential for stereotyping. There appears to be a lack of extensive investigation by researchers other than the developers to support the model's sweeping assumptions or the theory that culture is the source of behaviors that make up cognitive style.

The above questions negate the model as a possible alternative theoretical framework from which to view intrinsic cultural variables. However, the approach utilized with direct assessment of behavior, educational strategies to meet children's needs, and a broader consideration of culture is a step in the right direction. What is apparent is the need to explore other alternatives that reflect a comprehensive view of culture such as that of multicultural education suggested by Contreras (this volume). Such a view must include current cultural knowledge from disciplines other than psychology and education, such as sociology, anthropology, and others. Perhaps the close bond between education and psychology, and educators' reliance on psychology to answer pedagogical questions, accounts for the narrow, theoretical framework currently used to account for implicit cultural variables. A possible alternative that merits consideration is an approach similar to that suggested by Josue Gonzalez (1974) and utilized in research by Frank Gonzales (this volume). Such an alternative would need to consider specific student and teacher behaviors that are culturally related and relevant to classroom practice and should be based on extensive research. Preference for close physical contact has been used as the basis for classroom strategies, yet few studies of Mexican American children's actual interactions have been reported. Therefore, assumptions based on behaviors presumed to be culturally related must also be supported by research data. While it is evident that an all-encompassing theory to provide a framework through which to view implicit cultural variables is not currently available, continued efforts will more clearly codify thinking to that end. Important as such efforts may be, what is even more crucial is how resulting models are implemented in the classroom. Warm and caring teachers who deal with cultural differences, or any other differences, in an accepting manner are still the deciding factor in how successful educational programs are. This is especially true of programs dealing with sensitive matters such as implicit cultural factors.

REFERENCES

Aiello, J. R., and Jones, S. E. Field study of the proxemic behavior of young school children in three subcultural groups. *Journal of Personality and Social Psychology,* 1971, *19,* 351–356.

Baxter, J. C. Interpersonal spacing in natural settings. *Sociometry,* 1970, *33,* 444–456.

Berry, J. W. Ecological and cultural factors in spatial perceptual development. *Canadian Journal of Behavioral Science,* 1971, *3,* 324–336.

Buriel, R. Cognitive styles among three generations of Mexican-American children. *Journal of Cross Cultural Psychology,* 1975, *6,* 417–429.

Castillo, M. S., and Cruz, J. Special competencies for teachers of preschool Chicano children: rationale, content, and assessment process. *Young Children,* 1974, *29,* 341–348.

Coates, S., Lord, M., and Jakabovics, E. Field dependence-independence, social–nonsocial play and sex differences in preschool children. *Perceptual and Motor Skills,* 1975, *40,* 195–202.

De Avila, E. A., Havassey, B., and Pascual-Leone, J. *Mexican American children: a neo-Piagetian analysis.* Washington, D.C.: Georgetown University Press, 1976.

Edmonson, S. *Los Manitos: a study of institutional values.* New Orleans: Middle American Research Institute, Tulane University, 1957.

Escobedo, T. H. Field dependence-independence and language patterns of preschool Mexican American children. In T. H. Escobedo (Ed.), *Education and Chicanos: issues and research.* Los Angeles, Calif.: Spanish Speaking Mental Health Research Center, 1981, pp. 187–210.

Escobedo, T. H., and Huggans, J. H. Cultural differences and interpersonal spacing and cognitive style among black, Mexican-American, and Anglo children. Unpublished manuscript.

Garretson, O. K. A study of retardation among Mexican children in a small public school system in Arizona. *Journal of Educational Psychology,* 1928, *19,* 31–40.

Gonzales, F. Reinforcing culture in three bilingual programs. In T. H. Escobedo (Ed.), *Early childhood bilingual education.* New York: Teachers College Press, 1983.

González, J. M. A developmental and sociological rationale for culture-based curricula and cultural context teaching in early instruction of Mexican American children. Doctoral dissertation, University of Massachusetts, 1974. *Dissertation Abstracts International,* 1974, *35,* 2989 (University Microfilms No. 74-25836).

Hall, E. T. *The hidden dimension.* Garden City, N.Y.: Doubleday, 1966.

Heller, C. S. *Mexican American youth: forgotten youth at the crossroads.* New York: Random House, 1968.

Hernandez-Holtzman, E., Goldsmith, R. P., and Barrera, C. *Field-dependence, field-independence: educational implications for bilingual education.* Austin, Tex.: Dissemination and Assessment Center for Bilingual Education, 1979.

Holley, M. *Field-dependence-independence, sophistication-of-body-concept, and social distance selection.* Doctoral dissertation, New York University, 1972. *Dissertation Abstracts International,* 1972, *33,* 296B (University Microfilms No. 72-20,635).

Holtzman, W. H., Diaz-Guerrero, R., and Swartz, J. R. *Personality development in two cultures.* Austin, Tex: University of Texas Press, 1975.

Hoppe, C. M., Kagan, S. M., and Zahn, G. L. Conflict resolution among field independent and field dependent Anglo-American and Mexican-American children and their mothers. *Developmental Psychology,* 1977, *13,* 591–598.

Hulls, M. J., Melson, G. S., and Cohen, A. S. Situation and person factors in young children's communication. *Home Economics Research Journal,* 1980, *8,* 394–398.

Jones, S. E., and Aiello, J. R. Proxemic behavior of black and white first-, third-, and fifth-grade children. *Journal of Personality and Social Psychology,* 1973, *25,* 21–27.

Justice, M. T. Field dependency, intimacy of topic and interperson distance. Doctoral dissertation, University of Florida, 1969. *Dissertation Abstracts International,* 1970, *31,* 395B–396B (University Microfilms No. 70-12,243).

Kagan, S. Social motives and behaviors of Mexican-American and Anglo-American children. In J. L. Martinez, Jr. (Ed.), *Chicano psychology.* New York: Academic Press, 1977, pp. 45–86.

Kagan, S., and Buriel, R. Field dependence-independence and Mexican-American culture and education. In J. L. Martinez, Jr. (Ed.), *Chicano psychology.* New York: Academic Press, 1977, pp. 279–328.

Kagan, S. and Madsen, M. Experimental analysis of cooperation and competition of Anglo-American and Mexican-American children. *Developmental Psychology,* 1972, *6,* 49–59.

Kagan, S., Zahn, G. L., and Gealy, J. Competition and school achievement among Anglo-American and Mexican-American children. *Journal of Educational Psychology,* 1977, *69*(4), 432–441.

Knudsen, J. H. M., and Kagan, S. Visual perspective role-taking and field-independence among Anglo-American and Mexican-American children of two ages. *Journal of Genetic Psychology,* 1977, *131,* 243–254.

Laosa, L. M. Maternal teaching strategies and cognitive styles in Chicano families. *Journal of Educational Psychology,* 1980, *72,* 45–54.

Lomranz, J., Shapiro, A., Coresh, N., and Gilat, Y. Children's personal space as a function of age and sex. *Developmental Psychology,* 1975, *5,* 365.

Madsen, W. *Mexican-Americans of South Texas: case studies in cultural anthropology.* New York: Holt, Rinehart and Winston, 1964.

McNicholas, P. B. Responsive bilingual-bicultural instructional strategies: a prospectus. *Childhood Education.* 1976. *53,* 11–115.

Melson, G. F. Sex differences in proxemic behavior and personal space schemata. *Sex Roles,* 1977, *1.*

Murdock, G. P. The common denominator of culture. In R. Linton (Ed.), *The science of man in the world crisis.* New York: Columbia University Press, 1945.

Nelson, L. L., and Kagan, S. Competition: the star-spangled scramble. *Psychology Today,* 1972, *6*(4), 53–56, 90–91.

Ramírez, M. Cognitive styles and cultural democracy in education. *Social Science Quarterly,* 1973, *53,* 895–904.

Ramírez, M. and Castañeda, A. *Cultural democracy, bicognitive development, and education.* New York: Academic Press, 1974.

Ramírez, M., and Price-Williams, D. R. Cognitive styles of children of three ethnic groups in the United States. *Journal of Cross-Cultural Psychology,* 1974, *5,* 212–219.

Rodriguez, A. M., and Plank, C. C. Creating a culturally pluralistic classroom: theories and practice. In T. H. Escobedo (Ed.), *Education and Chicanos: issues and research.* Los Angeles: Spanish Speaking Mental Health Research Center, 1981, pp. 35–48.

Sanders, M., Scholz, J. P., and Kagan, S. Three social motives and field independence-dependence in Anglo-American and Mexican-American children. *Journal of Cross Cultural Psychology,* 1976, *7.* 451–462.

Scherer, S. E. Proxemic behavior of primary school children as a function of their socioeconomic class and subculture. *Journal of Personality and Social Psychology,* 1974, *29*(6), 800–805.

Trego, R. E. An investigation of the rod and frame test in relation to emotional dependence and social cue attentiveness. Doctoral dissertation, Texas Christian University, 1971. *Dissertation Abstracts International* 1972, *32,* 4910B (University Microfilms No. 72-7617).

Tuck, R. *Not with the fist: Mexican Americans in a southwest city.* New York: Harcourt, 1946.

Witkin, H. A. A cognitive style approach to cross-cultural research. *International Journal of Psychology,* 1967, *2,* 233–250.

Witkin, H. A., and Berry, J. W. Psychological differentiation in cross cultural perspectives. *Journal of Cross Cultural Psychology,* 1975, *6,* 4–87.

Witkin, H. A., and Goodenough, D. R. Field dependence and interpersonal behavior. *Psychological Bulletin,* 1977, *84,* 661–689.

Witkin, H. A., Moore, C. A., Goodenough, D. R., and Cox, P. W. Field dependent and field independent cognitive styles and their educational implications. *Review of Educational Research,* 1977, *47*(1), 1–64.

III | Classroom Strategies

9 | Mathematics and Young Bilingual Children

ALBERTA M. CASTANEDA
The University of Texas at Austin

To a newborn language means nothing. We can talk lucidly and cleverly to a newborn and impart no information. We can frighten him with a loud, harsh voice or calm him with a crooning tone, but we cannot sway him with words. At some point a change occurs. The developing child has acquired enough information, organized it into enough concepts, associated them with enough labels, that he can ask questions when he wants to know something and can acquire new information from another person through words. When this has happened, a new realm of education opens. The child is no longer tied to the here and now. He can learn about things that are not within his perceptual range. Although his ability to do so is severely limited by the language available to him, he can learn about things he cannot see, hear, taste, feel, or smell, either because they are distant in time or space or because they do not physically exist. This turning point, developing at about two and a half or three years for many children, establishes the lower bound identifying a group of children who have special educational needs.

From that time until they can read enough to acquire new information from printed words, at about seven for many, children are in a special period. To a greater extent than ever again, they are dependent on sensory information. To a greater extent than ever again, their language abilities are growing. Teachers must provide these children with:

1. Sensory information through physical experiences—the opportunity to observe, handle, and act upon objects, to observe, cause, and stop processes, and to participate in and observe events
2. The opportunity to hear proper language, associate it with conventional meanings, and use it
3. A climate that encourages them to attend, manipulate, and trust their own perception and cognition and to use language

There is a kind of teaching that is appropriate for most children from about two and a half to seven. I shall call these children "young children" and the teaching style "early childhood education." For some reason we tend to violate all three of the requirements of early childhood education when we attempt to teach young children mathematics. Rather than providing them with concrete materials and modeling and encouraging their use of proper language, we ask children to memorize and recite or make marks on paper.

Most programs for young children begin mathematics instruction with the association of spoken name to written symbol, the forming of written symbols, and the memorization of a sequence of number names—that is, naming and forming (not reading and writing) numerals and counting. Although we would not expect children to name and form words that have no meaning for them, we regularly ask them to name and form numerals that have no meaning for them. Indeed, many five-year-olds are asked to complete "3 + 2 = [   ]" when all they know about three, two, and five is that they are words that follow two, one, and four, respectively. Rarely is attention systematically paid to building meanings prior to the introduction of written mathematical symbols and names.

Anyone who has been in primary or intermediate classrooms recently has seen many children so dependent upon their fingers or other manipulatives that they resort to them to solve the simplest equation. They have seen children who cannot solve 3 + 2 = [   ] without a number line or counters and yet are doing pages of examples such as the vertical form of 3,255 + 2,123; who write 411 as the sum of 39 and 12, and 3 + 8 = 5 without discomfort; who count seven objects and eight objects and then recount the fifteen objects to solve 7 + 8 = [   ]. Many elementary school–aged children do not understand what they are asked to do in arithmetic. Uncomprehending, they participate by employing various procedures with counters, and they must be taught a new procedure for each type of computation.

Mathematics is a sequential discipline. The ability to understand and do each new level of mathematics is dependent upon the understanding and skill the learner brings from the last level. The whole structure rests upon the base formed when the learner is in preschool and the early primary grades. We should make that base as firm as possible.

In each of the next three sections of this paper, a characteristic of early childhood education is considered in the context of beginning mathematics instruction to build the argument that all teachers of young children, particularly teachers in bilingual programs, should be aware of the distinction between premathematics and mathematics in both content and language if they are to provide curriculum and instruction that are developmentally appropriate to young children.

CONCRETE MATERIALS

The need to provide concrete experiences for young children is generally accepted by early childhood educators. If we want a young child to learn about pecans, an object, we give him pecans to see, heft, feel, smell, taste; give him pecans in hulls, in shells, and shelled; arrange for him to see pecans develop on the tree, pick them up, hull, shell, chop, cook, and plant them. If we want a young child to learn about melting, a process, we arrange for him to observe, cause and stop, speed and retard, the melting of butter, chocolate, wax, ice, sugar, and other materials; to hear the words that describe the premelting and postmelting state of materials; to talk about what he sees and feels, what changes occurred, how the process started, what made it happen faster or more slowly, what was common and different in the cases of melting. In both examples we let him acquire information from concrete experience and associate it with the right labels, thus acquiring meaning and language.

If we want a young child to learn about a mathematical entity or process—the number five or the process of adding, for example—what do we hand him or arrange for him to see, do, and talk about? The number five cannot be perceived because it does not exist physically. It is an intellectual construct made up of value and position and possessing such characteristics as not being divisible by any whole number other than one and five; being the sum of three plus two, two less than seven, one greater than four; and being a factor of all whole numbers ending in five or zero. None of these characteristics can be perceived. Similarly, adding cannot be perceived. You can add within the sight of the child, but he cannot see the process because the adding takes place in your intellect, invisibly. Addition has commutativity, closure in the whole numbers, and an identity element, but it does not have temperature, mass, or any other physical property.

There are no physical referents for the simplest of mathematical concepts. Therefore, mathematical instruction cannot be made to fit the pattern of bringing the child into physical contact with the thing or process we want him to learn about, and there is virtually no place for mathematical content in a program for young children. Only at the upper bound, for *some* six- and seven-year-olds, is there a place for mathematics in early childhood education. That does not mean that we turn our back on the subject matter. It means, rather, that we use what we know about how young children learn and what we know about mathematics to find the real-world roots, the perceptible roots, of some mathematical concepts and plan instruction that will help children develop premathematical concepts and associate them with proper language. These concepts will provide a base of meaning and the words with which we can begin talking about the meaning of the mathematical symbols to come.

While the number five is not perceptible, a young child can perceive five objects—pecans, for example. He can see them in different arrangements, hear the series of sounds as each drops, feel one for each finger on one hand. He can move one aside and see four remaining; he can try to put them into two equivalent sets and observe the results. He can perceive the numerosity, the manyness, of a collection of five pecans. He can perceive a physical analogy to the cardinal property of the number five and, also, to the addition and subtraction facts with sums of five. What he knows about five objects will apply when he is required to symbolize relations between numbers and to complete addition and subtraction equations.

It is important that we distinguish between premathematical and mathematical concepts and learning. We who are responsible for what happens to young children in school settings must be aware of when we ask children to step across the chasm from concepts and language for which there are physical, palpable referents to those for which there are none, to concepts and language that can be learned about only through other languages. If we know that we are not teaching about the number five but rather five objects, we will be less inclined to move children to numerals and equations prematurely and be more willing to provide the time and instructional support needed for the child to move consciously away from the world of objects into the world of number.

The specific labels and concepts that precede the mathematical concepts— that is, premathematics or the perceptible roots of mathematical concepts and skills—are appropriate and significant content for five- and six-year-olds and some four-year-olds. While the distinction between premathematics and mathematics applies to other realms of mathematics, the examples used in this paper are drawn from whole number arithmetic.

LANGUAGE

Just as we should distinguish between premathematics and mathematics in concepts, so we should distinguish between premathematics and mathematics in language. In premathematics we are talking about objects. In mathematics we are not talking about objects. Often a change in language signals the difference, and yet we often fail to take advantage of this signal. The following are some examples (in English) of the contrast between the language of premathematics and mathematics and the problems that occur when the distinction is not made.

1. In the sentence "Five objects are more than three objects," the number word "five" is used as an adjective; it tells how many objects. "Are more than" describes the relationship between the manyness of five objects and that of three objects; that is, when the objects in any set of five are paired with those in any set of three, it is perceptible that there are two objects in the set of five without partners.

There is no test that will make perceptible the analogous relation between the numbers five and three. That relation is written "5 > 3," and is read "Five is greater than three." Now, the number word, "five," is used as a noun, and it takes a singular verb. It names a number; it does not tell how many.

The premathematical language is: "Five things *are more than* three things."

The mathematical language is: "Five *is greater than* three." The change from the plural to the singular verb cues the change in meaning of the word "five," and the change from "more than" to "greater than" cues the changed relationship. Both distinctions are important. The language supports the change in meaning, and we should make the most of it. We should use the proper language for the statement about objects and the proper language for the statement about numbers.

Contrast the common misreading of "5 > 3" as "Five *is* more than three." The words confuse the language of objects with the language of number. The singular verb and the number name used as a noun will not let the sentence be about objects; but what can it mean to say that the number five is "more than" the number three? It is even more troublesome to say, "Five is more than three" when talking about five objects. The subject "five objects" requires a plural verb. The use of "five is more than three" for both object and number deprives the child of a linguistic handle to the two ideas.

2. "Three and two (more) objects are five objects" is a valid general statement about the world of objects. When we move away from the world of objects into the world of number, we write the related equation "3 + 2 = 5." The proper oral language for the equation is "Three plus two is equal to five." Again the change in language signals that a change of meaning has occurred. The shift from "and" to "plus" says that we are talking about number, not objects: "plus" indicates the number operation of addition. The change from plural to singular verb is an important one, a cue that "3 + 2" names an entity. Out of that singularity the meaning of the equality sign grows. The equality sign is read "is equal to" or "equals" and means "is another name for." Three plus two "is another name for" the number five.

If teachers read the equation as "three plus two *are* five," the child receives confusing and misleading cues. The plural verb denies that "three plus two" names an entity and inhibits the development of the mathematical meaning of the equality sign. The very word muddies the meaning and gets in the way of the children's movement into the world of number.

When the object words "Three *and* two *are* five" or "Three *and* two more *are* five" are used for the equation, two basic arithmetic symbols are distorted. The plus symbol does not mean "and," and the equality sign does not mean "are." Reading "three *and* two more *are*" may be an attempt to cue the child into the related set operation, or it may be the usage of the teacher's vernacular, but it is faulty and misguided.

"Three *plus* two *is* five" could be considered a little better. At least the plus sign is read properly and the singular verb reinforces the information that "3 + 2" is an entity; but "3 + 2" is not "5": it *is equal to* five. There is a difference. We can help children by keeping the difference straight in our own thinking and in the language we use with them.

3. In some classrooms the equation "$7 - 2 = 5$," properly read as "Seven minus two is equal to five," is read as "Seven take away two are five." Although the number words seem to be used as nouns, the idea of "taking away" the number two from the number seven is meaningless. The plural verb contradicts the number nouns. Again, teachers may substitute the words "take away" for "minus," thinking that they are cueing children into the related set operation, that of set separation, and use "are" for "is equal to," thinking that they are simplifying the language and meaning. But in doing so they are making less obvious to the child the mathematical understanding that "$7 - 2$" names a number and that "seven minus two" is "equal to," or "another name for," the number five. If the reason for misreading the minus and equality signs is the immaturity of the child, we should put off teaching subtraction until the child can develop the concept and acquire the proper language.

There are proper words to describe and distinguish between premathematics and mathematics. They are proper because they make distinctions in meaning where distinctions occur. The proper words will serve the child well as he goes on with the study of mathematics, and the distinctions they preserve will help ensure that he *will* go on with it. But young children can learn only the words they actually hear. Teachers should, therefore, look beyond the words they learned as children and that occur in their vernacular. Those teaching in English should make an effort to use the wording set forth in the text above and summarized in table 1.

Table 1:   Object and Number Statements: English

Object Statements	*Number Statements*
1. Three apples *are more* apples *than* two apples. *(or)* Three apples *are more than* two apples.	1. $3 > 2$ Three *is greater than* two.
2. Two apples are *not as many as* three apples. *(or)* Two apples *are fewer than* three apples.	2. $2 < 3$ Two *is less than* three.
3. Three *and* two apples *are* five apples. *(or)* Three *and* two more apples *are* five apples.	3. $3 + 2 = 5$ Three *plus* two *is equal to* five. *(or)* Three *plus* two *equals* five.
4. If there *are* five apples and we *take away* two apples, there *are* three apples left.	4. $5 - 2 = 3$ Five *minus* two *is equal to* three. *(or)* Five *minus* two *equals* three.

Table 2:   Object and Number Statements: Spanish

Object Statements	Number Statements
1. Tres manzanas *son más que* dos manzanas.	1. 3 > 2 Tres *es mayor que* dos.
2. Dos manzanas *no son tantas como* tres manzanas. *(or)* Dos manzanas *son menos que* tres manzanas.	2. 2 < 3 Dos *es menor que* tres.
3. Tres manzanas *más* dos manzanas *son* cinco manzanas. *(or)* Tres manzanas *y* dos *son* cinco manzanas.	3. 3 + 2 = 5 Tres *más* dos es *igual a* cinco. *(or)* Tres *más* dos *igual a* cinco.
4. Cinco manzanas *menos* dos manzanas *son* tres manzanas.	4. 5 − 2 = 3 Cinco *menos* dos es *igual a* tres. *(or)* Cinco *menos* dos *igual a* tres.

Teachers of young children in bilingual programs must find and learn to use the words in the other language that will:

1. Help preserve the distinction between object and number expressions to cue themselves and the children when they have entered the world of mathematics
2. Emphasize the singularity of addition and subtraction expressions and of the numbers in inequality relations

For example, in Spanish the number statement "Tres *es mayor que* dos" is preferable to "Tres *es más que dos*," as a reading for "3 > 2" because it contrasts more clearly with the object statement "Tres manzanas *son más que* dos manzanas." Likewise, the number statement "Tres más dos *es igual a* cinco" or "Tres más dos *igual a* cinco," is preferable to "Tres más dos *son* cinco" as a reading for "3 + 2 = 5" because it specifies that "3 + 2" is an entity and contrasts with the object statement "Tres manzanas y dos *son* cinco manzanas" or "Tres manzanas más dos manzanas *son* cinco manzanas." Even "Tres más dos *es* cinco" is preferable to "Tres más dos *son* cinco" as the number statement. Object and number statements in Spanish that parallel the English statements of table 1 appear in table 2.

PARTICIPATION

I alluded above to the usual way in which young children are introduced to mathematics. As long as there is no distinction made between premathematics and mathematics, there will be little improvement in this area. If we believe mathematics begins with counting, numeral writing and reading, addition, and subtraction, we are likely to begin instruction there, and as number words have no physical referents, we will forever be asking children to use words whose meanings we cannot teach them. If, however, we consciously begin instruction with premathematics concepts, it is possible to devise instruction that is consistent with other aspects of early childhood education. As long as the content is premathematics (prenumber), the information needed is in the real world, and concrete materials open to manipulation can be provided; for prenumber the materials are collections of objects and the characteristics of the collections and the results of manipulations can be observed and described; and there is proper, precise wording to be modeled and used. Thus, the first two needs of early childhood education are met. The children can be actively engaged with the materials, responding on the basis of what they can see and come to know, and their trust in their own perception and cognition grows. They become inquirers and thinkers rather than memorizers, and the third characteristic of early childhood education is met.

Premathematics is perceptible and reconcilable with what children know. When based on *premathematical* understanding, *mathematics* can be learned by children as rational, verifiable in their own experience, and reconcilable with what they know. Early learning in mathematics need not consist of memorizing labels for and sequences of meaningless symbols.

INSTRUCTION IN MATHEMATICS AND YOUNG BILINGUAL CHILDREN

This paper has discussed mathematics and young children without reference to their ethnicity or first language because I believe that mathematical concepts are the same from culture to culture and from language to language and that, except for extreme examples and limited periods of time, children are developmentally the same from culture to culture and language to language.

Three may be considered a lucky number in some cultures and a jinx in others, but that is aside from the mathematical meaning. There is a whole number three that falls between two and four and has the same characteristics regardless of the orthography or phonology used to produce the name for the number. Written "III," "3," "11_2," "three," or "tres," the mathematical concept is the same. Achievement in mathematics by children may be more expected by some cultural groups than by others, and mathematics may be regarded differently in different cultures, but mathematical concepts and skills do not vary.

I have argued that to be developmentally appropriate, early childhood education, regardless of the ethnicity of its clientele, cannot begin with mathematics; instruction must begin consciously with premathematics—the real-world, perceptible roots of mathematical concepts. Culture is part of the perceptible world. Young children should learn—with objects and in settings meaningful to them—about "more than," about the numerosity of five objects (and of zero through ten objects), and about the results of joining a set of two to a set of three (and other actions on sets of objects). But the step away from objects *must* be taken. If they are to learn mathematics at all, all children must learn culture-free mathematics, and if a full panoply of career choices are to be open to them, children must learn mathematics.

Mathematics is a language, and early learning in premathematics and mathematics is language learning. Whether a child's instruction is in one language or another, or in a combination of languages, the distinction between the concepts and language of premathematics and those of mathematics should be maintained and the words used should support and emphasize that distinction.

10 | Language Proficiency and the Development of Mathematical Concepts in Hispanic Primary School Students

GILBERT J. CUEVAS
University of Miami

There is evidence that language learning and language use have implications for the acquisition of concepts and the development of the ability to think. Some suggest that language determines and defines thought; others, like Piaget (1956), tend to see only a limited effect of language on thought. Some of Piaget's coworkers argue that language development may be influenced by general cognitive development, since some major changes in language mastery occur at the same time as major cognitive changes. We may conclude that whatever theoretical approach one takes, language and thinking are probably strongly related, and especially so in the development of such concepts as those involved in mathematics. One, the concept of number, has long been a concern for mathematicians and mathematical philosophers, who investigate the nature of mathematics; for developmental psychologists, who investigate the cognitive skills that presumably underlie numerical competencies; and for educators, whose concern is constructing a curriculum for teaching numerical competence. In addition to this general concern, there is a special need to expand our understanding of children's development of number and numeration concepts when these are taught in a language that is the student's second language.

The purpose of this paper is to report the findings of a two-year study of the

The research presented in this report is part of a comprehensive longitudinal study conducted by the author and Jack Coffland, School of Education and Allied Professions, University of Miami, Florida, pursuant to NIE contract 400-77-0074 (1977–79).

development of mathematical concepts in children in a bilingual program. The discussion is organized into three major sections. The first gives the background of the study, including a review of relevant literature on language and mathematical learning, on bilingualism and cognitive development, and the acquisition of the concepts of number and numeration. The second section is a report on methodology and results, and the last is a discussion of results, conclusions, and suggestions for future research.

BACKGROUND

Aiken (1971), in a review of studies of verbal factors in mathematical learning, reports that researchers have long recognized the effects of language on mathematical performance. Studies indicate that there is a positive correlation between reading ability and scores on tests of problem solving in arithmetic, but most agree that the exact relationship between language factors and mathematical achievement is not clear. Aiken (1971) summarizes the results of studies of student-teacher verbal interaction in mathematics classes that show that the language used by the teacher may have an effect on students' computational ability. The language used in mathematical materials has also been reviewed. Hargis (1977) contends that all mathematical ideas are embedded in definite language statements, with clauses signaling relationships and nouns signaling ideas. He reports that while reading materials that match the child's language have been developed, the vocabulary of mathematics texts often fails to match the child's vocabulary.

Calhoun and Redmond (1974) analyze the key qualities of mathematical materials, in particular, conciseness, abstractness, and complex relationships. They present the following example: "When a mixed number is subtracted from a whole number, what number must you always borrow in the minuend?" (p. 806). Of the nineteen words in this sentence, eight have definite mathematical meanings that must be understood before one can understand the sentence. They also point out that many mathematical terms have different meanings in ordinary use; "set" and "order," for example, are used conventionally in sentences like "Set the table" and "This is an order." Children are often confused by such dual meanings, and this is especially true of children who are working in a second language. One may conclude from the preceding studies that for a student to master mathematical concepts, he or she must first master the language of the concepts.

Another area that bears on the variables under study is the relationship between bilingualism and thinking. The major issue is whether bilingualism helps, hinders, or has no effect on cognitive ability. It is certainly not easy to answer this question. Most studies involving children who became bilingual at an early age rely on data from individual children whose backgrounds and upbringings are very unusual. Probably the best large-scale studies of children who became bilingual to some extent during the early school years are those carried out by Lambert and his coworkers in Canada (Lambert and Rawlings, 1969; Lambert, Just, and Segalowitz, 1970). The results of these studies suggest some cognitive and affective advantages in early bilingualism, at least when both languages share the same level of prestige. It should be noted, however, that it is not always easy to compare the results of different studies in this area, since the nature and degree of bilingualism vary widely and researchers use a variety of criteria for bilingualism, ranging from the ability to produce complete and meaningful utterances in two languages (Haugen, 1953) to the possession of native control in two languages (De Avila and Duncan, 1975).

Peal and Lambert (1962), in a study dealing with intellectual development and school achievement, state:

> The picture that emerges of the French/English bilingual in Montreal is that of a youngster whose wider experiences in two cultures have given him advantages which a monolingual does not enjoy. Intellectually, his experience with two language systems seems to have left him with a mental flexibility, a superiority in concept formation, and a more diversified set of mental abilities, in the sense that the patterns of abilities developed by bilinguals were more heterogeneous. . . . In contrast, the monolingual appears to have a more unitary structure of intelligence which he must use for all types of intellectual tasks. (p. 20)

Other studies also suggest cognitive and affective advantages in early bilingualism. Given the complex nature of bilingualism, however, additional research efforts are needed to further clarify and develop a theoretical framework in this area.

Finally, we should consider the development of natural numbers. Three major theories explain this development. The first is based on the research of Piaget, which offers a number of descriptions of children's acquisition of mathematical concepts. Piaget states that children from five and a half to seven years of age are able to solve problems involving serial correspondence by using a perceptual method that involves trial and error. At around age seven, the child begins to use intellectual procedures to solve the problem. At this age, the student considers the whole arrangement to be seriated rather than considering small groups within the collection. This has implications for the development of the idea of ordinal number as it relates to cardinal number: To determine how many objects are in a collection, the objects have somehow to be ordered so that they are counted only once. Piaget (1956) states that it is not until around six or seven years of age that the child has a complete understanding of the relationship between ordinality and cardinality. He has also cautioned that it is a mistake to suppose that children acquire the notion of number and other mathematical concepts just from teaching; rather, to a remarkable degree, they develop these for themselves, independently and spontaneously. However, children must grasp the principle of conservation of quantity before they can develop the concept of number.

The Peano–Von Neumann theory gives an alternative explanation of the development of the concept of ordinal number. Beginning with the primitive numeral zero, the individual may add "one" any number of times, and all the natural numbers can be developed by this series of operations. This theory suggests that children develop their concept of numbers sequentially, starting with the understanding of small numbers and gradually working up to larger ones. The Russell-Frege theory, on the other hand, assumes that a number has classes such that any two elements of a set are similar to each other and no elements outside the set are similar to any inside the set. Obviously, this process produces a set of classes representing each number in the number system (Brainerd, 1973).

Each of these theories predicts that children will derive their understanding of the natural number system through a series of sequentially developed concepts. Research data on the acquisition of number concepts are extensive and sometimes contradictory. The complexity of the development of the concept of number is illustrated by Siegel (1971a, 1971b), who found that children's ability to recognize ordinal position develops later than the equivalence attribute of conservation. This finding was reversed by D'Mello and Willemsen (1969), who found that children were able to count the number of objects with another set having the same number of objects. Thus, the ordering of the acquisition of numerical skills is by no means well established.

An additional report helps to illustrate the problems children can have learning number concepts, especially when working in a second language. Ginsberg (1977), working from the case studies of several children and from some of the older literature on counting, has made several general statements about the way in which children learn the sequence of counting. He begins by suggesting that the names of the numbers from one through nineteen are basically memorized. This is a laborious, time-consuming task that occupies many of the child's preschool years, and the child will have many frustrating experiences attempting to ascertain what is meant by the adult who says, "Count these!" or "Here are three cookies." Some time will elapse before the child is able to count items or name the numbers in order. Once the child has learned to count through nineteen, however, Ginsberg hypothesizes that subsequent abilities are based upon the learning of specific rules. He believes that children do not memorize the order of numerals over nineteen; instead, they obtain several rules that can be used in working them out. As evidence, he observes that a child will count from twenty-one to twenty-nine and ask; "What comes next?" He will then count from thirty-one to thirty-nine and again ask, "What comes next?" According to Ginsberg, this demonstrates that the child is memorizing a general pattern or rule for constructing large numbers, although he still needs to memorize the order of the numerals representing multiples of ten.

Despite the lack of agreement about the order in which the basic numerical skills emerge, there is little doubt that such skills must be acquired before an understanding of the decimal system can take place. Central to understanding the nature of the decimal number system is an understanding of the nature of symbolic substitution systems. Before algorithms for the operations may be learned, the child must understand the relationship between a number, its numerical symbol, the place value system, and the rules for representing multiple place numbers.

The concept of place value involves symbolic substitution. That is, given a number system with base n and working from right to left, each place represents n^0 units, n^1 units, n^2 units, and so on. One area of research into the development of numeration systems studies numeration through the use of other number base systems. Most of the studies in this area report no significant difference in performance between groups given instruction in base ten and those given instruction in other bases (Jackson, Robinson, and Dale, 1976; Lerch, 1963; McCormick, 1965), though they do point out the usefulness of analog numeration systems in teaching children rules for grouping that are similar to those of the base ten numeration system.

It appears therefore that readiness studies must be made for mathematical concepts themselves. At what age can a child understand and work with number sentences? At what age can a child understand and work with a number sentence that is missing an addend? Questions such as these are not immediately answerable from the existing literature on the development of number concepts in young children. We must expand our understanding of children's development of number and numeration concepts, and this is particularly important in cases where the language of instruction is not the student's native language, since very little research has been done in the area of bilingual instruction in mathematics.

RESEARCH AND METHODOLOGY

The research reported here attempted to provide answers to the following questions:

1. Are number and numeration concepts presented to Hispanic children before they are developmentally prepared for those concepts?
2. What language should be used in teaching mathematical concepts to students whose native language is not English?

The study focused on Hispanic primary school students in three linguistic groups: Spanish monolingual, English-Spanish bilingual, and English monolingual. Using a descriptive-analytical approach, the pupils' development of number and numeration concepts was followed over a two-year perioa that covereJ the early stages of their involvement with formal instruction in arithmetic. By identifying students' problems in this area, the study attempted to gain a clearer picture of Hispanic children's acquisition of concepts and to provide some insights into the effects on them of the use of English in mathematical instruction.

Sample

During the first year of the study, twenty-five students, assessed at various levels of limited English proficiency, in a first-grade classroom at a selected public elementary school (School A) were chosen as participants. The school, in Dade County, Florida, was selected because of its predominantly Hispanic population. During the second year, the majority of the original students were followed into the second-grade year, and another twenty-five first-grade students were included in the sample. This group (from School B, also predominantly Hispanic) was a higher-achieving group than the first year's sample. The first-year group was chosen expressly to examine the problems children with limited English proficiency encounter in learning mathematics. The second-year group was chosen to explore the successes of Hispanic children, both bilinguals and English monolinguals, and the relationship of language to the learning of number and numeration concepts. The two groups revealed the broad spectrum of performance in mathematics found among Hispanic children.

The teachers at both schools were female and had the same number of years of experience. Both were competent professionals and were highly rated in professional activities by their principals. They were both monolingual English-speakers.

Instrumentation

Various achievement, Piagetian, and language tests were administered to the children over the two years of the study. Data were collected from student performance in the following tests.

1. Metropolitan Readiness Test: The MRT (Level II, Form P) was administered by the researchers to students at the beginning of their first-grade year to assess their level of development in prereading and premathematical skills.
2. Dade County Systems Mathematics Program Tests. Teachers administered a diagnostic/prescriptive program designed to guide instruction and verify children's success with number and numeration objectives.

3. Piaget tasks.[1] Tests developed by Piaget were used during the first-grade year to establish the children's cognitive development at the pre-operational or operational level. Four tasks involved the conservation of length, area, volume, and mass; in addition, the students performed class inclusion and classification tasks. All six of the Piaget tests were given in one sitting, which lasted from twenty-five to thirty minutes. Each child was tested individually.

4. Language assessment. The Language Assessment Scales (De Avila and Duncan, 1975) was administered in order to assess the level of students' language skills and classify them as Spanish monolingual, bilingual, or English monolingual.

5. Language development tests. The language development of first graders was assessed, focusing on two general areas: their knowledge and use of common language structures, especially those that might be used in a mathematical situation or a mathematics class, and their knowledge of the terms of mathematics, especially those used in the curriculum for the primary grades. The language-structure tests assessed the students' use of conditional and passive sentences and relativization in sentences, knowledge of mass and count nouns, and ability to follow sequential order and conceptualize the term "largest." Bilingual children were tested in both Spanish and English. Spanish monolingual children were tested in Spanish only.

Procedures

The major portion of the research involved visits to the classrooms selected for inclusion in the study. A case-study approach was followed for the purpose of making developmental inferences. In addition to the information yielded by assessment instruments, data were collected by observing children's interaction in the classroom during group and individual lessons. The investigators recorded the behavior of students and teachers as topics in number, numeration, and basic mathematical operations were presented in the class, focusing on the teacher's manner and language and the students' understanding of the material. Students were periodically tutored in problem areas and interviewed in order to obtain a description of the thinking patterns used in learning number and numeration concepts. Finally, the children's ideas, vocabulary, and use of mathematical concepts were recorded.

---

[1]The Piaget tasks and the language development tests (item 5) were administered by Ziva Peleg, associate professor of education at the University of Miami, who was a consultant and contributor to the research project.

RESULTS

The data were grouped by the children's grade and age level within each grade so that we could analyze their learning of number and numeration on a developmental basis. The children were divided according to the levels stated in table 1.

In terms of cognitive development, 9 percent of the "young" first graders were classified as being at the concrete operations stage; 31 percent of the older students were found to be at this stage. For the second grade group a similar trend was found: 75 percent of the older students were at the concrete operations stage, and 25 percent of the younger students.

Table 2 presents the results of our testing of the students' mastery of number and numeration concepts. The number of students reported reflect participant dropout during the study. As can be seen in the table, the performance of both groups was about the same for number concepts, but the older students tended to outperform younger ones on the numeration test.

A comparison of age groups yielded a mixture of results, some expected, others not. As one would expect, the percentage of children at the concrete operations stage increased with the age of the students, both within a single grade and between the two grades. The results presented in table 2 show no difference between the age groups in the understanding of number concepts. For numeration, the older group outperformed the younger group in both grades.

The results of the language development tests are given in table 3. It is apparent that the language skills of these first-grade children were not totally developed and that some language structures caused them difficulty. Many of the difficult language structures were used in mathematics instruction or involved concepts that were part of the mathematics curriculum. For example, the inability to differentiate between the physical and numerical uses of the word "biggest" could easily cause difficulties in the learning of number concepts.

The students' performances on the Language Assessment Scales (De Avila

Table 1:   Grade- and Age-Level Divisions

Grade	School	Minimum age[a]	Maximum age
First grade	School A (young)	6 years 6 months	6 years 9 months
	School B (old)	7 years 3 months	7 years 6 months
Second grade	School A (young)	7 years 6 months	7 years 9 months
	School B (old)	8 years 3 months	8 years 6 months

[a]Ages were computed from the student's birthdate to 1 June 1979, the date on which the project ended.

Table 2: Summary of Mastery Scores for Number and Numeration

	GRADE 1		GRADE 2	
SKILL AREA	*Young*	*Old*	*Young*	*Old*
	$N = 11$	$N = 13$	$N = 11$	$N = 9$
Number	11(100%)[a]	12(92%)	10(91%)	8(88%)
Numeration	7(64%)	11(85%)	6(55%)	8(88%)

[a]Figures indicate the number and percentage of students showing mastery of the skill. Mastery was defined as answering 75 percent of the questions correctly.

and Duncan, 1975) were analyzed, and monolingual (English or Spanish) and bilingual groups were compared on cognitive development and degree of mastery of number and numeration concepts. A chi-square computation indicated no differences among the three groups in the proportion of children assigned to the preoperational and operational stages of cognitive development. The

Table 3: Average Scores on Ten Language Tests
(N = 23)

Tests	Maximum possible score	Mean score achieved	Percentage of possible score achieved by sample
Biggest number task	2.00	.74	37
Use of "before"	2.00	1.48	74
Use of "after"	2.00	.96	48
Passive sentence: Inanimate agent Animate object	3.00	2.04	68
Passive sentence: Animate agent Inanimate object	3.00	2.17	72
Passive sentence: Animate agent Animate object	4.00	2.66	67
Passive sentence: Inanimate agent Inanimate object	2.00	1.48	74
Relativization	4.00	2.30	58
Use of mass/count nouns[a]	2.00	.83	42
Use of mass/count nouns[b]	2.00	1.04	52

[a]Use of nouns in answers to questions
[b]Use of nouns in phrasing questions

Dade County Systems Mathematics Program Tests revealed a larger percentage of bilingual students showing mastery of number (100 percent) and numeration (80 percent) than Spanish or English monolinguals. Of the three, the Spanish monolingual group had the smallest number of students mastering number and numeration concepts (75 and 38 percent respectively). This result was expected, since students were instructed in English, and it points to a possible need for instruction in Spanish for students in this language category.

DISCUSSION OF RESULTS

The Development of the Concept of Number

The majority of the participating first-grade students were found to be at the preoperational or transitional stage of cognitive development, even though they were tested toward the end of the school year, as many were approaching their seventh birthday. Of the children tested at School B, 80 percent were functioning at this level. By definition a preoperational child has a narrow range of operations available to him or her. Such skills as reversing and associativity, for example, are not in the preoperational child's repertoire.

As would be expected of preoperational children, many of those tested had difficulty with the conservation tasks. The most difficult of all was the one involving conservation of length. At first glance this task would not appear to be as important to the study of number as conservation of amount, but one tool for teaching the concept of number is the number line, and it could be argued that use of the number line depends upon a child's ability to conserve length. The child must relate the two parts of an addition equation with the total as they are pictured on the number line. Since conservation of length was the last of the conservation skills to develop, the use of the number line as an explanatory device in first grade may be somewhat premature.

One fact particularly impressed the researchers. Some of the Hispanic students' problems with number concepts at the beginning of the year were clearly language-related. That is, the source of their difficulty was the inability to discriminate among the English terms "fewest," "least," "greatest," "greater than," "less than." Once the concepts were presented in Spanish and a relationship was established between the English and Spanish labels, however, the students were able to demonstrate progress in the mastery of these relationships.

For a small group of Spanish monolingual students, difficulties in learning concepts related to number were found to have causes other than language. Even when instruction and classroom activities were carried out in Spanish, these children were unable to do the exercises and problems. The concepts were:

1. Identification of sets with the fewest/least/greatest number of elements
2. Use of "less than" or "greater than" to describe order relations between pairs
3. Identification of sets having one more (or one less) element than another set (no set had more than ten elements)

These students could count the elements in a set but were unable to indicate, to the teacher or the researchers, the relationship between two sets. The skill of counting had no relationship to the comparison of sets or the description of numerical relationships. All of these children were assessed as preoperational; they appeared to follow the classic description of the preoperational child and his or her mathematical abilities.

For the majority of Hispanic students, the concept of cardinal number did not pose a serious problem; 75 percent displayed mastery of the concept, even though mathematical instruction was provided in English, a language in which some students were not proficient. It can be hypothesized that this concept is not as language-dependent as others. The students' success may also be due to the fact that the instruction was basically manipulative. The students worked with blocks and other objects in an effort to visualize the idea of set equality—the one-to-one correspondence of elements in two sets—or set inequality. Such an approach is relatively language-free, as compared to instruction on a topic like numeration. Further evidence of the children's ability appeared in the results of a criterion reference test administered at the end of the project. The mean scores for this section of the test were quite high, for both first and second graders. Mastery was defined as the ability to answer 75 percent of the test items correctly, and 100 percent of the first graders and 91 percent of the second graders achieved this level. In addition, when the students were classified in Piagetian terms, 100 percent of those classified as concrete operational or transitional mastered the skills in the number section of the criterion reference test, and 81 percent of those classified as preoperational did so.

The lack of problems in the area of number may be due to the fact that number concepts are taught at the kindergarten level, and so the majority of first-grade children have had some previous exposure to them. Moreover, interviews revealed that many of the children obtained a good background in number skills at home. When students had difficulty, their problems appeared to be the result of instruction that was given too soon. All children showing failure on number concepts had been rated as preoperational; when instructed, all responded with typical preoperational behavior, when failing to generalize the ideas taught to them.

The Development of the Concept of Numeration

As with number, the topics included under numeration caused few difficulties for students as long as the numerals used in the exercises were kept small. The larger the numeral used, the more likely it was to cause difficulty. The results of all the tests indicated that children had more problems with numerals over ten than with numerals under ten. But by the end of the first-grade year, and despite some language problems, most students displayed mastery of numeration concepts.

However, a problem surfaced in one of the earliest numeration activities introduced. Many children had memorized the numbers from one to ten before they came to school. In an effort to add meaning to the memorized terms, children were given number/numeral matching exercises, order arrangement exercises (of the type "two is one more than one," "three is one more than two," "four is one more than three," etc.), and finally exercises dealing with the numeral coming "before" or "after" a given numeral ("What numeral comes before 6?" "What numeral comes after 9?"). Exercises of this last type, dependent upon the use of "before" and "after," caused a great deal of difficulty in the first-grade classrooms, especially those in which the majority of students were Spanish monolinguals.

Language testing made it evident that not all children were capable of dealing with activities that involved the use of the terms "before" and "after." Children, especially children working in a second language, may not be fully aware of the meanings of the terms and the related language structures. This problem is a language-development problem; mathematical concepts should not be presented if the linguistic ability to deal with them has not developed.

Our data suggest that the teaching of numeration relies heavily upon language. Spanish monolingual students either did not acquire certain concepts or did not acquire the English vocabulary to show mastery of them. This is an area where teaching in the native language of the student might be helpful.

CONCLUSION

The primary purpose of the study reported in this paper was to examine the manner in which first- and second-grade Hispanic students acquired number and numeration concepts. Two research questions guided the investigators. The first one dealt with the presentation of these concepts in relation to the cognitive development of the student. The second focused on the language of instruction.

The first question considers the implications of the findings of developmental psychology for the teaching of mathematics. While the mathematics curriculum in the primary grades is mathematically sound, it may not be psychologically sound. Should some of the concepts presented in the first-grade mathematics curriculum be delayed until the second grade? We found that many students had difficulty with "large numbers." Some first-grade children were still functioning at the preoperational or transitional stages for all mathematical concepts, and there is evidence in the literature that a child can be at the concrete operational stage when working with smaller numerals and yet at the preoperational stage with large numerals. This study supports that idea; children often performed a task successfully with small numerals and yet seemed overwhelmed by the same task when additional elements were placed in the set.

In addition, a task involving conservation of place value indicated that many children could not successfully relate grouped and ungrouped bundles of ten; consequently, teaching them the place value system for larger numerals seems questionable. Teachers also identified many numeration objectives dealing with expanded notation as difficult for their students. The presentation of these objectives would be delayed if the children were introduced to larger numerals in the second grade, rather than the first.

In the area of language, the study focused on two types of students: the non-English-proficient (Spanish monolingual) or limited-English-proficient student and the bilingual student (proficient in both languages). The literature reports that limited-English-proficient students will most easily acquire the basic concepts presented in the school curriculum if those concepts are taught in the students' native language. This approach would eliminate the burden of having to translate from an unfamiliar language to the native language at the time the student is trying to understand a new concept. Our results support the extension of this approach to mathematical instruction. The study indicates that Spanish monolingual and limited-English-proficient students had not mastered number and numeration concepts as well as bilingual and English monolingual students in our Hispanic sample. One obvious explanation for their poor performance is the fact that instruction was carried out completely in English, a language unfamiliar to them. Teachers may, in addition, have placed too much emphasis on verbal explanations of those concepts.

Language testing in English revealed that all students had some difficulty with the various verbal structures used in the tests. Some of the linguistic features tested involved concepts that were part of the mathematics curriculum (the use of "biggest" and mass versus count nouns), while others involved language structures used in the teaching of mathematics ("before" and "after," and passive constructions). Test results indicated that at least some members of every group had difficulties with every structure tested. Thus, the first-grade teacher cannot assume that all children will be interpreting his or her comments in the manner desired. The inability to differentiate between the two uses of the term "biggest" could easily cause difficulties in the classroom. The teacher who asks the children to name the largest numeral and then carelessly draws two numerals on the blackboard so that one is physically larger than the other has just caused a problem for well over half the children in a first-grade classroom.

The fact that the use of "before" and "after" had not been completely mastered, especially when the order of the actions described did not correspond to the order of the elements in the sentence, may present corresponding difficulties in the mathematics classroom. Teachers are prone to make such statements as "After you have written the one's figure in your answer, carry the ten's figure to the next column." A simple reversal of this statement—"Carry the ten's figure to the next column after you have written the one's figure in your answer"—may confuse children, and they may enter a figure in the wrong position. It is obvious that in mathematics changing the order of the actions often changes the result of the actions. The primary-grade teacher must be careful not to use constructions that the child has not mastered. The greater problems of Hispanic students in this area may well stem from unfamiliarity with the English language.

A greater number of students understood passive constructions when the sentences involved an animate agent and an inanimate object: (for example, "The boy was hit by the car") than when they involved an inanimate agent and an animate object ("The car was hit by the boy"). These results indicate that children are still relying on semantic cues at this age, and sentences that are reversible in nature may cause difficulties for the students when no semantic cues are given.

Mistakes in both relativization and passive sentences can cause confusion in mathematics class. Such sentences as "Three is subtracted from five" and "Eight is divided by three" are both passives of the reversible type that gave children the greatest amount of difficulty. The division by partition sometimes used in classroom activities dealing with sets is frequently phrased in the passive form ("Fifteen pieces of candy are divided equally among three children"). It is easy to slip into relativization when speaking orally, and teachers often insert dependent clauses between the actor and the action. Every time this is done, many children in a first-grade classroom become lost.

Finally, children did poorly on the use of mass and count nouns. Questions like "How many" and "How much" are often used in word problems, and children's difficulties with such problems may stem from unfamiliarity with the concepts or language associated with mass and count nouns.

These findings pose two general questions for future research:

1. What is the relationship between teachers' language patterns and children's mathematical achievement?

2. Are there specific language structures used in the teaching of mathematics that pose difficulties for students?

Finally, the literature indicates that bilinguals' wider experience in two cultures and languages gives them advantages that monolingual students do not enjoy. Peal and Lambert (1962), in the passage quoted above, cite the bilingual's "mental flexibility, . . . superiority in concept formation, and more diversified set of mental abilities" (p. 20). The present study's demonstration that bilingual Hispanic students outperformed Spanish monolinguals and Hispanic English monolinguals in the mastery of all number and numeration concepts supports Peal and Lambert's conclusion.

REFERENCES

Aiken, L. Language factors in learning mathematics. *Review of Educational Research,* 1971, *42,* 359–385.

Brainerd, C. J. Mathematical and behavioral foundations of number. *Journal of General Psychology,* 1973, *88,* 221–281.

Calhoun, C., and Redmond, L. A. Are you teaching kids to read mathematics? *Reading Teacher,* 1974, *27,* 804–808.

D'Mello, S., and Willemsen, E. The development of the number concept: a scalogram analysis. *Child Development,* 1969, *40,* 681–688.

De Avila, E., and Duncan, S. *Language assessment scale.* Palo Alto: Linguametrics, 1975.

Ginsberg, H. *Children's arithmetic: the learning process.* New York: Van Nostrand, 1977.

Hargis, C. H., and Knight, L. N. Math language ability: its relationship to reading in math. *Language Arts,* 1977, *54,* 423–428.

Haugen, E. *The Norwegian language in America: a study in bilingual behavior.* Philadelphia: University of Pennsylvania Press, 1953.

Jackson, N., Robinson, H. B., and Dale, P. *Cognitive development in young children: a report for teachers.* Washington, D.C.: National Institute of Education, 1976.

Lambert, W., Just, M., and Segalowitz, N. Some cognitive consequences of following the curricula of the early school grades in a foreign language. In J. Alatis (Ed.), *Monograph series in languages and linguistics.* Washington, D.C.: Georgetown University Press, 1970, pp. 229–262.

Lambert, W., and Rawlings, C. Bilingual processing cf mixed-language associative networks. *Journal of Verbal Learning and Verbal Behavior,* 1969, *8,* 604–609.

Lerch, H. H. Fourth-grade pupils study a number system with base five. *Journal of Educational Research,* 1963, *57,* 59–61.

McCormick, R. L. A comparative study of two methods of teaching a decimal system of numeration. Doctoral dissertation, Purdue University, 1965.

Peal, E., and Lambert, W. The relation of bilingualism to intelligence. *Psychological Monographs,* 1962, *76.*

Piaget, J. *The child's conception of number.* New York: W. W. Norton, 1956.
Siegel, L. S. The development of the understanding of certain number concepts. *Developmental Psychology,* 1971a, *5,* 361–363.
Siegel, L. S. The sequence of development of certain number concepts in preschool children. *Developmental Psychology,* 1971b, *5,* 357–361.

11 | Bilingual Reading in the Primary Grades: Some Questions About Questionable Views and Practices

ROSALINDA B. BARRERA
New Mexico State University

In many school bilingual programs in the southwestern United States, the teaching of reading is dominated by instructional beliefs and practices that may well be counterproductive to children's reading-language development. Consider the following comments by primary-grade teachers of Spanish-English bilingual education.

> Some of the children have not read much in their Spanish books so far this year; they're still learning their letters and sounds.

> I can't transfer him to English reading yet—his English score on the _____ [language proficiency] test is still too low.

> She really shouldn't be moved to a higher-level English book because she makes a lot of reading errors. . . . she doesn't pronounce all the words correctly.

Modern knowledge of children's language and learning exposes the considerable shortcomings in pedagogical thought and action reflected in the preceding statements: the simplistic strategy for initial reading instruction, the rigid guideline for determining introduction to second-language reading, and the unsophisticated assessment of nonnative oral reading performance. One has only to observe readers inside and outside of the classroom to confirm the unproductive outcome of these practices and views. Such instructional inclinations only serve to confuse what reading is and how it might be more effectively taught; unfortunately, they are common to many reading programs in

This paper was supported by a postdoctoral fellowship with the NIE-NMSU Project on Minorities and Women's Research, which was funded by the National Institute of Education (NIE), Department of Health, Education and Welfare (Grant No. NIE-G-79-0012, Project No. 8-1096). The opinions expressed herein do not necessarily reflect the position or policy of the NIE, and no official endorsement by the NIE should be inferred. Special thanks are extended to Lily Chu, project director at New Mexico State University, for her assistance and support.

164

bilingual education and are going unexamined by the majority of practitioners in the field.

This paper has been written to provide a critical, questioning look at various aspects of current reading pedagogy in Spanish-English bilingual programs. Specifically, I wish to scrutinize a number of pedagogical notions that have enjoyed considerable credibility and longevity in bilingual classrooms,[1] but that appear on closer examination to be of doubtful value to children's reading-language learning. These prevailing but misguided notions may, in effect, be serving only as stumbling blocks and barriers to more coherent, effective reading instruction for Spanish-English bilingual children. The misconceptions about the reading process and reading instruction that they embody are not unique to the bilingual classroom, but their manifestation there has not yet been subjected to an extensive examination. My intention is not to criticize teachers and schools but rather to urge a questioning attitude on their part about certain aspects of bilingual reading pedagogy. Clearly, we cannot afford to be complacent about the quality of reading programming in bilingual education or to allow dysfunctional or unproductive instructional features to go unchallenged. The observations central to this discussion are drawn from work with Spanish-English programs in the Southwest during the past decade of federally supported bilingual schooling, although I believe much of the commentary is applicable to the teaching of reading in other situations: that is, in bilingual reading programs employing other minority languages and in mainstream, English-only reading programs serving bilingual students.

The following widespread notions about reading-language teaching and learning in Spanish-English bilingual education demand immediate re-examination and re-evaluation by all of us who are committed to ensuring reading success for language-minority children:

1. Phonics is the best approach for teaching initial reading in Spanish.
2. First-language reading and second-language reading are disparate processes.
3. Second-language reading development is entirely dependent on oral language development.
4. Language-proficiency scores can predict "readiness" for second-language reading.
5. Language-based differences in second-language reading are reading problems to be eradicated.

---

[1]These classrooms represent programs along the whole spectrum of bilingual education approaches, from "native-literacy-first" models to "dual-language" models that utilize Spanish and English concurrently in initial reading instruction. Most of these programs, however, are transitional in nature, using the native language only until students achieve English proficiency.

6. The language arts are separate and mutually exclusive categories of instruction.

In no way is the discussion that follows intended to be exhaustive of these pedagogical beliefs or inclusive of all instructional directions in Spanish-English bilingual reading that might merit a more critical inspection. In fact, the notions treated in this chapter are not only closely intertwined and difficult to examine in isolation from one another, but also closely related to various other beliefs and practices in bilingual reading that we might do well to explore and analyze in our continuing efforts to improve reading instruction.

PHONICS HEGEMONY IN SPANISH READING

The teaching of grapheme-phoneme (letter-sound) relationships and synthetic sounding-blending procedures forms the cornerstone of many kindergarten and first-grade native-language reading programs in Spanish-English bilingual education today. In some schools the teaching of "las vocales y las consonantes" and their sounds, or of various syllables and sounds, is thought to be the one and only way to introduce children to reading in Spanish. So intense is the focus on phonics in Spanish reading methodology that in some bilingual education circles, any suggestion that Spanish reading be taught through another approach is akin to educational heresy. Nonetheless, despite its extensive popularity and reputed efficacy, this orientation leaves much to be desired.

Central to a Spanish phonics orientation is the belief that reading is primarily a simple, linear act in which letters are converted into sounds, sounds are fused or blended into words, and the spoken language is then linked to meaning. This lockstep representation of the reading process is related to two other key assumptions: (1) consistency or regularity in the relationship between the phonemes and graphemes of a language greatly facilitates the process of learning to read that language, and (2) the reading process differs across alphabetic languages as a result of differences in the phoneme-grapheme correspondence of the languages. From these assumptions are derived the various circuitous defenses of the emphasis on phonics in beginning Spanish reading: that phonics is ideally suited to Spanish reading because the language exhibits a relatively high phoneme-grapheme correspondence (Herbert, 1971; Michel, 1977); that it is easy to learn to read in Spanish because the reader has only to associate letters and sounds that match closely (González, 1980; Thonis, 1976); and that reading in Spanish is different from reading in English—that is, much easier—because of the greater regularity of the Spanish sound-letter system (Lado, Hansen, and D'Emilio, 1980; U.S. Commission on Civil Rights, 1975). At times, it is even asserted that because of its sound-letter consistency, Spanish reading does not engender learning difficulties (Andersson and Boyer, 1970; Michel, 1977).

This view of initial reading instruction in Spanish considers only the orthographic aspects of language, the spelling system, at the expense of other, more important considerations. In the first place, it tends to slight the importance of meaning or understanding in reading, giving first place instead to the code and its mastery by the learner. Second, this view encourages the presentation of reading to the child as a language-parts phenomenon, a presentation inconsistent with the contextualized, holistic, and connected forms in which the young child is likely to first encounter written language naturally. Third, it ignores the potentially powerful influence of such factors in reading as the learner's language knowledge and conceptual background. Finally, a Spanish phonics perspective fails to consider the possibility of universals in the reading process, basic commonalities that may transcend surface-level orthographic differences in languages.

The above-mentioned limitations of a Spanish phonics orientation are demonstrated by contemporary research into the reading behavior of native Spanish-speaking children. Ferreiro (1978, 1980) and Ferreiro and Teberosky (1979, 1981), in studies of three- to six-year-old Mexican children of varying socioeconomic backgrounds, provide intensive longitudinal data that reveal that children go through a number of modes of interpreting written language before arriving at final modes of interpretation compatible with the structure of the alphabetic system, despite the regularity of phoneme-grapheme relationships in Spanish. These findings clearly challenge the current supposition that children's ability to deal with phonic information is well established by the time they enter kindergarten or first grade. Ferreiro and Teberosky (1981) note that many young learners entering school have come to know intuitively that written language has meaning but cannot make sense of written language when it is presented to them as isolated letters and sounds. Instead of providing children with such "meaning-less" training, these researchers recommend that educators create classroom environments and conditions that will allow children to discover for themselves the important relationships between spoken and written language.

Evidence that Spanish reading is not a serial operation of identifying words letter by letter or syllable by syllable is provided by a series of recent investigations of the oral reading performance of native Spanish-speaking Mexican American children in the primary grades (Barrera, 1978; Hudelson-Lopez, 1975; Silva, 1979). These studies show that young readers of Spanish are able to use their stored thoughts and language knowledge along with the written context to identify unknown words and reconstruct the meaning of the text. As they read Spanish, young native Spanish-speakers, like other children reading their native languages, apply strategies that show them to be not merely engaged in creating spoken representations of print, but actively involved in a highly selective, multifaceted, and complex thinking process.

Further evidence to challenge a phonics-dominant or phonics-only route can be found readily in current bilingual classrooms: the numerous kindergarten and first-grade children in phonics-oriented Spanish reading programs who do not demonstrate any significant degree of fluency in Spanish reading, almost in flagrant disregard of their programs' central tenets. Such readers, whose difficulties often extend beyond the first grade, are not exceptional;[2] they constitute a sizable proportion of average pupils in average classrooms in various localities. These are children who are unable to "master" the Spanish symbol-sound sequences mandated by their school reading programs or who read in painstaking fashion, letter by letter, word by word, fixated on the identification of words and only vaguely concerned with the construction of meaning.

For these children, learning to read in Spanish through phonics is not the easy task it is reputed to be. Unfortunately, there is a tendency to overlook these less-than-successful cases, however numerous and persistent they may be, and for educators to continue to defend phonics as an efficacious and effortless way to learn to read in Spanish. Not surprisingly, it is frequently the learner or even the teacher who is blamed for the lackluster outcome of phonics instruction. After all, other children apparently "pick up" Spanish phonics without any discernible difficulty or long-term ill effect on their reading performance. But perhaps the successes should be explained away instead of the failures. Other researchers (Goodman, Goodman and Flores, 1979; Roser and Jensen, 1978), have noted that children who seem to learn to read effortlessly in phonics programs appear to be those with stronger reading roots, who are well on their way to reading success upon their entry to formal schooling. For children with minimal whole-language reading experiences, phonics training may be an unfamiliar, meaningless, and difficult activity. Thus, it may be that Spanish phonics is acquired best by children who already know a lot about reading or even already know how to read and understood least by children with limited exposure to natural, connected reading experiences.

Above all, the point to be made here is that Spanish phonics training does not guarantee simple and instant literacy for all children. Some children will become proficient readers of Spanish while enrolled in phonics-oriented programs; others will not. It seems imperative, therefore, that teachers in bilingual education make phonics teaching only one dimension of several in Spanish reading instruction. Knowledge of letter-sound relationships is only one of the cueing systems that should be available to the reader as she or he goes about identifying words to get at meaning. More than likely, then, the most effective and efficient reader, of either Spanish or English, will be the one who knows the various cueing systems available for word identification and knows how and

---

[2]It cannot be said, for example, that the real problem is one of inaccurate language assessment: that is, that the children's Spanish proficiency was overestimated and, therefore, they do not belong in a Spanish reading class at all.

when to use them, singly or in combination (Goodman and Burke, 1973; Southwest Educational Development Laboratory, 1980). It follows that in order to begin to address relevantly the native-language reading needs of Spanish-speaking children, we must expand beginning Spanish reading instruction to include extended, whole-language reading experiences that are meaningful and purposeful to young readers; we must reaffirm the importance of comprehension in Spanish reading; and we must provide learners with a balanced approach to word identification in place of the one-sided approach common today.

FROM FIRST-LANGUAGE READING TO SECOND-LANGUAGE READING

The assumption that English reading and Spanish reading are different processes and must, therefore, be taught differently is a common one in Spanish-English bilingual education. I frequently come across teachers in bilingual classrooms who hold the mistaken notion that the young reader of Spanish confronts a radically different task when she or he begins reading in English. Some concomitants of this line of thinking are the belief that exposure to English reading while the child is learning initially to read in Spanish will somehow "interfere" with native-language reading acquisition and the belief that some level of skill or proficiency in reading Spanish is required before instruction in reading English can begin. The latter concern is reflected in some schools' attempt to define optimum achievement levels in Spanish reading as prerequisites for the start of second-language reading. The former is detectable in program policies, sometimes unexpressed, that discourage any English reading activities during a so-called native-language reading phase. However, the reading behavior of children in bilingual classrooms does not uniformly support the general apprehension that reading in English at a time when first-language reading is beginning to unfold must inevitably set back or retard first-language reading growth. In addition, school efforts to keep the reading strands in the two languages separate and sequential in time may actually conflict with children's reading behavior.

Fillmore (1980) emphasizes that once language-minority children (bilingual as well as non-English-speaking) enter school, they encounter potent social forces that induce English learning in both monolingual and bilingual programs. It is a rare child who can resist these forces and not begin to learn English. I would add another dimension to Fillmore's observations: This powerful impetus toward learning English is not restricted to the oral form of the language; in many children it extends to the written form as well. In our print-dominated society, children participating in school Spanish-English bilingual programs, regardless of the extent of Spanish in their lives, also have significant and frequent encounters with written English, inside and outside school. It would be almost impossible, and contrary to young children's powerful learning drives, for them not to take notice of and want to learn about the highly visible written English that is part of their environment. In fact, language-minority children are driven quite naturally toward learning about written English.

During my work in schools, I have seen bilingual children responding to written language in their dual-language environments in a number of exciting ways. To begin with, some children prior to entering school have already begun to explore the ubiquitous forms of written English in their communities—signs, logos, labels, billboards, television—and can identify some English print. Largely as a result of these highly contextualized encounters with written English, children in "native-literacy-first" bilingual programs, even in kindergarten, frequently ask to read English words, phrases, and sentences familiar to them and subsequently demonstrate effective retention of these items by continuing to read them and even write them. During language experience activities in some bilingual classrooms, children dictate stories in Spanish and English and then proceed to reread their mixed texts facilely and accurately, unaware of or unbothered by the appearance of the two codes. In the second and third grades, it is not unusual to find young readers of Spanish who started reading (and writing) English successfully away from school, sometimes virtually on their own, as first graders or kindergarten pupils.

These observations suggest several intriguing conclusions, some of which depart markedly from presently dominant viewpoints in bilingual reading pedagogy. First of all, bilingual children when reading for understanding do not appear to approach reading, or learning to read, in Spanish and in English as separate, distinct processes. Strategies for processing the written text to get at meaning are carried over from one language to the other. Second, the beginning of second-language reading can be a natural, learner-initiated, and learner-controlled occurrence when children approach reading as a desirable, useful, and meaningful activity. This type of introduction to second-language reading is in direct contrast to the formally imposed, skills-focused process many educators now conceive of as the proper way to "transfer" from first-language to second-language reading. Third, these glimpses of bilingual reading behavior suggest that the inception of second-language reading need not be dependent on any definable level or degree of native-language reading proficiency; rather, second-language reading can commence soon after native-language reading begins, or develop virtually alongside it, as long as the learner is making sense of the written language he or she encounters. In essence, one reading process is operative across both languages, regardless of their surface forms, and is kept in motion by the reader's ongoing drive to gain meaning and understanding.

This proposal that first-language and second-language reading can codevelop should not be construed as an endorsement of simultaneous Spanish and English beginning reading experiences that are basically symbol-sound oriented. Unfortunately, in some schools bilingual reading instruction still takes the form of concurrent, back-to-back Spanish and English phonics training. It is questionable whether children are being taught reading efficiently or effectively when they are shuttled back and forth between symbol-sound instruction sessions that must sometimes be giving them limited or conflicting information about reading. And I am hardly suggesting that the beginning reader of Spanish can be thrust into an English basal reading program beyond his or her linguistic and experiential reach and interest and encounter only a modicum of difficulty. Some traditional English basal reading materials are grossly unsuitable for use with language-minority children; on the other hand, other materials of this sort may be useful if employed judiciously in a whole-language instructional model that emphasizes meaning. But merely attaching a beginning Spanish reading strand, especially one that is phonics-oriented, to a traditional English basal program that is not comprehension-centered is indefensible as bilingual reading programming.

It follows, however, that bilingual teachers presenting reading in a meaning-centered manner should not be preoccupied with rigidly separating first-language and second-language forms. Even bilingual children who are beginning readers can be provided with written material in both languages (or a mixture of the two) so long as the content is natural and meaningful to them. It is likely that in young children's minds, reading is not differentiated by language. Accordingly, our instruction need not construct artificial barriers separating first-language reading in Spanish and second-language reading in English; rather, we should stress the singularity of reading as a process of getting at meaning. The foregoing observations underscore the need for teachers' decisions about bilingual reading instruction to be of a highly individualistic nature, taking into account each learner's past and current language experiences within and beyond the classroom.

ORAL LANGUAGE AND SECOND-LANGUAGE READING

The traditional communication sequence of "listening, speaking, reading, and writing" has been indelibly impressed upon many bilingual education teachers as the only model for language arts instruction in the child's second language.[3] The message to teachers behind this strict ordering of the language arts has been well intentioned: No child should be asked to read a language unknown

---

[3] Elley (1981) traces this influence to the audiolingual school of language teaching, whose pedagogical principles and assumptions dominate English as a Second Language (ESL) instruction in many bilingual programs.

to him or her. Although one can hardly deny the importance of oral language development to reading, many educators in bilingual programs have come to believe as a result of this precautionary dictum that second-language reading must always follow a specific period of English oral language development, and, related to this, that there exists an optimum level of English oral language functioning for beginning to read in that language. Among the most noticeable by-products of these beliefs are the various oral language criteria that schools have imposed for admission to second-language reading instruction.

In the previous section it was noted that some bilingual children learn to read in their native language and the second language almost simultaneously. That this occurs implies that even a relatively limited oral English base may permit the development of second-language reading. Obviously some primary-grade children learning to read in their native language are motivated to read the second language and are able to do so with varying degrees of success even though their grasp of oral English is not advanced. Similar behavior is observable in bilingual and monolingual classrooms among older Spanish-speaking students from Mexico; many, already literate to some degree in their native language, display high motivation to read English and begin doing so as they are learning to understand and speak the language. Especially when presented with comprehensible and worthwhile second-language reading tasks, motivated students at all grade levels are able to merge second-language reading growth and second-language oral development. It is precisely this behavior that has been overlooked and perhaps at times even stifled in many bilingual classrooms as a result of ingrained beliefs that second-language reading should always be kept separate from, and successive to, second-language aural-oral development.

Other researchers have called attention to this somewhat symbiotic relationship between oral language development and reading in second-language learning. Goodman, Goodman, and Flores (1979) write about bilingual children who seem to be able to learn oral and written English simultaneously, using the two forms to support each other in developing their general control of the language. These authors point out that there are no general rules telling teachers when to begin instruction in reading in relationship to oral language, and that in many cases second-language reading can commence simultaneously with oral language beginnings.

Likewise, Elley (1981), on the basis of findings from an experiment on South Pacific bilingual children's ability to learn from second-language written materials, affirms that bilingual pupils can and do develop oral language and reading skills in the second language more or less simultaneously. Elley states that bilingual pupils are able to do second-language reading without an extensive repertoire of words and structures when their materials are meaningful. Under these circumstances bilingual learners can make sensible and correct predictions about unfamiliar language structures and can teach themselves the meaning of new language when they see it in print. Thus, they are able to learn more about their second language by reading it. Elley calls for a new and increased role for reading in order to improve instruction in English as a second language, a role that embraces second-language reading as an effective means for learning language, extending vocabulary, and figuring out new syntax.

In their efforts to relate second-language reading instruction to oral language development, many school bilingual programs evidently have looked at these components rather narrowly. In bilingual classrooms second-language reading usually is conducted through commercial reading materials, principally a basal reading series. This formal, sequential treatment overlooks the possibility that second-language reading can be undertaken in a more natural, less rigid manner. Common classroom interpretations of oral language development in the second language are also fairly restricted, often taking into account only the children's speaking fluency, or the productive side of oral language. Receptive language capabilities, more relevant to reading than oral production, are often not even considered. Tendencies such as these converge to produce rather limited views of the relationship between oral language and reading in the second language—for example, the belief that children's oral language production must be more or less commensurate with the textbook language to be used in instruction, and vice versa (Gonzales, 1981).

But some children in Spanish-English bilingual classrooms can and do begin to read in a second language, naturally and without either high English oral functioning or extensive familiarity with "book English." Some do so apart from any classroom instruction, right after they begin reading in their native language and are getting started in their English learning. Frequently, these children model themselves on or are assisted by other children, usually siblings, who are already reading English. Some children are thus able to develop considerable fluency in ESL reading after two or three years, not necessarily achieving up to their grade level, but satisfactorily gaining in reading proficiency. Although not entirely native-like in their reading performance and comprehension, these young readers are nevertheless able to begin and to progress in second-language reading without many of the trappings that usually accompany formal ESL reading instruction in the primary-level classroom: controlled language structures, controlled vocabulary, sequential materials, skills lists, and so forth. That they are able to succeed without these provisions suggests that they are not shackled in their second-language reading by the limits of their oral language knowledge; it is likely that these young second-language learners do indeed learn English by reading it in context. How else does one make sense of written language and structures that one has not yet heard or spoken aloud? In fact, this is not an unusual phenomenon: Native readers of English do just that as they read. It seems, therefore, that we should not marvel at or reject the possibility that bilingual children can pace their own second-language reading and successfully initiate it early in their learning of the second language. Instead, we should recognize this achievement as a natural outcome of language learning in our print-oriented society. A more puzzling matter meriting our attention is what the schools can do to capitalize on this situation so that these children can become effective and efficient users of written English.

LANGUAGE TESTS AND BEGINNING
SECOND-LANGUAGE READING

Educators in Spanish-English programs usually consider several criteria in deciding when to begin formal second-language reading instruction. In more and more programs, however, the sole criterion actually employed has come to be the child's performance on a language assessment instrument, usually a commercially produced language-proficiency test. Teachers' informal judgments of children's English functioning and potential for second-language reading—and children's own beginning endeavors in second-language reading—continue to play a minor role in the decision to introduce formal second-language reading instruction. Typically, classroom instruction in second-language reading begins only after the child (or children, as group placement prevails) has attained a certain score, or level of performance, on the language test the school has chosen for this purpose. For a variety of reasons, some of which have been alluded to in previous sections, this overreliance on oral language measures as indicators of "readiness" to read in a second language should be abated.

Increasingly, language researchers have stressed that there is more to processing and understanding a written text than oral language knowledge (Goodman, 1979; Fillion, Smith, and Swain, 1976; Smith, 1979). It has been noted repeatedly that the more familiar children are with "book language" and its elements—story structure, the conventions of formal written language, variations in writing style, and so on—the greater their chances of success in book reading and comprehension (Applebee, 1979; Goodman and Watson, 1977; Guthrie, 1977; McCormick, 1977; Mandler and Johnson, 1977). Therefore, one must consider familiarization with or sophistication about "book English" a desirable prerequisite for ESL textbook-centered reading. In short, oral productive ability in and by itself, which is what school-adopted or school-developed oral language measures tend to emphasize (Sanchez, 1976), is not as valid as indicator of readiness to do ESL textbook reading as one might wish. Apparently, then, the practice of basing the introduction of second-language textbook reading on the attainment of oral English proficiency as measured by these kinds of tests is not well grounded.

Without delving into ongoing controversies concerning the adequacy of currently available language tests to assess even oral language functioning, one can find sufficient classroom evidence of a general lack of correlation between oral language test scores and second-language reading placement. It is not uncommon to find children who have scored at the desired level on an oral language test and yet do not display adequate comprehension in second-language textbook reading, although they can do a satisfactory job of calling out words. Conversely, one can find children who have not scored at the required level on a school-employed language test but nonetheless have high receptive control of English and read English quite successfully away from the classroom.

More than likely these discrepancies between oral language test results and second-language placement are undetected and tolerated in many bilingual classrooms because of a general lack of emphasis on comprehension in beginning second-language reading instruction. This inattention is apparent in such instructional practices as assigning children to initial ESL reading by way of "transitional" classes in which core materials are English linguistic reading products that emphasize phonetically regular words. Comprehension development in these materials, which often require phonological control exceeding that of many bilingual children, is at best difficult and at worst impossible. There is also the practice of having children progress through second-language reading sequentially, starting out in the very first books in an English basal series—the first preprimer or even the readiness workbook—in which story content is minimal or is conveyed mainly through pictures. When comprehensionless practices like these characterize the initial stages of formal second-language reading instruction, chances are that incongruencies between oral language test scores and reading instructional placement will go unnoticed.

The most serious consequence of the use of oral language measures, however, is the lack of development, or even the erosion, of the teacher's decision-making power in this important area of second-language teaching. The acceptance of a quantitative index based on a highly limited language sample as an indicator of second-language reading potential reflects a pessimistic attitude toward the teacher's ability to make this judgment and a serious misunderstanding of the relationship between oral language and reading. I remain convinced that the teacher's personal assessment should be the ultimate criterion here, with all formal tests relegated to a limited, secondary role. If doubts exist about teachers' observational competence or judgment, then we should provide the kind of training that will increase their sensitivity to the highly individualistic and dynamic nature of second-language learning in general and second-language reading in particular. The use of formal tests does not in any case eliminate the need to help teachers learn to interpret and better understand children's language learning and reading. In the end, the introduction to second-language reading instruction should be viewed as a matter for individual consideration and second-language reading as more than a school-centered, test-determined, group-assigned undertaking.

Given that most bilingual education programs depend on an English basal reading series as the hub of second-language reading instruction, a more appropriate way to determine whether a child understands the language well enough to benefit from instruction in these materials would be an inventory of the child's aural comprehension of the contents of such textbooks. This could be accomplished by reading excerpts aloud to the child and then asking him or her to retell what has just been read. This type of informal procedure is a much more sensitive indicator than an oral language test of the child's preparedness for ESL reading for several reasons: it assesses readiness for reading book language by actually using samples of book language; it focuses on the child's understanding of book language and not on the production of oral language; and it allows the child's comprehension of book language to be expressed through retellings in English or Spanish or both.

It should be pointed out that this procedure is not intended to limit texts for second-language reading to those possessing linguistic features that "match up" with the child's oral production, as some have proposed (Gonzales, 1981). The use of this procedure should be grounded in the belief that learners can improve their control of the second language by reading it and can tackle unknown aspects of the language in meaningful print contexts. When applied with these ideas in mind, this type of inventory can serve to separate reading material that is clearly beyond the child's linguistic or conceptual knowledge and thus most likely unsuitable for instruction at that time from material that is linguistically and conceptually comprehensible and thus potentially useful. An obvious benefit is that this procedure can be applied to all written materials under consideration for second-language reading. Educators need to remember, however, that such an assessment cannot account for all the diverse factors influencing the reader-text relationship and that it certainly does not replace the remarkable ability of many conscientious young readers to self-select materials close to or at their instructional functioning levels.

LANGUAGE INFLUENCES IN ESL READING

In more Spanish-English bilingual reading programs than not, it seems that the only standard for monitoring and evaluating the ESL reading progress and performance of bilingual children is a native-English-speaking model. As a rule, one can detect little awareness of the developmental aspects of children's second-language learning and their influence on ESL reading. Concomitantly, first-language influences on children's second-language reading are not adequately understood. English instructional and evaluative materials, essentially designed for mainstream, monolingual English-speakers, continue to be used indiscriminately with bilingual children. It is indeed reprehensible that in some bilingual classrooms there has been so little movement toward understanding the effects of children's language background on their second-language reading behavior.

Language-influenced differences in second-language reading are dealt with in various inappropriate ways in the bilingual classroom. By far the most overt example is the undue attention that continues to be paid to pronunciation in oral reading. Surface phonological variations in oral reading are categorically assumed to reflect a disruption of meaning and loss of comprehension. For example, it is assumed that "sheep" pronounced as "cheep" will be misunderstood by the reader as "cheap"; that "yellow" produced as "jellow" will be taken to mean "jello." When these pronunciation differences also affect syntactic features, resulting in the deletion of inflectional morphemes such as those indicating past tense, plurality, or possession, they are even more likely to be considered meaning changes by teachers.

Although recent research has shown that such language-based pronunciation differences do not automatically interfere with the comprehension of meaningful, connected texts (Barrera, 1978; Goodman and Goodman, 1978), many bilingual teachers continue to treat all such features as errors disruptive of meaning and therefore spend important teaching time eliminating these "problems" from pupils' oral renderings. Teachers neglect to recognize the compensating effects of context and other cues in connected written discourse that offset many pronunciation variations in the reading of both native and nonnative speakers. Similarly, many teachers fail to recognize that redundant features of the language of written texts, such as the occurrence of multiple cues to indicate tense or plurality, also minimize the effects of these differences. More than likely it discourages or defeats the young reader's efforts to extract meaning from the text when reading is halted by the teacher to "correct" language-based miscues. Meaning is sidetracked while valuable time is expended on unnecessary and frequently ineffectual pronunciation drills.

This is not to say that language-based differences in bilingual children's ESL oral reading might not lead at times to confusion; they can and they do. But it is erroneous and counterproductive to assume that all such variations will disrupt meaning at all times; instead, teachers need to learn to distinguish when these differences do in fact impede comprehension and necessitate assistance for the reader in clarifying and deriving the intended meaning of the text. Teachers of bilingual children especially need to recognize that reading is not a precise process in which meaning is lost if one word or several words are altered by the reader. Moreover, teachers of ESL reading need to recognize that other characteristics of learners, such as differences in the areas of conceptual schemata and cultural background, might present more formidable barriers in ESL reading than pronunciation patterns (Joag-Dev and Steffensen,

1980). Undoubtedly we need to direct attention away from pronunciation accuracy in ESL reading to these potentially more important variables.

Apart from "misreading" the effects of language-based pronunciation variations during ESL oral reading, many teachers in bilingual education also appear to misunderstand bilingual children's language background when it comes to assessing reading comprehension. A "native-like" yardstick is also apparent here. It is frequently assumed that a bilingual student who has read an English text should be able to answer oral comprehension checks on that text entirely in English. If children's productive ability is not up to this task, as is sometimes the case, their comprehension may be grossly underestimated, and over a period of time, their instructional placement may be held at a much lower level than warranted. Even cursory work with bilingual children reading in English reveals that they are often able to read and understand much more in English than they can retell or write about in English. Retellings are sometimes done wholly in the native language or through a combination of both languages. If children are restricted to expressing their understanding of second-language materials in the second language, they are actually being tested on oral production and not on reading comprehension. Nor can one discount the influence of affective factors, such as inhibitions about speaking in the second language, that may prevent the child from responding to comprehension checks in that language. An inability to respond fluently in English, therefore, should not lead to a hasty conclusion that the child's English reading comprehension is lacking.

Many of the ESL reading "problems" of bilingual children are unwittingly created by their own teachers whenever these children are assigned to reading tasks and materials patently incompatible with their language background. A prominent example of this is the frequent imposition of English phonic instructional tasks and sequences on bilingual children with the expectation that they can progress through them as a native English-speaker might. Sadly, when children display rather predictable difficulties in this area—such as an inability to perceive and/or produce certain English sounds—the typical reaction is not to question the relevance or appropriateness of such training for Spanish-English bilingual learners but to respond with more instruction of the same kind. Another example of disregard for language background is the use of commercially produced English reading tests to measure pupils' ESL reading progress. It seems that some programs use without reservation vocabulary and phonic subtests requiring children to name items that are probably familiar to language-majority children but whose English labels are often unknown to children learning English as a second language. The same is true of language skills subtests that assume a knowledge of English grammar commensurate with native abilities but out of line for children developing second-language abilities.

The classroom practices described in this section make it clear that much work remains to be done if more effective ESL reading instruction is to be realized in Spanish-English bilingual education. Helping teachers to become aware of the developmental nature of second-language learning may limit the imposition of native-like standards on children's ESL reading. Teachers need to know, as Goodman and Goodman (1978) have noted, that children's ESL reading "will reflect not only their first language but the extent to which they are coming to control English phonology, grammar, orthography, lexicon, and idiom" (pp. 3–8). Obviously bilingual children are moving toward native-like command in ESL reading, and until they achieve this, their reading behavior should not be expected to conform to a native English model, and particularly not an adult one. Needed work in this area includes helping teachers to sort out differences in children's ESL reading that are a natural outcome of their language background, and that do not hinder comprehension, from genuine reading problems requiring instructional attention.

A FRAGMENTED VIEW OF THE LANGUAGE ARTS

The unnecessary fragmentation of the language arts is an even more pressing problem in bilingual classrooms than it is in monolingual English ones. This problem is compounded when potentially valuable components of language arts instruction, in both languages, are omitted from classroom practice. Splintered or incomplete instructional efforts in the language arts do not have a favorable effect on the reading-language growth of bilingual children.

The Spanish language arts program frequently is a program in name only. Perhaps this is because contemporary Spanish-English bilingual education programs are largely transitional in nature; that is, they employ the native language only as a bridge to English. In any case, language arts offerings in the native language tend to be meager and not as robust as they should be. There is a general lack of emphasis on expanding children's knowledge of oral and written Spanish. Simply stated, what should be a Spanish language arts program is often only a reading program with little or no complementary, systematic efforts in Spanish oral or written language development. To make matters worse, the reading program usually consists of a basal series, accompanying workbooks, and innumerable dittoed worksheets. The result is a sterile, one-dimensional reading program, heavily concerned with the recoding aspects of reading at the expense of reading comprehension and lacking a variety of activities to foster reading proficiency.

There is a real need in Spanish-English bilingual education for more abundant Spanish reading materials for use in primary-level programs, particularly materials of high predictability as are available in English (Bridges, 1979; Rhodes, 1981). The problem is often exacerbated when materials in supply are not fully used or adapted for use in much-needed reading-language activities.

For example, reading aloud to children in Spanish is frequently given low priority or even relegated to the "frills" category in Spanish language arts offerings. And yet the benefits of this activity, when it is an integral part of the language arts curriculum, are far-reaching and long-term: listening to the oral reading of a written text not only helps to acquaint students with the nuances of written language and its differences from the oral mode, but also aids in expanding their linguistic and conceptual knowledge. In most classrooms, moreover, children have no opportunity to participate in diverse communication events and so explore the different functions of language. Vocabulary development is of the decontextualized, dictionary variety, with lists of words for children to locate but no meaningful oral or print contexts to attach them to. Student reading in the content areas in Spanish, for example, social studies and science, or the reading aloud to children from specialized content area materials in Spanish is rarely observable. It is no wonder, then, that young Spanish-speaking readers in grades two and three sometimes have trouble understanding Spanish materials of a higher level of difficulty. A variety of factors probably are responsible for this: inadequate reading vocabulary, limited familiarity with written story features, and unknown textbook conceptual information. One cannot discount the possiblity that a large proportion of the Spanish books currently available for reading to and by children in bilingual classrooms may be irrelevant and overly difficult, but the fact remains that little is being done to expand children's knowledge of oral and written Spanish in current native-language programs.

We should not continue to overlook the marginal nature of most Spanish language arts programs in bilingual education or believe that they offer all there is to language arts instruction in the native language. Within the Spanish-reading strand, children need a broader base of connected written-language experiences. The scope of activities in the rest of the Spanish language arts program should be expanded to acquaint children with and help them learn the many different ways of using Spanish. At the same time, the various language arts forms must be presented not as unrelated, isolated skills, but rather as indivisible aspects of a communication whole.

A piecemeal approach also characterizes ESL instruction in the language arts curriculum. The spoken and written forms of the second language are generally separated for instruction purposes. In many programs periods for ESL instruction are wholly oral, their primary focus being the development of children's control over language structure and phonology. Little attention is directed toward presenting the written language in context during oral ESL activities. In fact, I have observed that when written English was incorporated into oral ESL periods, these occurrences have almost always been followed by apologetic comments from teachers about their inclusion of such material. This tendency to separate the spoken and written forms of the second language has a number of ramifications for second-language reading development.

Because the oral ESL strand is almost exclusively devoted to the development of grammar and pronunciation, efforts to acquaint children with written English are minimal. A systematic program of reading aloud from English textual materials prior to the introduction of formal ESL reading instruction is the exception and not the rule in bilingual classrooms. Such a program could easily be initiated, using stories and tales with which the children have some familiarity in Spanish and so providing a rich and familiar context in which they can begin to interact with written English structures and vocabulary. In some classrooms that I have visited, however, English books are banished from the ESL period or class until a decision has been made, usually on the basis of formal language-proficiency testing, that the children involved can begin to read in English. In the end, what many schools offer in the way of ESL language arts is a disjointed effort consisting of an isolated oral ESL strand with a fixed focus on oral productive ability and few ties (or none) to reading and a separate ESL reading strand, whose content is a "textbook English" for which the learner has received little preparation.

Smith (1979) asserts that the various divisions in language arts programs are arbitrary categorizations of the schools and not a reflection of categories in the learner's mind. He points out that the central question is not how the language arts should be brought together in the learner's mind, but why they should ever be separated. The same question can also be posed of language arts instruction in bilingual classrooms, not only with respect to each language, but also across languages. Many of the traditional and rigid slots we have created for such components as oral ESL, "transitional" ESL reading, Spanish reading, and so forth may be more dysfunctional than salutary where the literacy development of bilingual children is concerned. Furthermore, in most schools we have done little or nothing to relate for students the language arts and the content areas, such as social studies and science. It has been stated that bilingual education is in need of bold innovation in curriculum design (Goodman, Goodman, and Flores, 1979); surely we will be taking a step toward answering that need by working to integrate the language arts in bilingual education.

CONCLUSION

At the outset I observed that myopic notions about the reading process, reading development, and reading instruction are not to be found only in bilingual classrooms; they permeate monolingual English reading education as well. However, there is no consolation, bittersweet or otherwise, to be derived from this observation by those in bilingual education. It is an unfortunate paradox that in the continuing struggle to root bilingual education as a viable answer to the reading-language needs of language-minority children, many associated with these programs have resisted new and alternative perspectives on traditional reading-language pedagogy. For all Spanish-English bilingual education

programs in the Southwest, one can ask whether any substantive advances have
really occurred in the teaching of reading to native-Spanish-speaking students.
Admittedly the language of reading instruction has changed—the native language is used to introduce the child to reading or used alongside English in
beginning reading—but in the classroom underlying attitudes about language
have not changed much, and knowledge about children's language learning and
reading has not significantly increased. It is unlikely that use of the native language by itself will ensure improved reading instruction for bilingual children
if the pedagogical base for reading remains virtually unchanged. To move
toward more effective and relevant reading programs for these children, we
must begin to discard instructional beliefs and practices that overlook the
highly individualistic and dynamic aspects of children's language learning, and
we must begin to appreciate the range of contexts, social and functional, in
which reading begins and develops.

REFERENCES

Andersson, T., and Boyer, M. *Bilingual schooling in the United States: volume one.*
  Austin, Tex.: Southwest Educational Development Laboratory, 1970.
Applebee, A. N. Children and stories: learning the rules of the game. *Language Arts,*
  1979, *56*, 641–645.
Barrera, R. B. Analysis and comparison of the first-language and second-language
  oral reading behavior of native Spanish-speaking Mexican American children.
  Doctoral dissertation. University of Texas at Austin, 1978.
Bridges, C. Predictable materials for beginning readers. *Language Arts,* 1979, *56,*
  503–507.
Elley, W. B. The role of reading in bilingual contexts. In J. T. Guthrie (Ed.), *Com-
  prehension and teaching: research reviews.* Newark, Del.: International Reading
  Association, 1981.
Ferreiro, E. What is written in a written sentence? A developmental answer. *Journal
  of Education,* 1978, *160,* 25–39.
Ferreiro, E. The relationship between oral and written language: the children's view-
  points. Paper presented at a preconvention institute of the International Reading
  Association, St. Louis, Missouri, May 1980.
Ferreiro, E., and Teberosky, A. Los sistemas de escritura en el desarrollo del niño.
  Mexico: Siglo XXI Editores, 1979.
Ferreiro, E., and Teberosky, A. La comprensión del sistema de escritura: construc-
  ciones originales del niño e información específica de los adultos. *Lectura y Vida,*
  1981, *2,* 6–14.
Fillion, B., Smith, F., and Swain, M. Language "basics" for language teachers:
  towards a set of universal considerations. *Language Arts,* 1976, *53,* 740–745.
Fillmore, L. W. Learning a second language: Chinese children in the American class-
  room. In J. E. Alatis (Ed.), *Current issues in bilingual education.* Georgetown
  University Round Table on Languages and Linguistics 1980. Washington, D.C.:
  Georgetown University Press, 1980.

Gonzales, P. C. Beginning English reading for ESL students. *Reading Teacher*, 1981, *35*, 154–163.

González, G. A. Bilingual/bicultural reading instruction (Introduction in Teacher's Manuals for *Spanish Reading Keys*). Oklahoma City: Economy Company, 1980.

Goodman, K. Quoted in NCTE to you: convention report. *Language Arts*, 1979, *56*, 202.

Goodman, K., and Burke, C. Theoretically based studies of patterns of miscues in oral reading performance (final report, Project No. 9-0375). Washington, D.C.: U.S. Department of Health, Education and Welfare, Office of Education, Bureau of Research, 1973.

Goodman, K., and Goodman, Y. Reading of American children whose language is a stable rural dialect of English or a language other than English (final report, Project NIE-00-3-0087). Washington, D.C.: U.S. Department of Education, 1978.

Goodman, K., Goodman, Y., and Flores, B. *Reading in the bilingual classroom: literacy and biliteracy*. Rosslyn, Va.: National Clearinghouse for Bilingual Education, 1979.

Goodman, Y., and Watson, D. J. A reading program to live with: focus on comprehension. *Language Arts*, 1977, *54*, 868–879.

Guthrie, J. Research views: story comprehension. *Reading Teacher*, 1977, *30*, 574–577.

Herbert, C. Initial reading in Spanish for bilinguals. (ERIC Document ED 061-813.) Paper presented at the Conference on Child Language, Chicago, Illinois. Quebec: Laval University, International Center on Bilingualism, 1971.

Hudelson-Lopez, S. A study of the use of context by native Spanish-speaking children when they read in Spanish. Doctoral dissertation, University of Texas at Austin, 1975.

Joag-Dev, C., and Steffensen, M. S. Studies of the bicultural reader: implications for teachers and librarians. Reading Education Report no. 12. Champaign, Ill.: Center for the Study of Reading, 1980.

Lado, R., Hansen, I., and D'Emilio, T. Biliteracy for bilingual children by grade 1: The SED Center preschool reading project. In J. E. Alatis (Ed.), *Current issues in bilingual education*. Georgetown University Round Table on Languages and Linguistics 1980. Washington, D.C.: Georgetown University Press, 1980.

McCormick, S. Choosing books to read to preschool children. *Language Arts*, 1977, *54*, 543–548.

Mandler, J. M., and Johnson, N. S. Remembrance of things parsed: story structure and recall. *Cognitive Psychology*, 1977, *9*, 111–151.

Michel, J. Learning to read Spanish: the case of the Spanish dominant bilingual child. Unpublished paper, University of Texas at San Antonio, 1977.

Rhodes, L. K. I can read! Predictable books as resources for reading and writing instruction. *Reading Teacher*, 1981, *34*, 511–518.

Roser, N. L., and Jensen, J. M. Real communication: key to early reading and writing. *Childhood Education*, 1978, *55*, 90–93.

Sanchez, R. Critique of oral language assessment instruments. *Journal of the National Association for Bilingual Education*, 1976, *1*, 120–127.

Silva, A. D. Oral reading behavior of Spanish-speaking children taught by a meaning-based program. Doctoral dissertation, University of Texas at Austin, 1979.

Smith, F. The language arts and the learner's mind. *Language Arts,* 1979, *56,* 118–125, 145.

Southwest Educational Development Laboratory. Bilingual reading study: some preliminary findings. Mimeographed paper, November 1980.

Thonis, E. W. *Literacy for America's Spanish-speaking children.* Newark, Del.: International Reading Association, 1976.

United States Commission on Civil Rights. *A better chance to learn: bilingual bicultural education.* Clearinghouse Publication no. 51. Washington, D.C.: U.S. Government Printing Office, 1975.

12 | The Spanish Reading Process and Spanish-Speaking Mexican American Children

AURELIA DÁVILA DE SILVA
Intercultural Research Development Association,
San Antonio, Texas

Since the introduction of the Bilingual Education Act of 1968 and the Bilingual Education Act of 1974, questions and hypotheses about the process of learning to read in Spanish have resulted in research that may help in resolving several controversies. Before this time research into Spanish reading was nonexistent. A 1980 survey of Texas teachers indicated that many questionable assumptions regarding the Spanish reading process are still widely held:

1. It is easier to learn to read in Spanish because (1) beginning reading is principally a process of phonetic "code cracking," and (2) Spanish is more "phonetic" than English.
2. Children learn to read by acquiring many different, separate skills. Good readers don't miss words, and when they do, it is because they: (a) don't know the word, because of a lack of word-recognition skills or vocabulary; (b) don't know phonics; or (c) are not being careful— for example, they are reading too fast or not paying attention.
3. Fluency is one of the most important signs of a good reader. Once a student learns to read without mistakes, with good expression and correct pronunciation, he or she will be a good reader and will understand what is being read. In other words, correct oral reading automatically implies good comprehension.
4. One of the most important goals in reading is to enjoy reading. In order to learn, however, students need to work: for example, to go through their workbooks page by page and be drilled in new vocabulary before reading it in a story.
5. Learning to read is a sequenced process that begins with learning the sounds and the alphabet. Since these are different in Spanish and English, a child who has learned to read in Spanish needs to start all over in learning to read English.

6. Some command of English is necessary to learn to read, but a teacher has to help students catch up with their native-English-speaking counterparts—for example, to read the basal series at grade level. Therefore children should be placed in English reading as soon as they begin school.
7. It is nice for children to learn to read in Spanish because it maintains cultural and family ties, but it is much more important to learn to speak and read English because English is the language they will have to use to make a living and survive as adults.

Much controversy surrounds the notion of teaching children to read in their native language. As a result, many children who speak a language other than English are expected to read in English before they have been given an opportunity to obtain competence and performance skills in it. Spanish-speaking children in the Southwest, in particular, have been expected to read a language they neither understand nor speak. The basic fear is that teaching children to read in their native language will take up time that should be used for reading in English and learning school subjects. Teachers therefore feel pressured to start English reading exercises early in a child's school career. Some even fear that a child taught to read Spanish may not attain English reading strategies at all. Moreover, assumptions about the teaching of Spanish reading, like those listed above, may interfere with the process of learning to read. Until recently we have not had research to guide us in making decisions about the teaching of Spanish reading. Recent research can give us a better insight into the reading process as it occurs in Spanish and help us determine practical and effective classroom teaching strategies.

This paper summarizes current research on the process of learning to read Spanish as it is experienced by Spanish-speaking Mexican American children. Specifically, studies involving readers' miscues (deviations from the text as the child reads aloud) will be reviewed. Next, a study involving Spanish reading will be presented at length, along with a discussion of its results and instructional implications. Finally, the results of all these studies will be related to the teacher survey referred to above in the hope of answering some of the concerns of teachers in bilingual classrooms.

READING MISCUES

Six research studies (Barrera, 1978; Eaton, 1979; Flores, 1982; Goodman and Goodman, 1978; Hudelson-Lopez, 1975; Silva, 1979) have offered insights into the phenomenon of Spanish reading. These studies were based on K. Goodman's work of the 1960s with English-speaking children. Prior to Goodman's investigations (1965, 1969), children's reading errors were perceived as reflecting what the child did not know. The research of Goodman and other investigators (Goodman and Burke, 1968, 1973; Goodman, 1967) shows that miscues give insights into the reading process by revealing the strategies used by the reader. It was Goodman (1965) who initiated the concept that a miscue does not carry the negative connotations of an error. The investigations revealed how children used their language to help them move through print. Other research studies have confirmed that English reading is a language-related process (Allen, 1969; Goodman, 1967; Menosky, 1971; Page, 1970).

Miscue Analysis of Spanish Reading

Hudelson-Lopez (1975) explored how Spanish-speaking Mexican Americans from a South Texas border town utilized context and prediction as they read Spanish print. She examined seventy-five Spanish-speaking Mexican American children from second and third grades as they read isolated words in a list. These children, who ranged in reading levels from preprimer through third grade, were then asked to read a selection in which every seventh word was covered (this strategy is called clozure). A significant number of words missed in the list were read correctly in the passage, a result that supports Goodman's (1965) findings. Some words that were read correctly in the list, however, were missed in the passage. Hudelson-Lopez concluded that children were using their phonics skills when they were asked to read the word list and their contextual strategies when they were reading the passage.

Students predicted the covered words correctly or substituted a semantically equivalent word 50 percent of the time. This finding, which illustrates that children were reading for meaning and anticipating information, is also supported by Goodman (1965). This study is evidence against the contention that Spanish reading is simply a matter of sounds and syllable patterns. Hudelson-Lopez concluded that children should be given practice in developing their contextual strategies, that words should be introduced in context, and that children should not be interrupted while they read but instead be allowed to use the context to self-correct.

Miscue Analysis of Spanish and English Reading

Barrera (1978) examined the first- and second-language reading miscues and retellings of fourteen Spanish-speaking Mexican American third graders. Her subjects received initial instruction in Spanish reading until the beginning of third grade, when English reading was introduced. The subjects all read the same passage in Spanish and different passages in English, which ranged from the second-grade to third-grade reading levels. Barrera noted several findings. As the children moved through the Spanish print, they deviated or miscued.

Children's miscues commonly had the same syntactical characteristics and functions in the text. Miscues involving inflectional or intonation changes in some words caused inflectional changes in the words that followed. Miscues involving omissions did not affect the meaning of the text. Omissions often created a more natural language than appeared in the text. Readers substituted words from their own experiences that did not change the meaning of the text, and they corrected miscues that disrupted the meaning, indicating a continuous interaction between meaning and print. No relationship was found between comprehension scores and the number of miscues. Finally, children reading in Spanish produced many miscues that were semantically acceptable.

While reading in English, children demonstrated the use of the graphophonic cue system (the correspondence between letters and sounds) by producing a large number of miscues involving graphic and phonemic similarity. Barrera concluded that the native language influenced second-language reading at a phonological level. The miscue patterns revealed in the English reading were similar throughout the whole range of basal readers from second- to third-grade reading levels. Characteristics of first-language reading, such as predicting, confirming, and rejecting information were also present in second-language reading. Barrera concluded that the miscues produced indicate that children do not process information in a precise, letter-by-letter manner, but rather use their language to help them confirm and anticipate information as they read Spanish and English print. They use the graphophonic, syntactic, and semantic systems as they read in both languages. Spanish reading, according to Barrera, is more than the deciphering of sound-to-symbol correspondences; it is a meaning-getting process. Barrera therefore advocates an emphasis on language and contextual clues in Spanish reading programs. She proposes language experience activities and pocket chart strategies, such as clozure (Guszak, 1978) as particularly appropriate for such programs, since they emphasize contextual material. Clozure strategies that would help children anticipate and confirm information, would also be appropriate.

Barrera also noted some implications of her study related to the timing of second-language learning. Since Spanish and English reading are language-related processes, learners must have the background to carry out such language-related strategies as predicting the next word in a given language. Reading in an unknown language could lead to mere "word calling" without comprehension. Barrera also concluded that since reading strategies in the child's native language and second language are similar, it is unnecessary to relearn reading strategies for the second language.

Children occasionally deviated from the printed text and altered pronunciation and grammatical features without affecting the meaning. This suggests, as Barrera points out, that time devoted to changing children's pronunciation and grammar through drills and exercises would be better spent in expanding language and concepts. According to Barrera, this can be done successfully by interrelating reading and the content areas.

Eaton (1979) studied the oral reading behavior of a sample of eighteen Mexican American first graders from a southeastern Texas border town. The subjects were identified as field-dependent (FD), field-dependent/independent (FD/I), or field-independent (FI) in cognitive style on the basis of their performance on the Children's Embedded Figures Test (Witkin, 1950). Eaton defines FD individuals as those whose perception is characterized by an inability to perceive parts of a field as separate units. FI individuals see items as separate from the surrounding field instead of fused with it. FD/I individuals are those whose perception is neither FD nor FI but somewhere in between. Half of Eaton's subjects had received Spanish reading instruction in the first grade along with instruction in English sound-to-symbol correspondence. At midterm these children were transferred to English reading, and Spanish reading was covered when time allowed. The other half of the subjects received English reading instruction from the beginning of the year and Spanish reading instruction starting at midyear. Children were asked to read selections in both Spanish and English and to retell the story. Using the Reading Miscue Inventory (Goodman and Burke, 1972), their miscues were analyzed.

The study produced a number of results with implications for early bilingual education. Among them was the finding that despite other differences between the cognitive-style groups, both FIs and FDs were able to retell more of the passage read in Spanish than in English, an indication of greater comprehension of Spanish print. In comparing the children's behavior in the two languages, Eaton found that all were more efficient readers in their native language. Nevertheless, the children were utilizing the same strategies across languages, indicating that only one reading process exists. It is therefore unnecessary to reteach strategies to initiate English reading if children know how to read in their native language.

Goodman and Goodman (1978) conducted a study that involved eight populations. The eight populations consisted of four second language groups and four dialect groups. Second language groups included Texas Spanish, Navajo, Hawaiian Samoan, and Arab. Dialect groups included downeast Maine, Appalachian white, Mississippi rural black, and Hawaiian pidgin. Of interest in this review is the Spanish group who have lived in the same geographic area, Southeast Texas, for generations.

Subjects were selected by asking teachers to eliminate poor readers and good readers. Ten average readers from the second, fourth, and sixth grades were selected for taping. The subjects were asked to read a selection they had not previously seen. One goal was for each group to read a common story. Another goal was that students read culturally and linguistically relevant material.

Readers were asked to retell their story. Some subjects retold their stories in their first language to a local aide. After taping the reading and retelling, researchers coded the first fifty nondialect, nonrepeated miscues and all dialect miscues within the same selection according to the Goodman Taxonomy.

Results from the study indicated that the subjects were bilingual. Miscue patterns of the subjects were similar to those of native English speakers. The subjects could also discuss what they had read in either English or Spanish.

In general, it was concluded that great differences exist in bilingual populations. Children who are learning to speak and understand a language can read and write the language to gain further control of it. Thus, children learn a language by reading and writing it as well as by speaking and listening to it. For teachers, the implication is that in order to plan instruction, support the learner, and determine linguistic competence, they must be informed about the reading process.

Flores (1982) examined the concept of language interference as applied to Spanish English bilingual Chicano children. Data utilized in this study were obtained from the miscue study by Goodman and Goodman (1978) in which the reading of four American English dialect groups and four bilingual groups in the United States was examined. The subjects selected were twelve Southeast Texas Spanish English bilingual children from grades two, four, and six. Flores' main focus in the study was the assumption in the "habit formation" view. The "habit formation" view is that when a child learns a second language, points of differences will arise which in turn will cause difficulties or interferences. This view purports to begin instruction at these points of difficulty. Dropping of the "-ed" or "-s" morphemes or the "confusion" between "sh" and "ch" have been identified as phonological, morphological, and syntactic differences in the first and second language. Therefore, Spanish speaking children learning English will eventually have language learning "problems" arising from the differences in the two languages.

Flores reported that the data from the study demonstrated that the language differences do not always interfere or cause difficulties in the construction of meaning and that the use of the term "language interference" is a misnomer. She concludes that the findings indicate that instructional practices based on teaching the differences between two languages must be questioned and re-examined.

STUDY OF ORAL READING

Silva (1979) analyzed the oral reading behavior of thirty Spanish-speaking Mexican American children as they read from first-grade Spanish reading materials. The miscues were coded at three different reading levels: preprimer level, primer level, and first reader level. Each miscue category was assigned a degree number that told, for example, how graphically similar it was to the original text. In the first part of the study each miscue category was analyzed in terms of how it varied from one reading level to another. The first part of the study compared two reading levels at a time, from the standpoint of one miscue category. For example, for graphic similarity, the first reader level was compared to the preprimer. The Goodman Taxonomy of Reading Miscues (Goodman and Burke, 1972, 1973) was the source of criteria for each degree.

The second part of the study was a comparison of the degree to which students rely on various miscues, thus exploring the possibility that students may rely more heavily on one miscue category than another. The comparison was done within each group. For example, the preprimer students' miscues were examined to determine the degree to which this group relied on various miscue categories (graphic and phonemic similarity, syntactic and semantic acceptability). Each group was examined internally, but no attempt was made in the second part of the research model to compare the three groups with each other.

The study addressed six major questions:

1. To what extent do these post-first-grade students use graphic information at their respective reading levels?
2. To what extent do they use phonemic information?
3. To what extent do they use syntactic information?
4. To what extent do they use semantic information?
5. What type of correction do they use?
6. Are there significant differences in the use of the four miscue categories (graphic similarity, phonemic similarity, syntactic acceptability, and semantic acceptability) by students reading at the three reading levels?

Research Methods

The subjects of this study were thirty post-first-grade Mexican American children whose primary language was Spanish. None had been taught to read in English; all had been taught to read in Spanish.

The instructional level of potential research subjects was determined by an informal reading inventory, and ten subjects were selected by a stratified sampling procedure from each of the three reading levels. The subjects then read at their instructional level while the researcher kept a record until twenty-five miscues had been committed. The oral reading was taped to avoid errors in coding the miscues. The miscues were analyzed according to the Goodman Taxonomy of Reading Miscues (Goodman and Burke, 1973).

The reading material selected was intended to give the reader some difficulty in order to facilitate the examination of the strategies the students used in dealing with unknown and unexpected words. The students were then evaluated on the basis of the strategies they used and the degree to which they used them.

The independent variables in this study were the three reading levels: pre-primer, primer, and first-grade. The dependent variables were the correction of miscues and the degree of similarity or acceptability of the four miscue categories: phonemic similarity, graphic similarity, semantic acceptability, and syntactic acceptability. These were measured as they varied from one reading level to another in the first part of this study. In the second part, the degree of the four miscue categories were compared with each other at each of the three reading levels. In part one the Kruskal-Wallis one-way analysis of variance by ranks was used to determine whether two groups being compared were distinguishable by their scores or represented a normal variation within one population. In part two the Friedman two-way analysis of variance was used to determine whether there was any significant difference between the degree of the four types of miscues within each reading level.

Summary of Findings

Part one of the study showed that the syntactic and semantic acceptability of miscues and the correction of miscues were not significantly different from the preprimer to the primer to the first-grade level. Graphic and phonemic similarity, however, showed significant increases in mean degree from the preprimer to the primer level and from the primer level to the first grade.

Part two showed, at the preprimer level, that graphic and phonemic similarity of miscues were not significantly different and that both categories were significantly lower in degree than syntactically and semantically acceptable miscues. Syntactic and semantic acceptability categories were not significantly different.

At the primer level there was still no significant difference between the degree of graphic and the degree of phonemic similarity. Graphic similarity was still significantly less than syntactic acceptability. However, there was no significant difference at this level between the phonemic similarity and semantic acceptability categories. Syntactic acceptability had become significantly greater than semantic acceptability.

At the first-grade level, the syntactic acceptability category was still greater than the graphic similarity and semantic acceptability categories. There was no significant difference between the following miscue categories: graphic compared with phonemic, graphic compared with semantic, phonemic compared with syntactic, and phonemic compared with semantic. A total of six comparisons were made. Two comparisons showed significant differences, four others did not.

DISCUSSION

Graphic and Phonemic Similarity

The second part of the study showed no significant differences between phonemic and graphic similarity miscues, perhaps indicating that the readers found a strong relationship between graphic and phonemic information. Both categories began at low levels compared with the semantic and syntactic categories, and both were significantly greater at higher reading levels than at lower ones. This low level is to be expected in a program that gives the student much experience with the graphophonic cue system in context. What is surprising is the amount of difference between reading levels. The graphic and sound similarity differed so greatly from the preprimer to the primer level that at the latter stage there is no significant difference between the phonemic similarity and semantic acceptability categories.

One can speculate that the students bring to the reading task a vast experience with the syntax and sounds of the language. At the outset they are unfamiliar with the graphophonic cue system, but they quickly become adept at grasping sound-symbol relationships. The general conclusion to be drawn from the progress of graphically and phonemically similar miscues is that the students appeared to learn to use the graphophonic system by being exposed to contextual reading without a separate module of phonics instruction.

Syntactic and Semantic Acceptability

The first part of the research model indicates that syntactically and semantically acceptable miscues did not undergo any significant differences from one reading level to the next. In light of the increasing complexity of the texts in terms of lexical items and T-units (the number of words included in a main clause and all its subordinate clauses), the results suggest that the higher-level readers may in effect be increasing their knowledge in the areas of syntax and semantics of the language and improving their strategies to extract meaning from the text. A significant difference was found at the primer and first-grade levels between the degree of syntactic and semantic acceptability of miscues. This finding may have been influenced by the research tool and the restrictions imposed by oral reading, such that syntactic acceptability could not be coded higher than semantic. A miscue may not be judged semantically acceptable unless it is also syntactically acceptable. The reason for this decision-making principle is that one can have syntax without semantics but not semantics without syntax. To make judgments about whether nonsyntactical utterances have semantics would involve arbitrary decision making. A parallel between the two categories continued to exist, in that neither syntactically acceptable nor semantically acceptable miscues decreased or increased significantly. This research produced the same result for Spanish readers that K. Goodman and all other miscue researchers had found for English readers: Learners are aware of syntax and semantics. The second part of the model found no significant difference between the syntactic and semantic acceptability categories at the preprimer level. Syntactic acceptability was significantly greater than semantic acceptability at the primer and the first-grade reading level.

The study did not reveal any significant increase in the semantic acceptability of miscues from one level to the next. This finding is surprising, since the children in this study were taught to read through a meaning-based program. Several reasons can be suggested. First, the study did not explore the miscues which were syntactically acceptable but not semantically acceptable. The retelling of the story in the child's own words was not taken into consideration. The retelling, part of the Goodman Taxonomy, would have made it possible to examine miscues that were syntactically unacceptable in the text but might have made sense to the child, as evidenced by the retelling. This study utilized questions instead of a retelling.

A second possible factor is an increase in syntactic and semantic complexity in the reading material, as indicated by an increase in T-units and lexical items. Finally, the information necessary to make semantically acceptable guesses may appear in later portions of the text. This means that more miscues would be semantically acceptable at the end than at the beginning of the story, and that as students approach the end of the story, the context would become more meaningful. Semantically unacceptable miscues may therefore be quickly and silently self-corrected by readers as they finish the story. Although they may appear in the study as having produced many semantically unacceptable miscues, such readers may in fact understand the story quite well.

Limitations

Some of the limitations of this study were referred to in the previous section. First, it was necessary to have the children read orally in order to mark miscues. There are differences between silent and oral reading; for example, silent reading is generally much faster. The retelling of the story in the children's own words, eliminated in this study, would have provided information about their oral and silent reading processes. Some children may produce few miscues but be unable to retell the story, indicating that they may not have understood it. Other children may produce many miscues and still be able to retell the story.

Although questions were utilized, the retelling was omitted. For this reason, this study may have assessed only the reading strategies related to oral reading and not the psychological reality of silent reading. There was also no way of determining whether children who were reading orally were silently correcting miscues in their minds. With the retelling, it would have been possible to estimate which of the children's syntactically unacceptable miscues were meaningful to them. The absence of the retelling therefore biased the results of this study toward a higher degree of syntactic acceptability than semantic acceptability.

Information on the individual students' educational backgrounds was not made available, and therefore such important data as attendance at kindergarten, previous exposure to print at home, and concepts about words and letters upon arrival in first grade were not included. Nor was it possible to obtain descriptions of the instructional methods used between the time the children entered school and the time they started to read. This researcher was not closely involved with the sample of children used in this study. Reading to a total stranger may have caused some children anxiety and affected their reading. The children's oral reading was taperecorded, and this unnatural situation might also have affected the results of the study.

The analysis of miscues to study children's handling of unknown elements requires that children not have seen the reading material previously. In some cases the children were reading material that was very difficult for them, but adjusting the material—using a lower-level basal reader—would mean that they would be reading a text they had seen before. In such cases and in others where children had already read the test material, the alternative basal series, Santillana, was used. To the extent that the two basal series, published by Laidlaw and Santillana, are not comparable, the results of the study were affected by this substitution.

PRACTICAL CLASSROOM IMPLICATIONS

This study demonstrates that beginning Spanish-readers are well aware of the syntax and semantics of their language and that this knowledge aids the Spanish reader in moving through the text. Further evidence suggests that the absence of graphophonic instruction will not disable beginning Spanish-readers.

It is a common practice in many beginning Spanish reading programs to attempt to teach graphophonic relationships before the child is allowed to read contextual material. Contrary to this practice, the readers in this study had been taught sight-word strategies such as clozure and allowed to read contextual material from the outset. Because of this program's emphasis on meaning, the results suggest, the readers may have learned graphophonic strategies in context. Among the practical implications of the study are the following:

1. It may be worthwhile to teach beginning readers sight-word strategies utilizing sentences that they will encounter in their texts.
2. The development of the graphophonic cue system may be done with the use of contextual material.
3. The teaching of graphophonic relationships before contextual material is introduced may not be necessary, since readers seem to learn about the relationships inductively from contextual material.

The observation of the correction strategy across all three levels revealed that children would attempt to correct by backtracking when something did not make sense and/or did not retain the structure of the language. The practical implications of this finding include the following:

1. Children who make errors while reading should not be corrected immediately; rather, they should be allowed to backtrack in order to correct miscues if they find that what they are reading does not make sense to them.
2. In order to correct themselves, children have to realize that what they read did not make sense. They should therefore be encouraged to ask themselves questions about the sense of their texts.
3. Observations of the reading behavior of Spanish-readers in this study indicated that they transformed print into their own dialect. Readers usually would not correct miscues that shifted language into their own dialect because they made sense to them. Such dialect miscues did not change the author's meaning. This indicates that beginning readers are ready for and can benefit from exposure to materials in different language styles. A gradual and conscious effort should therefore be made to expose beginning Spanish-readers to such materials.
4. Miscues involving dialect appear to be a positive way for children to transform the author's language into their own, and they are not detrimental to their understanding of the passage.
5. Teachers should be aware of the dialect differences in their classrooms so that they will not confuse miscues involving dialect with a reading weakness.

The findings in this study clearly demonstrate a knowledge of the structure and meaning of the language by readers at all three levels. Beginning readers bring this knowledge from home. Providing reading materials in the children's native language may be a practical and effective way of teaching reading, as such texts exploit the children's intuitive and well-developed knowledge of their language.

The Spanish-reader utilized three cue systems: graphophonic, syntactic, and semantic. This observation has several practical implications:

✕1. Beginning Spanish reading programs should include contextual reading to develop in students the ability to utilize the three cue systems. Materials have been developed to teach the graphophonic cue system, but children using these may learn the graphophonic system at the cost of not developing their use of the syntactic and semantic systems. Moreover, the language of graphophonic materials is often artificial and very unlike natural language.

2. The development of isolated skills, such as the teaching of word recognition through word lists or the teaching of sounds, should be replaced by the teaching of all three cue systems in context.

3. It may not be profitable to introduce children to new words in isolation. They can be given the opportunity to develop their reading strategies by using the cue systems to figure out new words.

4. The goal of developing strategies may require the teacher to develop or choose materials that offer children the opportunity to use the three cue systems.

5. A child's weakness in any of the necessary strategies should be diagnosed in a setting in which the reader reads contextual material, rather than through an assessment of his or her skills in isolation. It is important to find out how the child copes with the three cue systems in a connected text, where all the cues are available, rather than in isolated word lists, where some are absent. This assessment will give insight into the strategies used by children as they read.

FIRST- AND SECOND-LANGUAGE STUDIES OF MISCUES

A review of miscue studies (Hudelson-Lopez, 1975; Barrera, 1978; Goodman and Goodman, 1978; Eaton, 1979; Silva, 1979; Flores, 1982) reveals that Spanish reading is not a word-by-word process but rather a language-related one to which children bring their backgrounds of experience. Children reading in Spanish can be described as involved in a cyclical activity. As they are reading, they predict what will come next. They read on to test their predictions. If these prove to be wrong, they will regress to find out what they have misread and then proceed. A reader can move along without correcting or noticing misread or overlooked words unless they affect the meaning of the text. Spanish reading involves the sampling, predicting, testing, and confirming of information. A reader who is not told unfamiliar words and not corrected or otherwise interrupted while reading orally has an opportunity to work through the meaning of text. It is this process of working through that develops the reader's ability to obtain meaning from the text.

In contrast to the widely held views that good reading involves not missing words, the six studies reviewed here indicated that even when children's reading was not word-perfect, they were nevertheless very much involved in the interaction with meaning. One can conclude, then, that children do not have to read without mistakes in order to comprehend. Rather, children sometimes deviate from the print because they are trying to make sense out of what they read. Their insertions, omissions, and other alterations often result in a shift to more natural language. Only miscues that change the meaning of the text should be of concern to teachers.

The studies also reveal children's simultaneous use of graphophonic, syntactic, and semantic information while reading contextual material, drawing from their experiences and their knowledge of language to interpret the print. It would therefore be more profitable for teachers to use contextual material rather than develop isolated skills through workbook drills. Evidence, contributed by all the studies, that reading is a cyclical activity means that readers need language as a source of information before they can successfully use strategies like prediction and self-correction. Teachers, therefore, will help to advance and expand children's reading strategies by exposing them to reading in their native language. Asking children to read before they have acquired certain language-related strategies can lead to their resorting to calling out words instead of focusing on the meaning of the text.

All six studies demonstrate that the strategies for English and Spanish reading are the same. The concept that Spanish reading is easier than English reading is not supported by any of the studies. The studies all provide evidence that a child must be reading in a language that he or she understands in order to use strategies like prediction. It is therefore to the child's advantage to learn to read in his or her native language in order to develop language and concepts thus allowing time to learn the second language. Children will not *need to relearn reading* in the second language and will not fall back in conceptual development.

The following general considerations for teachers have been derived from the six studies:

1. Because reading is a language-related process, the meaning of a text has to be accessible for a reader to interact with it. A reader needs to read in a familiar language to interact successfully with an author's message. Unless a child reads in a language that he or she understands, the language-related strategies necessary to obtain meaning cannot be utilized.

2. The reading process is identical in Spanish and English. A child who learns to read in Spanish does not need to relearn to read in English. Teachers need not worry about time spent reading in Spanish if reading strategies for obtaining meaning are being developed in Spanish.

The same language-related strategies are being used for English reading.

3. Neither Spanish nor English reading is a precise process wherein every element is identified. Reading in both languages is a meaning-gathering process requiring the taking of risks. Unless challenged and encouraged to take risks, a child may turn to a word-calling routine that discourages understanding. One reading strategy that allows children to take risks by predicting information is clozure, the elimination or covering of words in a text.

4. Readers' miscues provide information on their use of graphic, phonemic, syntactic, and semantic information; thus, they offer important information on which to build a reading program.

5. Readers should not be told words when they hesitate, or be corrected when they deviate from the printed text. Rather, they should be allowed to regress, predict information, and self-correct.

6. Such materials as language experience stories, which utilize the language children bring from home, help beginners develop reading strategies.

REFERENCES

Allen, P. D. A psycholinguistic analysis of the substitution of miscues of selected oral readers in grades two, four, and six and the relationships of these miscues to the reading process: a descriptive study. Doctoral dissertation, Wayne State University, 1969.

Barrera, R. B. Analysis and comparison of the first-language and oral reading behavior of native Spanish-speaking Mexican-American children. Doctoral dissertation, University of Texas at Austin, 1978.

Eaton, A. J. A psycholinguistic analysis of the oral reading miscues of selected field-dependent and field-independent native Spanish-speaking Mexican-American first-grade children. Doctoral dissertation, University of Texas at Austin, 1979.

Flores, B. *Is the concept of language interference valid?* Paper presented at the International Reading Association Annual Conference, Chicago, April 1982.

Goodman, K. S. A linguistic study of cues and miscues in reading. *Elementary English,* 1965, *42,* 639–643.

Goodman, K. S. Analysis of oral reading miscues: applied psycholinguistics. *Reading Research Quarterly,* 1969, *5*(1), 9–30.

Goodman, K. S. What we know about reading. In D. Page and D. J. Watson (Eds.), *Findings of research in miscue analysis: classroom implications.* Urbana, Ill.: Clearinghouse on Reading and Communications Skills/National Council of Teachers of English, 1976, pp. 57–70.

Goodman, K. S. Windows on the reading process. In K. S. Goodman (Ed.), *Miscue analysis: application to reading instruction.* Urbana, Ill.: Clearinghouse on Reading and Communication Skills/National Council of Teachers of English, 1978, pp. 3–14.

Goodman, K. S., and Burke, C. L. *Study of children's behavior while reading orally.* U.S.O.E. Final Report, Project No. S425, Contract No. OE-6-10-136. Washington, D.C., U.S. Department of Health, Education, and Welfare, March, 1968.

Goodman, K. S., and Burke, C. *Theoretically based studies of patterns of miscues in oral reading performance.* Final Report, Project No. 9-0375, Grant No. OE-G-09-320375-4569. U.S. Department of Health, Education and Welfare, Office of Education, Bureau of Research, April 1973.

Goodman, K. S., and Goodman, Y. *Reading of American children whose language is a stable rural dialect of English or a language other than English: final report.* Project NIE-C-00-3-0087. U.S. Department of Health, Education, and Welfare. National Institute of Education, 1978.

Goodman, Y. M. A psycholinguistic description of observed oral reading phenomena in selected young beginning readers. Doctoral dissertation, Wayne State University, 1967.

Goodman, Y. M., and Burke, C. L. *Reading miscue inventory.* New York: Macmillan, 1972.

Guszak, F. J. *Diagnostic reading instruction in the elementary school.* New York: Harper & Row, 1978.

Hudelson-Lopez, S. J. The use of context by native Spanish-speaking Mexican-American children when they read in Spanish. Doctoral dissertation, University of Texas at Austin, 1975.

Menosky, D. M. A psycholinguistic description of oral reading miscues generated during the reading of varying portions of text by selected readers from grades two, four, six, and eight. Doctoral dissertation, Wayne State University, 1971.

Page, W. A psycholinguistic description of patterns of miscues generated by a proficient reader in second grade, an average reader in fourth grade, and an average reader in sixth grade encountering basal reader selections ranging from pre-primer to sixth grade. Doctoral dissertation, Wayne State University, 1970.

Silva, A. D. Oral reading behavior of Spanish-speaking children taught by a meaning-based program. Doctoral dissertation, University of Texas at Austin, 1979.

Witkin, H. A. Individual differences in ease of perception of embedded figures. *Journal of Personality,* 1950, *19,* 1–15.

13 | Cognitive Style and Mexican American Children's Perceptions of Reading

OLIVIA N. SARACHO
University of Maryland

Children's understanding of the nature of the reading process influences the way they learn to read, and they may have a better chance to learn to read if they understand the process. Thus, it would be helpful to find out what the children believe the reading process is in order to help them rectify misconceptions and develop a proper understanding of the process. A limited number of studies of children's perceptions of reading have been conducted. Muskopf (1962) attempted to relate first-grade children's reading achievement to two conceptions of reading: functional and formal. "Functional reading" refers to materials that pupils need to learn to read in order to function and survive in society: such materials as medicine labels, danger signs, road signs, and warning notices (Wilson, 1981). Formal reading is taught by presenting learning activities in some arranged, sequential order. Methods of instruction that create a desire to learn to read are used to teach formal reading. The results of Muskopf's study were inconclusive; he suggested that it might have been better to question the children directly about their conceptions of reading.

A later study examined the same topic. Reid (1966) questioned children about their conceptions of reading but instead of trying to discover whether one or two particular concepts were predominant, examined children's general level of concept formation in relation to reading and writing as embodied in the technical vocabulary, the growth of the developed concepts, and the role that these concepts play in the actual learning of the skills. The results indicated that the five-year-old children were aware that they could not read and had very little understanding of the nature of reading. They perceived it as a mysterious activity and had only the vaguest of expectations before they experienced it.

Tovey (1976) investigated children's perceptions of reading in the light of several psycholinguistic concepts. Thirty children, five each from grades one through six, participated in the study. Tovey found that teachers used the

201

word-recognition approach as the reading model. The results showed that the children had been taught to think of reading as an oral activity involving the pronunciation of words either immediately after recognizing them or after carefully examining every letter in each word. Such a technique suggests that reading is a word-calling process, not a thinking process. The thinking process was later included in a later study.

Myers and Paris (1978) analyzed second- and sixth-grade children's meta-cognitive knowledge about reading to provide a broader description of their conceptualizations. They defined metacognitive knowledge as general information that provides effective guidance in selecting and implementing task-relevant skills. Second-grade children were aware of the influence of some reading dimensions, such as interest, familiarity, and length, but they were less aware than the sixth graders of the semantic structure of paragraphs, the goals of reading, and strategies for solving comprehension failures.

Rawson (1979) proposed an approach to reading instruction derived from studies of Piaget, linguists (such as Chomsky and Halle), and others. It included an integration of cognitive growth, such as understanding of basic structures for language and reading. Competency in thinking was to be the objective of reading instruction. Young children learn to discover specific operations by simultaneously reflecting, thinking, and manipulating concrete materials. This process will help children to make a transition from concrete thinking to abstract thinking. For example, children learn similarities and differences as they manipulate objects. In reading they abstract distinctive features of consonant sounds, associating them with a symbol and recognizing classes of consonants (voiced and whispered). Then they learn to classify them into consonant clusters, vowels, suffixes, and so on. They consolidate and extend these and other operations in thinking to new conditions. The meaning of a word is determined as a class name and its relationship between the structure and meaning in the sentence. To help children understand the reading process, Rawson suggested the development of reading programs using cognitively oriented questions. The questions would elicit operations in thinking, and children's responses would then be considered in terms of the cognitive development and the understanding they represent. For instance, a response might indicate a need for a new challenge in thinking or, alternatively, a need to consolidate and extend to reading the thinking strategies they were currently discovering.

Below is a report of a study that examined children's understanding and perceptions of the reading process and analyze that understanding through cognitive-style mapping. The subsequent discussion reviews the cognitive styles of Mexican American children and cognitive mapping itself. The study presented here is part of current efforts to identify factors that influence the reading performance of bilingual bicultural children. The alarming failure in schools of children who have a first language other than English has prompted interest in helping these children to improve their overall academic performance. The possibility that there are cultural differences in cognitive styles is one area of recent emphasis.

COGNITIVE STYLE

Cognitive style is an individual's mode of perceiving, thinking, remembering, and problem solving. While all people react according to the situations in which they find themselves, they vary in their manner of reacting. These differences are in part a function of cognitive style. The distinctive modes of functioning known as cognitive styles are highly consistent and stable (Saracho and Spodek, 1981; Witkin, Moore, Goodenough, and Cox, 1977); they are also thought to be culture-bound.

Cognitive Style in Mexican American Children

The culture of Mexican American children and its relationship to cognitive style has been a concern of many researchers (Kagan and Buriel, 1977; Ramírez and Castañeda, 1974; Saracho, 1983). All have utilized the field-dependence-independence dimension of cognitive style, and most believe that the processing of environmental events is based upon the interaction of experience and such cognitive activities such as thinking, learning, language, and cultural transmission. Studies that have compared Mexican American and Anglo American children in terms of this dimension of cognitive style have found that Mexican American children are more global, while Anglo American children are more analytic (Kagan and Buriel, 1977; Kagan and Zahn, 1975; Ramírez and Price-Williams, 1974). Witkin (1973) attributes these differences to cultural differences in child-rearing practices and deference to authority. Saracho (1983), however, suggests that there is insufficient evidence to support the contention that all Mexican American children are global thinkers.

The abovementioned studies have focused on the culture and language of Mexican American children in relation to one dimension of cognitive style. Cognitive mapping, a way of displaying cognitive style as a whole has seldom been used with these children, although Baecher (1973) employed cognitive-style maps of Mexican American and Puerto Rican fourth and fifth graders to demonstrate the use of educational cognitive style analysis as a diagnostic-prescriptive technique. Since it is believed that both culture and language require multi-dimensional skills that can be organized to a conceptual framework, it may be helpful to assess Mexican American students along these lines. In the study reported below, the cognitive styles of various age groups were mapped and analyzed in terms of field dependence and independence. For example, students who were influenced by their associates and family in their interpretations of symbols in reading were characterized as field-dependent; students who were mapped under individuality—that is, who depended on themselves for symbolic meanings in reading—were characterized as field-independent.

Cognitive Mapping

Cognitive mapping is a way of ordering the numerous elements that make up individuals' cognitive styles. It is a relatively simple way of developing a profile of a child's cognitive style. Responses to descriptive statements are tallied and then weighted and combined into categories to yield a profile of the student as a learner, thinker, and reader. Thus, a cognitive map is a graphic description of a set of self-descriptive statements.

An individual's style encompasses various elements and basic structures (Baecher, 1976):

> *Symbols and their meanings.* Two kinds of symbols, theoretical (such as words and numbers) and qualitative (such as sensory or programmatic symbols and codes), are used to develop knowledge and derive meaning from milieu and personal experiences.
>
> *Cultural determinants.* For every individual there is an influence that dominates his or her interpretation of symbols. These are: (1) individuality, in which children use their own interpretations; (2) associates, in which children use their peer group's interpretation; and (3) family, in which children use their family members' interpretation.
>
> *Modalities of inference.* People make inferences by categorizing information; comparing and contrasting information; analyzing, questioning, and evaluating; and using evidence to make deductions.

These three categories describe (1) how people receive and process stimuli and information, (2) how their learning is affected by others, and (3) how they reason to conclusions. The first element includes spoken and written words and numbers, the response to sensory stimuli, and the setting. The second element indicates the degree to which students are influenced by peers and by authority. The third element provides clues about their modes of inference: Do they most often reason through the use of rules, through logical proofs, through comparisons? (Kusler, 1979). When a student's responses have been weighted and arranged, they yield a cognitive map, a relatively quick graphic view of his or her learning "terrain." The profile indicates the degree to which each of the cognitive elements is significant in the student's cognitive style. Three levels of significance can be determined: major, minor, and negligible. At the major level, the element in question exists in the student's statements more than half the time. At the minor level, it exists in the student's statements less than half the time. At the negligible level, the element is rarely found.

The present study was conducted to describe the children's perceptions of reading and relate these to the children's cognitive style through the use of a cognitive style-map. Research questions and subquestions addressed were as follows:

What are young children's perceptions of the reading process?
1. What is reading?
2. What behavior do young children associate with young children who like reading?
3. Which behavior do they associate with young children who do not like reading?
4. Where does reading occur?

What age-related differences exist in the cognitive-mapping categories?
1. What are the cognitive maps of the different age groups for symbols and their meanings?
2. What are the cognitive maps of the different age groups for cultural determinants?
3. What are the cognitive maps of the different age groups for modalities of inference?

METHODOLOGY AND PROCEDURES

The children were randomly selected from a pool of a hundred volunteers. There were sixty children (thirty boys and thirty girls), ten from each age group: three-, four-, five-, six-, seven-, and eight-year-olds. The ethnic background of all of the subjects was Mexican American, which was determined by the children's last names, information from teachers or parents, and the children's knowledge of the Spanish language.

An open-ended interview was used to obtain the children's perceptions of reading and identify the elements that were present in their cognitive style. The Guide to Cognitive Mapping developed by Bowman, Burch, Hill, and Nunney (cited in Baecher, 1976) was used to map the children's cognitive styles.

The subjects were interviewed individually in a quiet place, using English and Spanish, by a female interviewer of the same ethnic background as the children. After a preliminary introduction, an open-ended interview was individually administered in a conversational, relaxed, and informal manner. The interviewer explained to the children that she needed some information from them about reading, emphasizing that there were no "right" or "wrong" answers to her questions.

All interviews were taperecorded, and each child's responses were later transcribed. Two judges checked the transcriptions and used content analysis to develop categories from the responses. There was a 93 percent inter-coder reliability. Frequency distributions were tallied for elements in the children's responses that fit into each of the categories. Percentages for each category were computed, based on the total number of responses collected rather than on the number of respondents; thus, the unit of analysis was each category. These frequency distributions were also used to determine how the response frequencies varied among the different age groups. A chi square was calculated to examine each question.

A similar procedure was used to map the children's cognitive styles. Frequency distributions were tallied for the children's descriptive statements, taken from the transcript, which were assigned to one of the following categories a· d subcategories (Bowman, Burch, Hill, and Nunney, cited in Baecher, 1976):

SYMBOLS AND THEIR MEANINGS. Children use symbols to obtain knowledge and meaning. For example, they use:

1. *Theoretical visual linguistics* to derive meaning from words they see
2. *Theoretical auditory linguistics* to derive meaning from words they hear
3. *Theoretical visual quantitative* to obtain meaning from numbers they see
4. *Theoretical auditory quantitative* to obtain meaning from numbers they hear
5. *Qualitative auditory* to obtain meaning through hearing
6. *Qualitative olfactory* to obtain meaning by smelling
7. *Qualitative savory* to obtain meaning through taste
8. *Qualitative tactile* to obtain meaning through feeling
9. *Qualitative visual* to obtain meaning using sight
10. *Qualitative proprioceptive (fine)* to synthesize symbols to perform a complex task using fine muscles (such as playing a musical instrument or typing) or to immediately become aware of a possible set of interrelationships among symbolic mediations
11. *Qualitative proprioceptive (gross)* to synthesize symbols to perform a complex task using gross muscles (such as throwing a baseball) or to immediately become aware of a possible set of interrelationships between symbolic mediations
12. *Qualitative proprioceptive dextral (fine),* provided the child has a predominance of right-eyed, right-handed, and right-footed tendencies (as a right-handed person has), to synthesize a number of symbolic mediations to perform a complex task using fine musculature (such as writing with the right hand)

13. *Qualitative proprioceptive dextral (gross),* provided the child is right-handed, to synthesize a number of symbolic mediations to perform a complex task using gross musculature (such as throwing a ball with the right hand)

14. *Qualitative proprioceptive kinematics (fine)* to synthesize a number of symbolic mediations to perform a task using fine musculature to monitor a complex physical activity

15. *Qualitative proprioceptive kinematics (gross)* to synthesize a number of symbolic mediations to perform a task using gross musculature to monitor a complex physical activity

16. *Qualitative proprioceptive sinistral (fine),* provided the child has a predominance of left-eyed, and left-footed tendencies (as a left-handed person has), to synthesize symbolic mediations to perform a complex task involving fine musculature (such as writing with the left hand)

17. *Qualitative proprioceptive sinistral (gross),* provided the child is left-handed, to provide symbolic mediations to perform a complex task involving gross musculature (such as throwing a ball with the left hand)

18. *Qualitative proprioceptive temporal (fine)* to synthesize symbolic mediations to perform a task requiring the use of fine musculature to monitor a complex physical activity involving timing

19. *Qualitative proprioceptive temporal (gross)* to synthesize symbolic mediations to perform a task requiring the use of gross musculature to monitor a complex physical activity involving timing

20. *Qualitative code emphathetic* to be sensitive to the feelings of others

21. *Qualitative code esthetic* to enjoy the beauty of an object or idea

22. *Qualitative code ethic* to make a commitment to a personal set of values, a group of principles, obligations, and/or responsibilities

23. *Qualitative code histrionic* to deliberately perform an action to produce a particular effect on other persons

24. *Qualitative code kinesics* to understand and communicate using nonverbal behavior (such as smiles and gestures)

25. *Qualitative code kinesthetic* to perform motor skills in an acceptable way

26. *Qualitative code proxemics* to be sensitive to the degree of physical and social proximity other persons permit oneself

27. *Qualitative code synnoetics* to have personal knowledge of oneself

28. *Qualitative code transactional* to maintain positive interactions to influence other persons

29. *Qualitative code temporal* to respond according to expectations imposed on an activity by members in the role-set associated with that activity

CULTURAL DETERMINANTS. These were described at the beginning of this section.

1. Individuality
2. Associates
3. Family

MODALITIES OF INFERENCE. These are elements indicating ways of making inferences. Children use:

1. *Magnitude* to define norms or categorical classifications in accepting or rejecting a hypothesis
2. *Difference* to contrast or compare selected characteristics or measurements
3. *Relationship* to synthesize a set of dimensions or incidents into a unified whole or to analyze a situation to discover the other related parts
4. *Appraisal* to use magnitude, difference, and relationship in analyzing, questioning, or appraising something in the process of reaching a conclusion
5. *Deduction* to work out logical proofs, as in geometry or syllogistic reasoning

The combination of these elements makes up an individual's cognitive style, and a map of an individual's cognitive style indicates how he or she learns and acquires meaning. For instance, children who like to have stories read to them have a tendency to seek information through listening. This response would be categorized under "qualitative auditory" in the area of "symbols and their meanings." If the child's response indicated a preference to learn from a family member, it would be categorized under "family" in the area of "cultural determinants." Some children's responses indicated that they used a variety of resources (such as pictures, letters, and numbers) to classify, analyze, and interpret information before internalizing a message. Such responses would be categorized under "magnitude" in the area of "modalities of inference." This categorizing process was used to produce maps of cognitive styles.

Cognitive styles were mapped for each child and then collapsed by age group. The children's perceptions of reading were used to identify elements in their cognitive styles. For each age group a frequency distribution among the different cognitive elements was tallied from the children's responses. The total for each frequency was ranked on the nine-point scale developed by Nunney (1975) to determine the degree of strength for each element. The following principles were employed (Baecher, 1973):

1. A rank of 5–9 in the point scale means that the element is dominant in the population that exhibits it; a major orientation toward the element is found in that population.

2. A rank of 3–4 means that the element is a minor one.
3. A rank of 1–2 means that the element is in the lower quarter of the distribution; a negligible orientation toward the element is found. A negligible orientation does not mean that the element does not exist, but rather that its strength in the cognitive style of the Mexican American child is insignificant.

RESULTS

The results are presented in two parts. The first part presents the children's perceptions of reading, and the second maps their responses onto their cognitive style.

Perceptions of Reading

The children's responses indicate that age determines young children's perceptions of reading. The data were grouped in relation to four questions, and the children's responses were categorized using content analysis. Responses of children of different ages are shown in figures 1 to 4.

Figure 1 shows the responses of each age group to the first question: "What do you see in reading?" For three-year-olds, reading is still a mysterious activity; the four-year-olds are beginning to relate the meaning of reading to what is being read; the five-year-olds are beginning to associate reading with print; the six-year-olds are becoming more aware of print; the seven-year-olds see reading as essential to learning; and the eight-year-olds interpret "reading" as "reading books" as well as "learning to read." Some of the eight-year-olds are becoming aware that reading includes an analysis of words. The differences in responses varied significantly by age ($\chi^2 = 74.41$, $p < .01$).

The second question was: "How do boys and girls act when they like reading?" The data are presented in figure 2. Many of the three-year-olds named people who could read and many named a book; the four-year-olds described a feeling of liking to read; the five-year-olds uniformly associated liking to read with proper behavior; the six-year-olds perceived it as reading many things (such as stories, reading books, letters, and numbers) and experiencing happiness when reading; the seven-year-olds thought of it as enjoying an activity involving mostly reading (such as listening to others read, learning to read, or liking to study through reading) and exhibiting good behavior; and the eight-year-olds viewed liking to read as showing good behavior. The age differences in these responses were significant ($\chi^2 = 77.65$, $p < .01$).

The third question was: "How do boys and girls act when they do not like reading?" Figure 3 presents the data. The three-year-olds answered this question mainly by identifying behavior (misbehaving or nothing); the four-year-olds described a feeling (unhappy and sad) and a behavior (misbehaving); the

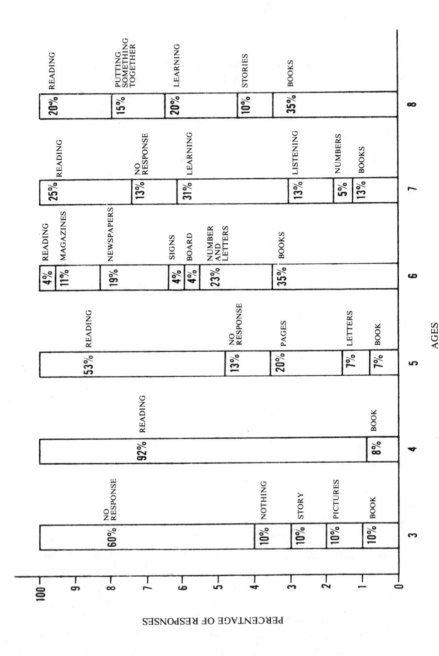

Figure 1: Children's Responses to Question 1: What Do You See in Reading?

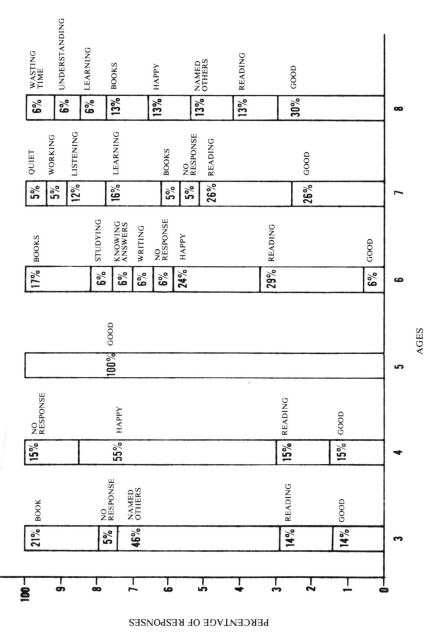

Figure 2: Children's Responses to Question 2: How Do Boys and Girls Act When They Like Reading?

211

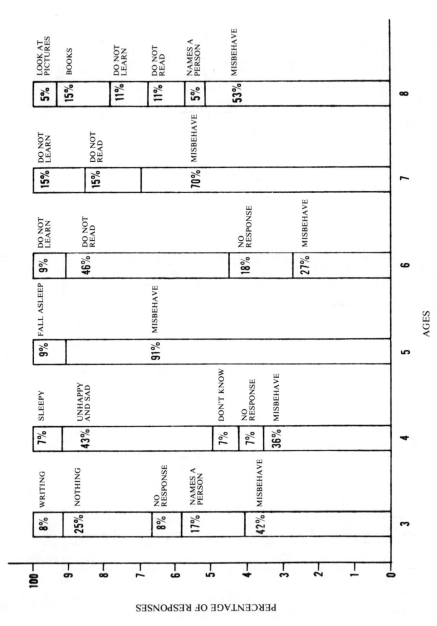

Figure 3: Children's Responses to Question 3: How Do Boys and Girls Act When They Do Not Like Reading?

212

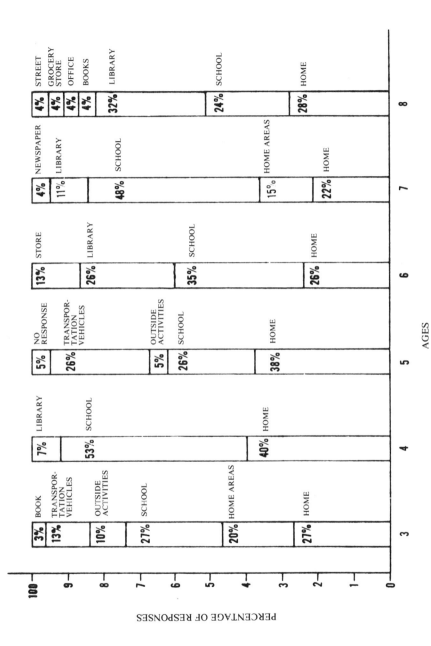

Figure 4: Children's Responses to Question 4: Where Do Boys and Girls Usually Read?

213

five-year-olds overwhelmingly saw such children as misbehaving; the six-year-olds perceived them as not reading and as misbehaving; the seven-year-olds also described them as misbehaving; and the eight-year-olds viewed them as misbehaving or doing things other than reading. A comparison of responses across the ages again yielded significant differences by age ($\chi^2 = 26.85$, $\rho < .05$).

The fourth question asked: "Where do boys and girls usually read?" These responses are presented in figure 4. The three-year-olds saw children's reading as occurring mostly at home and in school. They identified home areas where children read, including the kitchen, the couch, and, for the majority, bed. They assumed that children read in school because this was the major purpose of going to school. The four-year-olds also viewed reading as occurring mostly in school and secondarily at home. Some of these children had experienced reading in the public library. The five-year-olds thought children read mostly in the home and secondarily in school. However, they usually took a book with them when they traveled with their mothers, and so many of them responded that they read in the car, bus, or airplane. The six-year-olds named the school, the library, and the home. The seven-year-olds named school, the home, and, like the three-year-olds, various home areas. The eight-year-olds seemed to read mostly in the library and at home (as they did their homework), and they read at school, but, according to them, mainly during reading lessons or when they were working at their desks. These responses too indicated significant differences among the various age groups ($\chi^2 = 52.55$, $\rho < .01$).

Cognitive Mapping

In the second part of the study, the data were grouped according to the elements in cognitive style mapping. Profiles of the age groups indicated the degree to which each cognitive element was significant in the students' cognitive style. Table 1 displays the cognitive mapping of the children's responses.

The three-year-olds have a limited ability to derive meaning from printed words. However, they can process the meaning of spoken words and things that they see. The synthesis of several symbolic mediations to perform a physical activity that requires the use of fine motor skills seems to be a major strength with this group. Three-year-olds also tend to enjoy beauty in their environment. There was evidence that children initiated their set of values, principles, and responsibilities at this age. They are becoming independent, although the family and peers have a major influence on their thinking. The three-year-olds are beginning to develop definitions, categorize their thinking, and test their ideas. They are also becoming aware of differences and learning to make comparisons. However, they have a minor capacity to synthesize these characteristics (such as "Santa Claus doesn't have time to read, he's busy making toys,"

Table 1: Scale of Responses for Age Groups

	Age groups					
Elements	3	4	5	6	7	8
SYMBOLS AND THEIR MEANINGS						
Theoretical visual linguistics	2	6	4	9	3	5
Theoretical auditory linguistics	7	—	—	—	9	7
Theoretical visual quantitative	—	—	—	9	2	5
Qualitative visual	6	1	4	9	2	—
Qualitative proprioceptive (fine)	—	—	—	9	—	—
Qualitative proprioceptive kinematics (fine)	9	—	—	7	—	—
Qualitative code esthetic	7	—	9	4	—	4
Qualitative code ethic	2	2	5	2	7	4
Qualitative code transactional	—	—	—	9	—	—
CULTURAL DETERMINANTS						
Individuality	1	5	9	3	3	2
Associates	9	6	3	6	5	5
Family	9	6	6	4	6	4
MODALITIES OF INFERENCE						
Magnitude	5	7	9	7	5	—
Difference	5	7	9	7	5	—
Relationship	4	6	9	7	4	—
Appraisal	2	2	—	2	2	9

Note: The scale is based on the nine-point scale developed by Nunney (1975).

Percentage ranges for orientations:
negligible   0–25   1 to 2
minor   26–49   3 to 4
major   50–99   5 to 9

"picks out a book by themselves," or "gets a book and reads it") and a limited ability to assess them (such as "all kids love to read" or "sits and does nothing").

Although the four-year-olds are able to obtain meaning from written words, they are limited in their ability to perceive meaning through observation. Like the three-year-olds, they are at the initial stage of developing their own set of values, principles, and responsibilities. They are influenced by their own interpretations as well as their family's and associates'. They make inferences by classifying, making comparisons, and synthesizing dimensions (components which are discovered by analyzing a situation such as "sits down, being quiet, behaves, being nice, listens to teacher read, likes it") and analyzing incidents into an organized meaning. They are, however, at the initial stage of appraising their inferences.

The five-year-olds have a limited ability to perceive meaning in written words and through sight, but they are able to enjoy the beauty of an object, idea, or environment. They have also developed a set of values, principles, obligations, and responsibilities. They are highly individualistic but are greatly influenced by their family and, to a minor degree, their peers. They make inferences by defining their own terms, testing ideas, and comparing characteristics or measurements, and they synthesize these inferences to draw conclusions about their world.

The six-year-olds seem to be good readers and to have the ability to derive meaning from written words, sight, numerical symbols, relationships, and measurements. They can perform and synthesize several symbolic mediations and have physical skills that they can apply to complex tasks, such as playing a guitar or typing. They are also able to synthesize several symbolic mediations while monitoring a complex activity through motion. They have a minor orientation toward the enjoyment of beauty in their environment. They are also beginning to establish their set of values, principles, and responsibilities. Maintaining a positive communication is a major concern for them, and it has a strong influence on their goals. Their decisions are influenced by their peers and family (in that order), and they have a minor orientation toward individuality. Six-year-olds are able to use their reasoning to define, categorize, compare, and synthesize facts and ideas of a situation. To a small degree, they appraise their inferences.

The seven-year-olds have a minor orientation toward obtaining meaning from printed words. The acquisition of meaning through hearing was a major element in their cognitive style; numerical symbols, relationships, and measurement, however, had a negligible influence. Seven-year-olds have developed values, principles, and responsibilities. Their decisions are influenced by their family and their associates; individualism is a minor element. Their inferences are based on classification, comparison, and appraisal; they have a minor ability to synthesize incidents and ideas.

The eight-year-olds are best able to derive meaning through listening. To a lesser degree they acquire information from written words and through observation. They have minor orientations toward establishing their own set of values, principles, and responsibilities and toward enjoying beauty. Their decisions are mainly influenced by their peers, though they have a minor tendency to be influenced by their families and a negligible tendency toward individualism. Their ability to make inferences is at a higher level than that of any of the other children in this study. Eight-year-olds are strong on appraisal, a mode of inference that synthesizes the other modes. They are able to categorize, classify, compare characteristics or measurements, and synthesize dimensions (components of specific situations) to organize their information and assess their performance.

CONCLUSION

Young children in this study were insensitive to or unaware of many important dimensions of reading. To them, reading was a mysterious activity. A four-year-old child said, "Why are you asking me these questions? You know I am in nursery school. We do not have reading there!" Since knowledge about reading is necessary for the acquisition of reading skills, educators may need to incorporate programs to teach young children to realize that the main purpose of reading is to abstract meaning from the written word. Reading aloud to nonreaders may be of great value in developing this understanding, since this involves children in the reading process even before the acquisition of formal reading skills. Work by Hoskinson (1977) and Chomsky (1979) suggests ways to help children understand the reading process. Hoskinson recommends a process he refers to as "assisted reading," where at approximately when the child is four or five years old, the adult (teacher or parent) reads phrases or sentences, then the child repeats these. Books and stories are read and reread in this manner while the adult simultaneously moves his or her finger slowly under the lines she or he is reading. When the adult feels the children are ready, he or she will encourage the children to read words they recognize before he or she reads them. The final stage of this process requires that the child be encouraged to read independently with the adults providing the words that they expect the child will not be able to read. Movement from the stage of *being read to* to *reading* takes place as a result of hypotheses children develop and test concerning the written language they continuously see and hear. Hoskinson's assisted reading can involve children in this process, while getting children to write even before they start learning to read, as Chomsky suggests, will allow them to see the communicative process that reading entails.

Teachers need to know the children's perceptions of reading in order to understand the characteristics that children attribute to the reading process, to make sure that they understand its purpose, scope, and requirements, and to implement situations that foster their reading performance. Teachers must have such insights into children's perceptions, formulate plans, generate hypotheses, check their behavior, and evaluate their progress (Myers and Paris, 1978). This information can help teachers select strategies to teach effectively.

The perceptions of reading held by the children studied here are more closely related to their experience with reading than to anything else. One of the most interesting findings is that at the age of five reading is suddenly and dramatically linked to proper behavior. Boys and girls are viewed as being good when they read and as misbehaving when they do not like to read. Undoubtedly this perception is linked to the importance ascribed to reading during the first years of schooling. Reading-readiness programs in the kindergarten have probably helped—perhaps without conscious intent—to create this perception, and the recent concern for early success in reading may have helped to reinforce it. They need to learn as soon as possible that reading is important not just because readers are considered good children and nonreaders misbehavers, but because reading can provide them with satisfaction and serve their purposes. As children move through the primary grades, they still link reading with being good or happy, but not to the same overwhelming degree. It is probably the increased contact with reading that allows children to begin to see it in more complex ways.

The other changes found in children's perceptions of reading are related to where they read. While home and school continue to be dominant settings, as children mature they recognize that reading occurs in other places as well. This change is probably the result of experience rather than any developmental shift. If more problematic situations related to reading had been presented to children, the interviews might have revealed the effects of shifts in intellectual development. For example, if children had been presented with a set of cards. Each card could have been unique and the complete set could have been composed of possible combinations such as shape (circles, triangles, squares), number (one, two, or three), or color (red, blue, or yellow). The child could have been presented the card illustrating the concept and the child would then select instances illustrating the concept. Another example would be where a set of cards was presented to the child with four problems that the child was required to solve. These situations would provide some insight on the relationship of the child's intellectual capacity and performance on concept-attainment tasks where materials consist of several perceptual attributes (e.g., shape, number, or color). The children's readiness to accept the relevance of attribute values of an initial exemplar of the concept would provide evidence of individual consistencies in perception. This approach could provide guidance to the identification of numerous cognitive style dimensions, one of the most prominent of which has been field dependence and independence.

Studies have characterized the cognitive style of Mexican Americans as more field-dependent than that of Anglo Americans. Since cognitive style is related to psychological and intellectual qualities, these studies have educational implications. Children's responses to different types of instruction depend on their cognitive styles. For instance, field-dependent children favor group and exploratory experiences, but field-independent children favor independent work and impersonal, direct forms of instruction. Knowledge of cognitive styles and their influence on methods of teaching and learning can help teachers of young students to improve teaching strategies.

In this study, field dependence and independence were assessed not in absolute but in relative terms. The different age groups studied can be characterized in relation to field dependence and independence according to the mapping of their cognitive style. It can be suggested that a predominance of associates and family dimensions in the cultural determinants section and the magnitude and difference dimensions in the modalities of inference section indicates a field-dependent cognitive style. Surprisingly, the five-year-old children were more field-independent than any of the other age groups. As table 1 shows, the five-year-olds were field-independent in terms of cultural determinants because they relied on their own interpretation of symbols (9); in contrast, the three-year-olds (1) and the eight-year-olds (2) were more field-dependent. The three-year-olds were influenced to a major degree (9) by both their family and their associates, and the eight-year-olds to a major degree (5) by their associates and to a minor degree (4) by their family members. In terms of modalities of inference, it seems that the five-year-olds used both field-dependent (magnitude and difference) and field-independent (relationship) cognitive styles to make inferences. However, they were unable to use the extreme modalities of inference (appraisal and deduction), which are characteristic of greater field independence. The field independence of the way children make inferences seems to increase as they mature. This is consistent with studies of cognitive style related to ethnicity (Saracho, 1983) and to age (Witkin, 1973; Witkin, Moore, Goodenough, and Cox, 1977).

The data are restricted to descriptions of age-related changes in children's responses. One can speculate, however, about further uses of cognitive mapping. Educational materials and teachers' strategies are usually oriented toward decoding and translating skills in beginning readers. Students' cognitive strengths are disregarded. Cognitive mapping is one method for assessing each student's cognitive strengths. It can help teachers identify the dynamics and growing search for meaning on the part of the bilingual bicultural students. Their strengths can be assessed and used to plan appropriate instructional strategies. If cognitive mapping can identify traits related to the acquisition of reading skills, then educators may be able to incorporate specific techniques related to the children's cognitive style into the reading curriculum.

Reading instruction and cognitive style have been investigated independently. In light of the work that has been done on cognitive style in relation to bilingual bicultural children, studies of the relationship between cognitive style and reading might be most productive.

REFERENCES

Baecher, R. E. An exploratory study to determine levels of educational development, reading levels, and the cognitive styles of Mexican American and Puerto Rican students in Michigan. Doctoral dissertation, University of Michigan, 1973.

Baecher, R. E. Bilingual children and educational cognitive style analysis. In A. Sim-ões, Jr. (Ed.), *The bilingual child.* New York: Academic Press, 1976, pp. 41–61.

Chomsky, C. Approaching reading through invented spelling. In L. B. Resnick and P. S. Weaver (Eds.), *Theory and practice of early reading* (vol. 1). Hillsdale, N.J.: Lawrence Erlbaum Associates, 1979, pp. 43–65.

Hoskinson, K. Reading readiness: three viewpoints. *Elementary School Journal,* 1977, *78* (1), 44–52.

Kagan, S., and Buriel, R. Field dependence-independence and Mexican-American culture and education. In J. L. Martínez (ed.), *Chicano psychology.* New York: Academic Press, 1977, pp. 279–328.

Kagan, S., and Zahn, G. L. Field-dependence and the school achievement gap between Anglo-American and Mexican-American children. *Journal of Educational Psychology,* 1975, *67,* 643–650.

Kusler, G. E. Cognitive mapping and prescriptive education. In National Association of Secondary School Principals, *Student learning styles: diagnosing and prescribing programs.* Reston, Va.: National Association of Secondary School Principals, 1979.

Muskopf, A. F. The beginning reader's concept of reading as related to intelligence, reading achievement and the method of introducing reading. Master's thesis, University of Chicago, 1962.

Myers, M., and Paris, S. G. Children's metacognitive knowledge about reading. *Journal of Educational Psychology,* 1978, *70,* 680–690.

Nunney, D. N. Educational cognitive style: a basis for personalizing instruction. *Educational Scientist,* 1975, *1,* 13–26.

Ramírez, M., and Castañeda, A. *Cultural democracy, bicognitive development, and education.* New York: Academic Press, 1974.

Ramírez, M., and Price-Williams, D. R. Cognitive styles of children of three ethnic groups in the United States. *Journal of Cross-Cultural Psychology,* 1974, *5* (2), 212–219.

Rawson, H. Cognition and reading: an approach to instruction. In T. G. Waller and G. E. MacKinnon (Eds.), *Reading research: advances in theory and practice* (vol. 1). New York: Academic Press, 1979, pp. 187–258.

Reid, J. F. Learning to think about reading. *Educational Research,* 1966, *9,* 56–62.

Saracho, O. N. The relationship of teachers' cognitive styles and ethnicity to predictions of academic success and achievement of Mexican-American and Anglo-American students. In E. García and M. Sam-Vargas (Eds.), *The Mexican American child: language, cognitive and social development.* Tempe, Arizona: Arizona University Press, 1983.

Saracho, O. N., and Spodek, B. The teachers' cognitive styles and their educational implications. *Educational Forum,* 1981, *45* (2), 153–159.

Tovey, D. R. Children's perceptions of reading. *Reading Teacher,* 1976, *29* (6), 536–540.

Wilson, R. M. *Diagnostic and remedial reading for classroom and clinic* (4th ed.). Columbus, Ohio: Merrill, 1981.

Witkin, H. A. The role of cognitive style in academic performance and in teacher-student relations. Paper presented at a symposium on "Cognitive Styles, Creativity and Higher Education," sponsored by the Graduate Records Examinations Board, Montreal, Canada, November 1972. Research bulletin 73-11, Princeton, N.J.: Educational Testing Service, 1973.

Witkin, H. A., Moore, C. A., Goodenough, D. R., and Cox, P. W. Field-dependent and field-independent cognitive styles and their educational implications. *Review of Educational Research,* 1977, *47* (1), 1–64.

14 | The Oral Reading Miscues of Field-Dependent and Field-Independent Mexican American Children

ARLINDA J. EATON
California State University, Northridge

Ramírez and Castañeda (1974) contend that a large proportion of Mexican American students are required to function in educational environments that are culturally undemocratic, environments that fail to consider the influences of home and community socialization on the students' preferred cognitive styles:

> Most bicultural-bilingual programs and other programs attempting to develop culturally democratic educational environments have focused exclusively on language and heritage and have ignored cognitive styles. . . . Seeds of failure and alienation exist in these environments, environments which appear superficially to be conducive to success for Mexican American children. The cognitive-styles component, then, must play a central role in the development of culturally democratic educational environments. (Ramírez and Castañeda, 1974, p. 129)

The low reading scores and high dropout rate of Mexican American students are recognized and well documented (Litsinger, 1973). This situation warrants serious attention, and I believe that research examining the processing of print by bilingual Mexican American students might offer insight into this area of concern. The need to study interactions between linguistic boundaries and individual cognitive differences has been emphasized and cited in the literature (Ohnmacht, 1970), and cognitive-style research may advance our understanding of reading underachievement in particular. Such research requires accurate descriptive data about the oral reading behavior and preferred cognitive styles of bilingual children.

From a psycholinguistic perspective, reading is one of the two active receptive language processes, the other being listening. Readers successfully complete this complex process when they reconstruct a message encoded by a writer in printed language. The interaction between writer and reader is shaped by the three dimensions of language: semantic, syntactic, and pragmatic. During an interaction with print, a person's reading behavior is influenced by different cue systems, operating simultaneously, that result in his or her supplying either the words in print or miscues, deviations from the print (Goodman, 1965). These cues appear within words, in the flow of language, in factors external to language and the reader, and, most important, in factors within the reader. According to Goodman (1965, p. 639), the last category includes:

His language facility with the dialect of his subculture
His idiolect (his own personal version of the language)
His experiential background (the reader responds to cues in terms of his own real or vicarious experiences)
His conceptual background and ability (a reader can't read what he can't understand)

Intimately involved in the study of reading behavior are the cognitive processes through which readers acquire, organize, and employ knowledge. Cognitive style is one's characteristic mode of mental functioning. That is, people have preferred and consistent ways of processing information and organizing what they hear, see, remember, or think about. They approach the task of reading with their own established patterns, which enable them to cope with the environmental stimuli that surround the task. These stylistic patterns influence the manner in which they process print in order to derive meaning from it (Davey, 1971; Readence, 1975).

Field dependence and independence are but one dimension of cognitive-style orientation. Witkin, Dyk, Faterson, Goodenough, and Karp (1962) have employed the terms "field dependence" and "field independence" to describe the extent to which a person perceives analytically and overcomes an embedding context. Field dependence is the mode of perception at one extreme of the performance range, where the prevailing field strongly dominates perception. At the opposite end of the performance range lies field independence, where items are experienced as more or less separate from the surrounding field. Measures of this dimension of cognitive style form a continuous distribution, indicating that classifications merely reflect a tendency, in varying degrees of strength, toward one mode of perception or the other. They do not divide the world into two types.

It was noted above that readers are active participants in the reading act. Consequently, readers' thoughts and language cue not only their expected responses (the printed words), but also their observed responses (deviations from printed words). This phenomenon leads one to believe that readers' miscues are not random. Readers use the interrelated cue systems of language—graphophonic (the symbol-sound relationship), syntactic (grammar), and semantic (meaning)—in conjunction with their conceptual and experiential background to reconstruct meaning from print. The ways in which they employ these cue systems may be referred to as their linguistic strategies.

When individuals approach a reading task, they are confronted with a situation of response uncertainty (Smith, 1973, 1978). As a means of reducing this uncertainty, they impose their own organization upon the task. They select only what they need from the cue systems in order to reconstruct meaning from the print. Their selection is necessarily influenced by their established patterns of coping with environmental stimuli. Cognitive-style patterns—and in particular field dependence and independence because of the perceptual factor involved—may very well influence the types of cues that readers select as well as the extent to which they use those cues.

The purpose of this exploratory study is to investigate individual cognitive processes, or styles, as they relate to the oral reading strategies employed by native Spanish-speaking Mexican American first graders as they read in both English and Spanish. These reading strategies are revealed by an in-depth analysis of miscues. The Reading Miscue Inventory (Goodman and Burke, 1972) permitted the analysis of miscues at different levels of linguistic organization.

Three general questions served as the basis for the research:

> Does cognitive style—particularly the dimension of field dependence and independence—influence an individual's way of processing written language?
>
> Do the reading strategies employed by a bilingual individual vary according to the language in which she or he reads?
>
> Are there separate Spanish and English reading processes?

A sample of bilingual readers was assembled, and members were identified and grouped according to their degree of field dependence. The following specific research questions were then addressed:

> Do all members of the sample employ the same linguistic strategies in their attempt to reconstruct meaning from print?
>
> Do they all employ linguistic strategies to the same extent?
>
> Do they all comprehend equally well while reading?
>
> Do they all express an equal understanding of the material they have read?
>
> Do they all produce miscues that involve:
>
> 1. dialect
> 2. intonation

3. graphic similarity
4. sound similarity
5. grammatical function
6. correction
7. grammatical acceptability
8. semantic acceptability, and
9. meaning change?

The study is basically descriptive, its goal being to describe linguistically, according to the categories outlined in the Reading Miscue Inventory, the behavior during oral reading of bilingual children with varying degrees of field dependence. Information regarding the cognitive styles of Mexican American children is important to educators—teachers, administrators, and curriculum specialists—involved in the teaching of young children. It is as important for educators not involved, or only minimally involved, in bilingual programs as it is for those presently working in this area, since many Mexican American children are not in bilingual programs.

METHODOLOGY AND PROCEDURES

Sampling Procedure

The sample population for this study was selected from the sample population for a larger research project,[1] which was composed of children from a southeastern Texas public school district characterized as largely rural with substantial numbers of Spanish-dominant students of low socioeconomic status. The larger study included all kindergarten and first-grade children in four classrooms in two schools within the district. For the purposes of the smaller study, the sample was restricted to the twenty-one first-grade subjects who were receiving reading instruction in both English and Spanish. This decision was based on the fact that the kindergarten subjects of the larger project did not receive reading instruction, and findings reported in the literature suggest that cognitive style has its greatest impact during the initial learning of particular skills (Stone, 1976). Two migrant students had moved from the community by the time the data were collected, and one subject could not generate the twenty-five required miscues while reading the test passages in either lan-

---

[1]Funded by the National Institute of Education, "Teaching reading to bilingual children: effects of interaction on cognitive style and reading methodology on the reading achievement of bilingual children" is a longitudinal study designed to examine the effects of the interaction of learner characteristics (cognitive style, degree of bilingualism, cognitive development) and type of reading instruction on the reading achievement of Spanish-English bilingual children.

guage. Thus, the sample ultimately consisted of eighteen subjects (eight girls and ten boys), four of whom were unable to generate twenty-five miscues while reading in Spanish. Hence, eighteen sets of responses were analyzed in English, while only fourteen were analyzed in Spanish.

An advantage in using these first-grade subjects, none of whom was classified as an English-dominant speaker, was that their educational backgrounds were very similar. Before entry into the first grade, none had received formal reading instruction in either language. Their first six months of instruction included a substantial amount of synthetic phonics, as revealed by *RAMOS II* (Calfee and Calfee, 1976), a real-time documentation of classroom instruction. Because children progress at varied rates, and because the primary purpose of this study was to investigate the ways in which cognitive style might affect the use of different linguistic cue systems in reading, a specified grade level of reading was not a criterion for the selection of subjects. Each child's oral reading behavior was analyzed on her or his own reading level.

Instruments

All subjects were administered the Children's Embedded Figures Test (CEFT), developed by Witkin (1950), and the Matching Familiar Figures Test (MFFT), developed by Kagan et al. (1964), in order to identify them as field-dependent (FD) or field-independent (FI) and as impulsive or reflective; language facility was evaluated according to the Language Assessment Scales (LAS), developed by De Avila and Duncan (1977). The CEFT provided scores that formed a continuous distribution ranging from 4 to 15. Unlike the larger project, this study considered only the dimension of field dependence or independence. The ten subjects whose scores fell within one standard deviation from the mean (9.8) were classified as field-dependent/independent (FD/I) because their scores indicated that their perception was neither predominantly FD nor predominantly FI. Subjects whose scores extended beyond one standard deviation from the mean were considered FIs; there were three in this sample. Five had scores that extended beyond a negative one standard deviation from the mean. For the purposes of this study, these five were classified as FDs.

In addition to the CEFT, MFFT, and LAS, all subjects were administered De Avila's (1976) Cartoon Conservation Scales (CCS), a Piagetian-based measure of cognitive development including tasks that involve egocentricity and the conservation of number, substance, distance, identity, and length. The use of these nonverbal perceptual techniques to assess cognitive makeup helps avoid the penalty commonly imposed on students outside the mainstream culture by more traditional instruments for measuring IQ, which rely heavily on verbal-assessment procedures.

Total weighted scores for the eighteen subjects on Level 1 of the CCS ranged from a low of 22 to a high of 79; the sample mean was 46.9. Test results indicated that all subjects conserved on at least three of the six Piagetian-type tasks.

Materials

The textual materials used for both the English and Spanish test sessions came from the basal readers employed for reading instruction in the subjects' schools; the English selections were taken from the "Phonetic Keys to Reading" series (1972), while the Spanish selections were found in the basal readers of the Bilingual Oral Language and Reading Program (1973) developed by the Southwest Educational Development Laboratory. The materials for the study met certain general criteria; each selection: (1) followed a story format rather than an informational one; (2) contained a minimum of 300 words;[2] and (3) had not been read or heard previously by the subject.

Informal reading inventories in both languages were administered to the subjects by the examiners for the larger project during the final week of February 1979. All reading sessions were taperecorded by the examiners so that each subject's reading could be evaluated and her or his instructional level in both English and Spanish could be determined. Once a subject's instructional level was identified, the investigator went to the reader for the level just above it and selected a passage located at approximately the same point in the book as the inventory selection. This procedure allowed the reader to progress in the month between the time the inventory was administered and the time the oral reading samples for analysis were collected (last week of March 1979). Before these samples were collected, the classroom teacher and the subjects verified that the latter had not previously read or heard the passage selected by the investigator.

Data Collection and Analysis

No subject was required to read test stories in both English and Spanish during the same session. To avoid possible biasing effects due to unfamiliarity with the required task, a table of random numbers was used to select the ten subjects who initially read in English and the nine who initially read in Spanish.

The protocol established by Goodman and Burke (1972) was observed in collecting the data. The subjects were taperecorded in private, with only the subject and researcher present. Before the taping, the subjects were informed, in the language of the story to be read, that during the oral reading no help

---

[2]Sometimes more than one passage was read in order to meet this criterion.

would be forthcoming from the researcher when unfamiliar words were encountered. They were asked to employ the resources they normally used when reading alone, including predicting the unknown word or omitting it and going on.

The subjects were also informed that after reading the selection, they would be asked to retell everything they could remember about it in the language of the story. When the children preferred to use the other language, however, they were allowed to do so. Questions were asked by the researcher (in the language of the story) during the retelling in order to test comprehension or encourage a reluctant subject, but these were either open-ended or based on information the subject had already provided.

During the oral reading and taping, the researcher marked and recorded as much information as possible about the reading performance on a duplicated copy of the text. The marking system for miscue analysis described by Goodman and Burke (1972) was employed in noting the subject's reading behavior.

The task of analyzing the data began after the taperecording of the subjects' readings had been completed. The researcher listened to the tapes of the oral readings as many times as necessary to ensure that all deviations from the text could be precisely identified and added to the duplicate copies marked at the time of the reading sessions. The second step in the analysis involved the coding of those deviations that were counted as miscues for the purposes of the study. Miscues were included or excluded according to the guidelines set forth in the Reading Miscue Inventory (RMI) (Goodman and Burke, 1972).

Each of the subject's twenty-five miscues was analyzed in terms of each of the inventory's nine categories (dialect, intonation, graphic similarity, sound similarity, grammatical function, correction, grammatical acceptability, semantic acceptability, and meaning change). The researcher recorded the appropriate subcategories for each item on the Reading Miscue Inventory Coding Sheet. Descriptive statistics obtained for each language and for individuals and groups, identified by cognitive-style orientation, consisted of percentage frequencies and means.

The statistical analysis of the RMI includes a retelling score, which measures the reader's understanding of what he or she has read. This score is usually obtained by adding points designated to show the reader's awareness of character analysis, theme, plot, and events. In this study, however, the investigator used the same method the Goodmans have used in their most recent research: The 100 retelling points were divided between character analysis and events. Plot and theme were noted, but points were not assigned to them. Each story was analyzed in advance of the taping, and numerical points were assigned to story events and character analyses. Readers accumulated points as their retellings corresponded to the precalculated analyses. Retelling scores were integrated with the statistical data derived from the coding sheets for interpretation.

A comparative profile was compiled for each subject, summarizing all the statistical findings for each language. Additionally, group comparisons for each of the nine categories of the RMI in each language and across languages were analyzed.

RESULTS

It is difficult to generalize the conclusions of this study to a larger population, since an in-depth and thorough analysis of individual reading performance dictates a sample small in number. Moreover, the reading performance of Mexican American children whose language background is not predominantly Spanish cannot be compared with the behavior exhibited by these first-grade subjects. Unlike children involved in bilingual programs, where a considerable amount of time is spent in instruction in the native language before initiating reading instruction in the second language, the subjects of this study experienced a very brief exposure to Spanish reading. Their results pertain to the limited amount of narrative material read for this research project and are not necessarily reproducible with other types of reading material. Furthermore, the conclusions drawn from an oral reading environment cannot necessarily be generalized to a silent reading environment.

Nonetheless, several tentative conclusions can be considered. Among these native-Spanish-speaking Mexican American bilingual readers, FDs and FIs appeared in the study results as distinct groups whether they read in their first language or their second. The manner in which FIs and FDs processed printed material, however, looked very much the same across languages. In other words, the reading strategies employed did not vary according to the language in which the children read. FDs and FIs drew on the same linguistic cue systems in both languages—graphophonic, syntactic, and semantic. These data therefore support previous research findings that indicate that there is a single reading process.

On the other hand, the reading behavior displayed during the Spanish and English reading sessions revealed a difference between the FI and FD groups in the extent to which they employed these cue systems. FI readers generally drew on the cue systems to a greater extent than the FD readers did and were more likely to attempt words. Consequently their rate of miscues per hundred words was lower than that of the FD group, who tended to be overly cautious. FI readers made more substitutions and fewer omissions.

The FIs made more use of graphic cues to bring meaning to the printed text. A similar pattern was seen in the category of phonemic similarity; the substitution miscues produced by the FI subjects represented a greater degree of phonemic similarity than those produced by the FD subjects. Hence, the FI and FD readers maintained their unique patterns across both languages.

It was observed that all of the readers substantially relied upon the graphophonic cueing system, probably as a result of their classroom instruction and reading materials. Barr (1975), too, noted that the instructional methods, synthetic and sight-word, to which her thirty-two first-grade subjects had been exposed, significantly determined their print translation strategies; in fact, most of the children who initially used a strategy different from the one emphasized in their classroom altered their strategy to conform with the class method and/ or materials by the end of first grade. In the present study only the FD readers used the graphophonic system to the exclusion of the grammatical and semantic systems (Goodman and Burke, 1972). This overreliance may indicate weakened control over syntax; the literature characterizes FD readers as passively involved with their environment to the extent that they do not assimilate habits of grammatical usage as readily as more FI readers do (Schwartz, 1972).

This study's finding that the FIs produced more nonword substitutions than the FDs is at first glance inconsistent with other cognitive-style research reports, which indicate that FIs have better word-recognition skills and attend to meaning more carefully than FD readers do. No such inconsistency exists, however, if one compares the number of nonwords produced by the subjects with the number of their substitution miscues. Because the FIs generated considerably more substitutions than their FD peers, they actually produced a lower proportion of nonword substitutions.

FI readers were more successful in substituting words that corresponded identically in grammatical function with the expected responses. They were also more efficient in generating grammatically and semantically acceptable miscues, which in turn meant that there were stronger grammatical relationships among their miscues. As is consistent with the cognitive-style literature, FI readers were able to make more use of available syntactic and semantic cue systems to anticipate, predict, and verify unknown words during the reading. Although the same pattern was apparent for both languages, FD and FI readers were less successful in English (their second language) in generating miscues that had grammatical functions identical with the expected responses.

The more independent readers were of their perceptual field, the more successful they appeared to be in generating miscues that did not alter the author's intended meaning. Because the FD subjects omitted unknown words far more frequently than did the FI subjects, their passages suffered extensive changes in meaning more frequently. Insertions did not effect changes in meaning to the degree that omissions did. Schwartz (1972) indicated that FIs draw on their language environment, as well as attend to details, when reading. It might therefore be expected that readers identified as FI would average more insertions than the FD readers, and the data for this study fulfilled this prediction. On the other hand, the data contradicted the prediction that FI readers, because of their greater attention to detail, would make fewer insertions.

Consistent across the two groups was the generation of a considerably smaller percentage of meaningful miscues (those that result in no change in meaning) in English than in Spanish. In other words, the subjects were more efficient in producing such miscues in their native language.

Both groups displayed correction tendencies, and both immediate and delayed corrections, in which the subjects had to regress several words in order to correct the miscue, were observed. As is consistent with other miscue research, it was found that most miscues remained uncorrected. Nonetheless, the FI subjects, characterized in the literature as meaning-seekers, generated the higher percentage of successful corrections when reading Spanish materials. When reading in English, they corrected their miscues as often as did the FDs.

Even though frequency of correction formed no pattern in terms of cognitive-style orientation, the relationship between correction strategies and grammatical acceptability did. The more concerned with the grammatical acceptability of miscues the subjects were, the further their scores on the CEFT fell toward the FI extreme of the continuum. FI readers corrected a larger percentage of their grammatically unacceptable and partially acceptable miscues and left uncorrected more of their fully and partially grammatically acceptable miscues.

A parallel relationship was noticeable where semantic acceptability was concerned. The FI subjects demonstrated a greater awareness of a need to correct miscues that effected a change of meaning in the passage and were less inclined to correct miscues that were either fully or partially acceptable semantically.

Intonation miscues were minimal during Spanish reading sessions. The FI subjects generated a larger percentage of miscues involving intonation, but then the opportunity to do so was greater for this group, since the subjects read more words carrying orthographic accents signaling stressed syllables and more material containing dialogue. The percentages of second-language miscues involving intonation were smaller for both groups than their respective percentages in Spanish.

In accordance with other miscue studies, few miscues generated by the subjects of this study involved the influence of dialect and/or the first or second language. Dialect variations that were simply phonologic in nature were not included in the analysis. It was not uncommon for a reader to produce a phonologic dialectal variant at one point in the selection but not in another. Evidence of dialect was more prevalent in the subjects' oral retellings than in their reading.

The ability to extract meaning while reading was represented by comprehension scores. These indicated that the more relatively FI subjects were relying on their own knowledge of language in order to bring meaning to print rather than relying totally on the print itself. In both languages FI readers comprehended more than FD readers during the reading act, and their comprehension was substantially greater when reading in Spanish than when reading in English. Unlike the FI readers, the FDs did slightly better in comprehending their second language than their first. This last finding might be explained by analyzing the comprehension score itself, which is derived by interrelating the miscues that result in no meaning change with the miscues that are not semantically acceptable but are successfully corrected by the reader. It is possible that given their greater familiarity with Spanish, the FDs actually could have corrected some of their semantically unacceptable miscues silently but did not feel a need to do so overtly. Thus, it appeared that they were comprehending less. The FDs' higher retelling scores in Spanish seem to support this explanation. The FIs' retelling scores revealed that they could relate considerably more of what they had read than the FDs could. Both FIs and FDs were able to relate substantially more of their reading in Spanish than of their reading in English.

CONCLUSION

Several tentative conclusions can be drawn from an analysis of the reading behavior of the bilingual first-grade subjects who participated in this study, and these conclusions allow for certain suggestions for instructional programs to be made. Both FI and FD groups gained more meaning from reading in Spanish, a fact that seems to corroborate the notion that better oral control of a language provides better results in the beginning stages of the reading process. Thus, the study supports the native-language approach to beginning reading instruction for those students who are proficient speakers of Spanish with limited abilities in English. By initially reading in Spanish, these children are able to move from a known element, the oral form of Spanish, to an unknown one, the symbols that represent that spoken form. The introduction of English materials for beginning reading instruction requires these children to attempt to deal with an unknown, the symbols that represent the oral form of English, which is also an unknown to them. The latter option runs counter to learning theory (Ausubel, 1963).

As children begin to familiarize themselves with the reading process in Spanish, they also begin to develop their oral English in meaningful instructional settings. In the early stages of English as a Second Language (ESL) instruction, emphasis should be placed on the act of communication—that is, the messages that children are conveying—rather than the phonological characteristics of their form of English. The sooner children learn English syntax and semantics, the more successful they will be once they begin to read in English. Without knowing how words fit together in the English language, children will be unable to develop reading strategies involving the syntactic and semantic cueing systems. What is referred to as reading will become word calling, not comprehending.

Non-English-speaking and limited-English-speaking children starting to read in Spanish should be provided with ample opportunities to listen to both English and Spanish, especially stories, poems, riddles, and rhymes that contain a considerable amount of repetition and many predictable lines. Children readily catch on to the rhythm, refrains, and predictable lines and are soon able to participate by producing these parts. Dramatizations and role playing with puppets allow for further oral practice and fuller comprehension.

While reading Spanish and English stories to children, teachers will find it beneficial to pause when they come to highly predictable words and ask the children to guess the words, based on the surrounding context. If this method is introduced orally, the children should experience relative ease later in applying it to the printed page. Additionally, teachers should make use of every possible occasion while reading to children to elicit language from them. The children should be encouraged to discuss the illustrations, describe the characters, predict what will happen next in the story, tell whether or not they like the story and their reason, make up another ending for the story, and so on. Story-reading sessions of this nature allow for improved listening skills and oral expression, a deeper understanding of the story, and a holistic, meaning-centered perception of reading. With more knowledge about language and a broader background of experiences, children have less need to rely on the print, and they become more proficient readers.

Because the FI and FD readers in the study processed printed material (in both Spanish and English) in two distinct ways, it seems that once children's cognitive-style strategies have been ascertained, practice in their less developed strategies should be provided. This procedure would permit children to function successfully in both their preferred cognitive style and the cognitive style that is less familiar to them. Bicognitive children demonstrate their cognitive flexibility by using field-dependent and field-independent cognitive styles independently as well as simultaneously; they are comfortable when presented with a variety of academic tasks. Bicognitive development is a necessity for children whose values and identities differ from those of the mainstream American middle class (Ramírez and Castañeda, 1977).

In view of the fact that only the FD readers overrelied on the graphophonic cue system, it appears that they may have been more influenced than the FI readers by the type of instruction they received. Exposure to approaches other than synthetic phonics may be in order. Children who prefer a field-dependent cognitive style would benefit from more explicit instruction in the syntactic and semantic cue systems. Holistic language activities would provide them with this opportunity.

Children clearly see the relationship among thought, speech, and print when the language experience approach to initial reading instruction is used. Whatever they think about can be expressed; whatever they say can be written down; and whatever is printed can be read and shared by all. Dictated reading selections supply the students with the most familiar and predictable materials available—their own creations.

Published materials that are highly predictable are effective as beginning texts, especially if the teacher has employed similar materials to elicit predictions from students. Easy read-along books with accompanying cassette tapes are also useful. Using such materials, beginners perceive reading to be much like what they expected from having listened to others read to them.

Valuable instructional materials that require students to draw on their syntactic and semantic cue systems can easily be prepared by the teacher and used for both Spanish and English instruction. Small pieces of construction paper can be cut to cover several words on each page of a story and taped down at the top edge so that it is possible to lift the tabs from the bottom. ("Mary ——— Amy can hop.") Students should be directed to: (1) read to the end of the sentence, inserting "blank" or "hmmm" for the tabbed word; (2) predict the covered word and read it in the complete sentence; and (3) lift the tab to check their prediction against the printed word (Guszak, 1978b). Activities like this are most successful when students' independent reading materials are used—materials that can be read fluently and that require no assistance from the teacher in terms of word recognition and comprehension. Beginning assignments should have only the most obvious and predictable words covered so that students can concentrate on familiarizing themselves with the process of sampling, predicting, testing, confirming, and correcting by making use of syntactic and semantic cues.

This technique can be modified; for example, the teacher can cover all but the initial letter, consonant blend, or digraph ("The cat ran into the str———.") so that students can utilize all three linguistic cue systems—graphophonic, syntactic, and semantic. Once students feel comfortable with this procedure, the concept can be applied when they read from their instructional-level materials or materials that challenge them to the extent that they require assistance in recognizing some of the words and understanding some passages. When students encounter a word that they do not immediately recognize, the teacher should cue them to say "blank" or "hmmm" for that word, read to the end of the sentence, and then predict the unknown word. A meaningful follow-up cue to this one is: "Does that sound right? Does it make sense?" If students agree that the predicted word does not sound "right," then the teacher should encourage them to suggest another word that fits the context. Students are thus continually reminded that reading should be meaningful and sound like the language they know, rather than simply providing them with a word-calling task.

Scrambled word cards containing the same vocabulary as the beginning textbook offer students practice in word-recognition skills. During the initial stages, the activity can be structured so that students are presented with only the word cards needed to construct a given sentence. Once this skill has been mastered, students may select word cards from a larger pool to develop their own sentences.

With such instruction, children are more apt to view reading as a meaning-centered, language-centered process. They will come to recognize their non-meaningful substitutions as disruptive of the sense of the passage and will consequently correct themselves. They will learn to become risk-takers and predict unrecognized words, rather than omit them, by employing graphophonic, syntactic, and semantic cues.

Since reading strategies were shown to be the same across languages in this study, these strategies need not be retaught when reading instruction commences in the other language. Children learn to read only once; then they transfer reading skills from one language to another. Cohen (1980) has discussed the importance of appropriate initial placement in a Spanish-reading program. Transference will be successful only when developed reading skills—developed in a language of strength—are transmitted to a weaker language. If children who are not linguistically and cognitively stronger in Spanish are inappropriately assigned to beginning reading instruction in Spanish, transference will prove ineffective.

Effective transference, then, is linked to accurate identification. Cognitive strengths as well as linguistic strengths should be considered in determining the language in which the child will learn best (Cohen, 1980). Several of the widely used measures of language proficiency identify a child's dominant language on the basis of vocabulary and/or syntax; cognitive strengths and weaknesses remain unassessed. Yet the latter area is of primary importance; only when reading skills are acquired in the cognitively stronger language will children successfully transfer them to their cognitively weaker language. Thus, an identification of the child's dominant language, based on a cognitive assessment, is recommended before reading instruction begins.

Any reading difficulties experienced by children in their native language will be dealt with best in that language. Should transfer to the second language be attempted at this time, the reading problems will persist and may even become more severe (Cohen, 1980). Children need to be provided with the opportunity to utilize their cognitive strengths and familiarity with the native language to ameliorate any reading difficulties.

Because children learn language and acquire reading skills at varying rates, teachers must time their transfers to second-language reading individually. The importance of diagnostic-prescriptive instruction cannot be overemphasized in this setting. Some children may acquire reading skills in Spanish at a rate that surpasses their acquisition of oral language skills in English; other children may experience the reverse situation. It is unlikely that transferring a group such as this, that began reading instruction in their native language at the same time, will result in positive and successful experiences in second language reading for all children involved.

When the transfer to English reading occurs, teachers must not forget that English is not nearly as regular as Spanish in terms of grapheme-phoneme correspondences. An overreliance on the graphophonic cue system in English will prevent a child from becoming a proficient reader. Moreover, phonological features of Spanish frequently appear in children's oral English. Communication is not hindered, but certain English sounds have yet to be discriminated by the children, and until they are discriminated, they cannot be produced. Little progress will be observed if major emphasis is placed on phonics instruction and children are expected to associate symbols with sounds that are not yet distinct for them. The focus of initial reading instruction in English should be on whole words presented in meaningful contexts. The language experience approach allows for an exact match between the children's spoken form of English and the print they read because they dictate the stories that serve as initial reading material. Guszak (1978a) recommends seven techniques for teaching words in context. When modeling, framing, matching, substituting, closing, composing, and dialoging are practiced, children always see words in context, never in isolated lists.

The study clearly indicates a need for further research, including investigations of the hypothesis that initial reading instruction has more influence on beginning readers' strategies than does their cognitive-style orientation and the hypothesis that cognitive-style preference is influential only in the beginning stages of reading. Studies should also consider whether or not readers' cognitive-style orientation, as measured by the CEFT, changes with changes in reading strategy. The importance of cognitive-style preferences to reading progress should be comparatively examined at different levels of reading proficiency and maturity. Also needed is an investigation of the way children identified as FD and FI process informative textual material in contrast to narrative material. Does the influence of cognitive-style orientation vary with the material? Finally, a study that would weigh the effects on the reading process of different instructional materials would be meaningful. Is there a noticeable difference between the way readers with a particular cognitive style preference process the books in the "Phonetic Keys to Reading" series (1972), which are heavily phonetic in emphasis, and the way they process language experience stories?

REFERENCES

Ausubel, D. *The psychology of meaningful verbal learning.* New York: Grune & Stratton, 1963.

Barr, R. The effect of instruction on pupil reading strategies. *Reading Research Quarterly,* 1975, *10,* 555–582.

Bilingual Oral Language and Reading Program. Austin, Tex.: Southwest Educational Development Laboratory, 1973.

Calfee, R., and Calfee, K. H. *Reading and mathematics observation system, RAMOS II.* Palo Alto, Cal.: Stanford University, 1976.

Cohen, B. *Issues related to transferring reading skills from Spanish to English.* Los Angeles: National Dissemination and Assessment Center, 1980.

Davey, B. A psycholinguistic investigation of cognitive style and oral reading strategies in achieving and underachieving fourth grade boys. Doctoral dissertation, Case Western Reserve University, 1971.

De Avila, E. A. *Cartoon conservation scales.* Corte Madera, Cal.: Lingua Metrics Group, 1976.

De Avila, E. A. and Duncan, S. E. *Language assessment scales, level 1* (2d ed.). Corte Madera, Cal.: Lingua Metrics Group, 1977.

Goodman, K. S. A linguistic study of cues and miscues in reading. *Elementary English,* 1965, *42,* 639–643.

Goodman, Y. M., and Burke, C. L. *Reading miscue inventory.* New York: Macmillan, 1972.

Guszak, F. J. *Diagnostic reading instruction in the elementary school.* New York: Harper and Row, 1978a.

Guszak, F. J. *Individualizing your reading program in 23 days.* Manchaca, Tex.: Sterling Swift, 1978b.

Kagan, J., Rosman, B., Day, D., Albert, J., and Phillips, W. Information processing in the child: significance of analytic and reflective attitudes. *Psychological Monographs,* 1964, *78.*

Litsinger, D. *The challenge of teaching Mexican-American students.* New York: American Book Company, 1973.

Ohnmacht, F. W. Psychological research: a psychometric point of view. *Journal of Reading Behavior,* 1970, *3,* 213–220.

"Phonetic Keys to Reading" series. Oklahoma City: Economy, 1972.

Ramírez, M., and Castañeda, A. *Cultural democracy, bicognitive development, and education.* New York: Academic Press, 1974.

Ramírez, M., Herold, P., and Castañeda, A. *New approaches to bilingual, bicultural education.* Austin, Tex.: Dissemination and Assessment Center for Bilingual Education, 1977.

Readence, J. E. A psycholinguistic analysis of the oral reading miscues of impulsive and reflective third grade children. Doctoral dissertation, Arizona State University, 1975.

Schwartz, E. N. The effect of field dependence–field independence upon the word recognition ability of second grade subjects. Doctoral dissertation, Hofstra University, 1972.

Smith, F. *Psycholinguistics and reading.* New York: Holt, Rinehart and Winston, 1973.

Smith, F. *Understanding reading*. New York: Holt, Rinehart and Winston, 1978.

Stone, M. K. *Correlates of teacher and student cognitive style*. Beginning teacher evaluation study, Phase II, 1973-74. (ERIC Document Reproduction Service ED 131-120), 1976.

Witkin, H. A. Individual differences in ease of perception of embedded figures. *Journal of Personality*, 1950, *19*, 1–15.

Witkin, H. A., Dyk, R. B., Faterson, H. F., Goodenough, D. R., and Karp, S. A. *Psychological differentiation*. New York: Wiley, 1962.

About the Contributors

LUIZA B. AMODEO is the director of the Educational Research Center, College of Education, New Mexico State University, and an assistant professor in the Department of Curriculum and Instruction. She received her Ph.D. in psychological studies and early childhood development from the University of California, Los Angeles. Her research interests include language acquisition, bilingualism, teacher education, educational technologies, and rural educational issues.

ROSALINDA B. BARRERA, assistant professor of reading/bilingual education, is presently teaching graduate and undergraduate courses in reading/language arts education in the Department of Educational Specialities, New Mexico State University. She has a doctorate in reading education and has served as an elementary teacher, reading consultant, and public school administrator. Her primary research interest is the language-literacy development of nonnative English-speaking children.

MANUEL CÁRDENAS received a M.A. in mathematics from Texas A&I and a Ph.D. in statistics from Texas A&M. He is presently a research consultant in the Department of Experimental Statistics at New Mexico State University.

ALBERTA M. CASTANEDA is an associate professor in the Department of Curriculum and Instruction at The University of Texas at Austin, where she teaches courses in early childhood education. Her particular interest is the development of early concepts in mathematics. She has developed, taught, and tested programs for young children in mathematics and other curriculum areas.

GLORIA CONTRERAS is an associate professor in the Department of Curriculum and Instruction at The University of Texas at Austin, specializing in social studies and multicultural education. She received her doctorate from the University of Georgia at Athens and has worked in Latin America as a curriculum specialist. Dr. Contreras is coeditor of *Racism and Sexism: Responding to the Challenge,* chairwoman of the Publications Board for the National Council for Social Studies, and a member of the Board of Directors of the American Association of Colleges of Teacher Education.

GILBERT J. CUEVAS is an associate professor of education in the Department of Educational Leadership and Instruction at the University of Miami. He has graduate degrees in mathematics and educational research, and is codirector of the Mathematics Bilingual Education Materials Development and Training Project. Dr. Cuevas's research interests are language and mathematics, and student evaluation in the context of bilingual education.

ARLINDA J. EATON is associate professor of education in the Department of Elementary Education at California State University, Northridge, where she teaches undergraduate and graduate courses in reading. The editor of *Reading Beyond the First R,* a newsletter published by the School of Education, she is also a member of the executive board of the San Fernando Valley Reading Council. Dr. Eaton received her Ph.D. in curriculum and instruction from The University of Texas at Austin.

THERESA H. ESCOBEDO received a doctorate in education with an emphasis on early childhood education and is currently an associate professor at The University of Texas at Austin in the Department of Curriculum and Instruction. She teaches courses in early childhood, multicultural education, and parent involvement. She has received research grants from the National Institute of Education, National Council for Chicanos in Higher Education, Texas Committee for the Humanities, and the University Research Institute. Her research and publications have focused on early childhood education programs and learning styles of children from a multicultural perspective, as well as on equity issues related to minority women. Dr. Escobedo's most recent book, *Education and Chicanos: Issues and Research,* is published by the Spanish-Speaking Mental Health Research Center, University of California at Los Angeles.

LINDA ESPINO has been a special research assistant with the Southwest Educational Development Laboratory in Austin, Texas. She has a background in anthropology and field research. Her current research interest is in the cultural antecedents of cognitive style and subsequent observable behaviors.

EUGENE E. GARCIA is director of the Center for Bilingual/Bicultural Education and professor of education at Arizona State University. He received a B.A. in psychology from the University of Utah, a Ph.D. in child development from the University of Kansas, and served as a postdoctoral fellow in development psycholinguistics at Harvard University. He was a faculty member at the University of Utah and the University of California, and was an elected member of the Salt Lake City Board of Education (1972–76). Dr. Garcia has published extensively in the area of bilingual development. His most recent book, *Early Childhood Bilingualism,* is published by the University of New Mexico Press.

FRANK GONZALES, who has a doctorate in bilingual education, is director of bilingual education at Texas Tech University. He has served as a training resource specialist at the Bilingual Resource Center in Austin, Texas, and as a teacher on the college level and in public schools. Dr. Gonzales has focused on Mexican American culture in the classroom as his major research interest, and has developed educational materials for teaching conversational Spanish.

SARAH HUDELSON received a Ph.D. in curriculum and instruction, with concentrations in reading education and bilingual education. As a member of the faculty at Arizona State University, she researched and published in the areas of bilingual reading, bilingual children's writing development, and second language development. She is currently a faculty member at Florida International University, where she is developing courses for the bilingual education program and doing case study research. Dr. Hudelson has been an elementary school teacher in Texas and Michigan.

ANA HUERTA-MACÍAS received a Ph.D. from The University of Texas at Austin. She is presently a research associate with the Southwest Educational Development Laboratory in Austin, Texas. She has conducted research in childhood bilingualism and bilingual education and has published articles related to linguistic analysis, bilingual language acquisition, and code switching. She was the recipient of a National Endowment for the Humanities Research Grant, as well as grants from the Ford Foundation and The University of Texas.

JOHANNA H. HUGGANS is the director of the Child and Family Laboratory at The University of Texas at Austin. She received a M.S. in family relations and child development from Oklahoma State University and a Ph.D. in child development and family studies from Purdue University. Dr. Huggans is active in the American Home Economics Association, in national associations concerned with young children, and in child development research. She has written articles for child development and early childhood publications and is a frequent speaker at early childhood and parent education conferences.

STEPHAN L. JACKSON received a Ph.D. in elementary and early childhood education. He is currently an educational specialist with the Intercultural Development Research Association in San Antonio, Texas. Prior to this position, he was a principal investigator for research projects for the Southwest Educational Development Laboratory in Austin, Texas, and was an education consultant for the Education Service Center, Region XIII, Austin. Dr. Jackson also received Montessori training in Mexico City, and is certified by the Association Montessori International. He was instrumental in founding La Escuela Montessori de Montopolis, in Austin, in 1974, which is still in operation.

OLIVIA N. SARACHO is an assistant professor at the University of Maryland. She received a Ph.D. in early childhood education from the University of Illinois at Urbana-Champaign. She previously taught Head Start, preschool, kindergarten, and elementary classes in Texas, and was the director of the Child

Development Associate Program at Pan American University. Her current research and writing are in the areas of cognitive style, academic learning, and teacher education in relation to early childhood education.

AURELIA DÁVILA DE SILVA received a Ph.D. from the Department of Curriculum and Instruction at The University of Texas at Austin, where she has also done postdoctoral work in educational research. She is presently affiliated with the Intercultural Research Development Association in San Antonio, Texas. She is active in the International Reading Association and is an appointed member of that organization's committee on multiliteracy in multicultural settings. Her research interests include Spanish reading and Spanish children's literature, and her publications have been in the area of the acquisition of Spanish reading strategies.

Index